Fly-fishing the Arctic Circle to Tasmania

Fly-fishing the Arctic Circle to Tasmania

A Preacher's Adventures and Reflections

James W. White

FOREWORD BY
Brian McLaren

RESOURCE *Publications* · Eugene, Oregon

FLY-FISHING THE ARCTIC CIRCLE TO TASMANIA
A Preacher's Adventures and Reflections

Resource Publications
An Imprint of Wipf and Stock Publishers
199 W. 8th Ave., Suite 3
Eugene, OR 97401

www.wipfandstock.com

PAPERBACK ISBN: 978-1-5326-6548-6
HARDCOVER ISBN: 978-1-5326-6549-3
EBOOK ISBN: 978-1-5326-6550-9

Manufactured in the U.S.A.

Dedicated To
Bruce A. Kuster
Incomparable Friend

Contents

Foreword

Brian D. McLaren

I'VE ALWAYS PAID ATTENTION to folks a few years older than me. When I was eight, I watched eleven-year-olds. When I was eleven, I studied sixteen-year-olds. After I turned about twenty, I focused on folks fifteen to twenty years my senior. That habit continues today.

I guess I've always had a mentor-shaped hole in my heart. I've always been interested in people who model maturity, and I've always wanted to get an idea in advance of how life is to be done at the next stage.

That explains, in part, my appreciation for Jim White. I wish I had known him when I was a newly minted pastor in my late twenties. I feel the same way about when I was a young fly-fisher.

Even now, with me over sixty and Jim crossing eighty, I look at him as somebody I hope to be like when I grow up.

Ah, but I feel I am only telling a half-truth so far. The whole truth is that it's not Jim's maturity that I find most affable. To be frank, it's his incorrigible immaturity.

Although Jim is my senior, he is also still a boy at heart. You'll feel it in the first paragraphs of chapter 1 when he recounts memories from his boyhood. You'll realize that the little boy watching his dad loading earthworms into a coffee can still resides inside Jim. A few pages later, you'll feel that within Jim that young boy is still eating sardines in a boat and turning the tin into a toy boat in a stream.

I suppose that's something I hope I'll still have when I'm eighty and beyond, if I live that long: that boy-aliveness, that innocent joy in simple things, that pure passion for the next adventure.

Of course, I also share with Jim the wholesome addiction to fly-fishing, and that shared delight makes this book all the more a pleasure for me. It will do the same for you, I promise, if you know the meaning of the term "tight lines."

But even if you haven't (yet) been hooked (sorry) by the fishing lure (apologies again), I know that you have discovered delights of your own, and as you read Jim's far-flung adventure stories, you'll find it easy to relate his delights to yours.

For you, landing a little white ball on the green of a golf course might bring the same thrill that landing a Royal Wulff on the seam of a stream does for Jim. For you, the memory of your first set of Great Chef knives may bring the same pang of joy as that first split-bamboo fly rod did for Jim. For you, opening a new novel or memoir (like this one) may be your version of stepping into a new river. You'll soon see how a well-casted PMD fly descending toward a promising riffle shares something in common with a well-crafted prepositional phrase floating down toward that final period in the flow of a sentence. For younger folks, Jim's memory of a stream-cut landscape may evoke a pang similar to the one they feel when they hear the electronic soundscape that accompanies a video game.

Whatever the unique objects, I've come to believe that our delights and loves resonate.

You'll find a deeper lure in these pages too, an enticement to think about the m/Mysterious delight that moves in the deep hidden springs and pools of our lives. Rest assured, however, never once are Jim's spiritual reflections grim or guilt-ridden, proselytizing or doctrinaire.

You will enjoy his self-deprecating humor, such as the comment involving sideburns and hemorrhoids, and you will appreciate his theological insights. In one of the tales, a fishing buddy raises this question: "Is it better to be out fishing thinking about God or to be in church thinking about fishing?"

I may wonder how theologians Thomas Aquinas or John Calvin or the Niebuhr brothers would answer, but I don't doubt what Jim himself would say, at least now that he's retired from preaching!

At the end of the book, Jim lists the many friends with whom he has fished. I was honored to find my name there. We already have dates set to meet up again next year. There will be lots of joking and laughing, lots of eating and drinking, and lots of fishing, and hopefully at least a little catching, followed by lots of storytelling and truth-stretching. Who knows . . . maybe we'll contribute to Jim's next volume?

Until then, you'll be glad when you turn this page and take opportunity to join Jim on his adventures and insightful reflections.

Brian D. McLaren
Marco Island, FL

Preface

I went out to the hazel wood,
Because a fire was in my head,
And cut and peeled a hazel wand,
And hooked a berry to a thread . . .

—William Butler Yeats, "Song of Wandering Aengus"

MAROONED ON A RIVER island above the Arctic Circle, caught by a flash flood in New Zealand, boated with a NFL cheerleader in the Caribbean, robbed in a British Columbia motel, and bunked with an almost-terrorist in Manitoba, this preacher from Colorado has had some interesting experiences, to say the least, when going "further out" to fish. Some of those trips north and south, east and west—beyond continental United States—are told in these pages.

Manitoba Fish Tail for the Tales

I invite you to go with me as I fly-fish and explore worldwide waters and lands. You will enjoy the adventure stories, plural, *and* one story that brackets and underlies the several. Stories and story, then, await you.

There is good destination information in this book. We'll go to almost twenty different countries. You'll learn about people-places-customs-things *ordinarily* encountered by tourists doing international travel. *And,* since my fish-a-logues are not so ordinary, you will find yourself in non-touristy locales, meeting not-run-of-the-mill characters, hearing strange expressions from different tongues, seeing things heretofore unseen, and laughing with—and at—the author and friends. You could be hearing "stuff" you may just as soon forget—fishing esoterica, for example.

The inquisitive angler, though, may appreciate—even use—pescadoral information. So it is here for him/her. Still, I try not to become too technical. Almost everyone, I believe, will understand the action when a Kamloops rainbow trout *skys, goes screaming out,* and gets you *into your backing.* We all "hold the pole" then.

These tales are put down to delight you, that you will come away of a mind with me and Hunter S. Thompson:

> Life should not be a journey to the grave with the intention of arriving safely in a pretty and well preserved body, but rather to skid in broadside in a cloud of smoke, thoroughly used up, totally worn out, and loudly proclaiming "Wow! What a Ride!"[1]

To change Thompson's imagery, I am proclaiming, "Wow! What a wade! What a float!"

At the same time that these adventure fishing and travel tales are being related, I am dealing with a deeper, existential concern: the relationship between fly-fishing with its special *spirituality* and Christianity, the *religion* to which I am committed. I don't think I am alone in this pondering. I shouldn't be. Let me tell you why.

In America today there are 324 million citizens. Of this number something like 50 million say they fish, and 3.3 million are fly-fishers. That's a lot of folks angling. Most, I bet, would say fishing is good for their souls, even that fishing has "spirituality" to it. At the same time, most Americans—90%—affirm belief in God, 78% say they are Christian, 60% have church membership, and about 40% are in worship once a week. As a clergyperson in this faith and a passionate fly-fisher, I wonder about the relationship of the two.

Some people have said to me that being a clergyman and an outdoorsman is an unusual combination. I'm not so sure about that (you can make

---

1. Quotation exists in Hunter S. Thompson's book *The Proud Highway: Saga of a Desperate Southern Gentleman.*

the call), but I do want to bring my theological orientation alongside my avocational passion. All my life the two have mingled, perhaps for this book. So, at the end I can say, "What's it all about, Alfie?" What may be the *meaning* of fishing?

David James Duncan in *The River Why* writes,

> Who hasn't heard—particularly from fly fishermen who flaunt their literacy more than their bait-fishing counterparts— references to anglers as the most meditative of sportsmen? We feather-daubers love to echo Izaak Walton's characterization of our pastime as "the contemplative man's recreation." Yet in none of the thousands of pages of modern fishing prose have I encountered even the most rudimentary philosophical speculations.[2]

Or "*theological* speculation," the book in your hand perhaps being an exception.

So, *Fly-fishing the Arctic Circle to Tasmania: A Preacher's Adventures and Reflections* has three primary readerships: persons liking international travel and adventure stories, anglers generally and fly-fishers in particular, and men and women interested in the spiritual quest. All will find the stories/story a "good read." I promise not to be boring.

Other things, besides fishing adventures and faith concerns, are here. For the nature enthusiast there is description of international flora, fauna, and rocks—I love geology. Attention to customs, practices, and language of visited countries and people is here. Occasionally one of "the forbidden four" topics—religion, politics, sex, and money—is broached. Probably too much talk about food and eating transpires.

(Let me say, too, that pictures, when available and capable of transmuting from color to black and white, have been inserted.)

Serious heart and soul matters are not excluded either. Why should they be? Not everything about travel, fishing, and life is light. So I share introspective ruminations, emotional moments, and deep-seated values.

Every one of the sixteen chapters (ten of them stand-alone adventure stories) and the twelve segues talk about the company with whom I have broken bread and tippets. The characters met, I believe, will delight and intrigue you. There is fireside, stand-up comic Bob Schluter and tall-tales-telling cowboy Johnny Stafford, to name just two. There is the sagacious, go-for-it "BAK," Bruce Arnold Kuster.

---

2. David James Duncan, *The River Why* (San Francisco: Sierra Club Books, 1983), p. 109.

Bruce Kuster "Hissef"

To ride with "the boys in the boat," come from Lake Wobegon, are "strong women": Jeanne Koeneman, Sunny Moorhusen, and Patti Limpert White. [3]

Ah, to go a-fishing in distant waters with the "hazel wand," have memorable experiences, and reflect on it all, I have just loved. The voyages taken with friend's nonpareil to environs superlative, accompanied by the Spirit, have given this life of mine great meaning.

Thank you for page sojourning. Happy to have you in the boat. Grab a paddle. Dip in. Here we go.

James W. White
Colorado Springs
Winter 2018-19

Author Has Boat, Will Float-'n-Fish

3. For a full listing of people with whom I have fished, see the Appendix. Many readers will find their name included.

Acknowledgments

IF "IT TAKES A village to raise a child," it has taken a "really, really big community"—of able and patient folk—to get this book into being.

I am grateful to hundreds with whom I have shared waters, travel, and reflections. Many compatriots are named in this book. *All* are mentioned in the appendix—that is, all whose names I can recall. Anglers with whom I have spent whole stories here—and remember vividly, as will you—include John Hallsten in Alaska, Ron Granneman in New Zealand, Gordon Honey in British Columbia, Jim Moorhusen in Ontario, Sid Shelton in Mexico, Jon Thomas on Kodiak Island, Glen Ogden in Tasmania, Brent Jakobson in Manitoba, Donn Erickson in Venezuela, Wayman Suwinton in Bali, and Milan Hladik in the Czech Republic.

Important theological thinkers—also fishers—contributing to this book include Andy Blackmun, Ron Dunn, Brian McLaren, Mark Miller, Ruben Rainey, Anthony Surage, and David Weddle.

Long-time friends, great fishers and solid church leaders themselves, include Dick Anderson, Gary Carbaugh, Joe Field, Stan Harwood, Bob Tucker, and Jim Vandermiller. Not to forget recent-decades fishing compatriots and churchmen Mike Emerson, Steve Ferguson, Neil Luehring, Mark Mahler, Norm Peterson, Howard Ray, Rick Shick, John Stefonik, and Bruce Warren. We have fished-worshiped-spoken-and-reflected together. Many have read sections of this book and offered helpful suggestions.

Bruce Kuster has made contributions to almost every page, often literally, sometimes by telepathic transfer.

Assisting in the assembly, writing, typing, correcting, proofing, and redoing re-doings of the accounts are others who shared computer-keyboard and editing skills graciously. Let me name some: Melissa White Addington, Lucy Bell, Peter Burford, Ethan Casey, Andy Kort, Lillian Dashiell-Mooney, Carolyn Dickerson, Betsy Field, Peter Hokanson, Hannah Hokanson, Steve Kern, Michelle Kuster, Robbie Limpert, John Machin, Kim Manuliak, Mo

Morrow, Lynne Stefonik, Paul Schwotzer, Sid Shelton, Jean Tidball, Jane Warren, Hermann Weinlick, Monica Weindling, Lauren Willson, Matthew Wimer, and Patti White.

The Patti White of "and Patti White" must be spotlighted. She saw the book's first rise to its being a catch and finally a release. On some occasions, when her novel being read got boring, she's put on the Simms waders and swished the Orvis rod. She's encouraged my trips, saying enigmatically, "Go! Get out here! How can I miss you, if you never go away?" Thank you, Pattigirl!

Not to forget Gilda the Golden, ever under the desk, ever in need of "walkings."

For me *all the above* have been ghillies without peer.

CHAPTER 1

Beginnings into Fly-Fishing

Author, 8, at YMCA Camp with Catfish on Fly Rod

NOW, WALKING ALONG A lush creek bank or through a moist garden in cultivation and getting a smell of loam, I am undone. There is something about rich, freshly turned soil that transports me to Cascade, Colorado, the summer of 1941. I am four years old. We have parked the '37 Chevrolet beside the road and from its trunk taken a spade, a red Folgers Coffee can, and "the fishin' pole," a four-foot long white casting rod with a level-wind Shakespeare reel. My father holds my hand and we make our way over the railroad tracks, down to the stream. He leans the rod against the smooth granite boulder that marks the place where Cascade Creek joins Fountain Creek. In this grassy, slightly open area, my father stomps on the shovel and begins to turn over dirt clods. With the back of the shovel, he smacks them

1

into smaller chunks and, with his hands (I'll never forget his wide, strong hands) breaks the clumps apart in search of earthworms. The smell is wonderful, clean, and pungent. I help with the search-and-find effort, knowing what comes next.

When we've counted out a hundred, my father says, "That oughta be enough, Jimmy. Ready?"

Oh, yes.

I stand beside the boulder and hand him the pole. He threads a reddish earthworm onto a snelled Eagle Claw hook—one with two small bait-barbs. Then he says, "Okay, here we go." He gets on his knees by the boulder and inches his way toward the hole where water comes over a half-sunken tree trunk, making a sparkling waterfall and a wide pool. He casts into the white spillover and, almost instantly, says, "I got one," and hands me the rod. I crank it—sometimes properly—and soon there's a colorful little brookie flopping in the grass.

That's how it all began for me, this passion for trout fishing.

That I love trout fishing *from a boat* may have something to do with a second experience a summer or two later. My father had taken me way up Cascade Creek and probably was well on his way to a full creel. He said, "Let's have lunch." The lunch was white soda crackers and canned sardines. He took the key that was spot-welded to the back of the can, lifted the tin tab, put the tab through the key's slot, and rolled it back to expose sardines in yellow mustard sauce. I still love sardines, probably because I loved being there with him. It made a bonding of love, which all the difficulties with his later-in-life drinking never broke. Anyway, next came the thing I shall never forget. He took the empty sardine can, pulled up the rolled lid, and said, "We have a sail boat," and he put it in the brook's slow current. It went down, came to a little shoot, sped down that, dipped in, popped up, and drifted to the bottom of the pool. I had never seen anything so wonderful in all my life. I retrieved the can, took it back to the "boat ramp" and launched it again. I must have done that a dozen times till he said, "Okay, captain, time to go." He packed my boat in with the creeled fish. I don't remember anything about fishing itself that day, but I'll never forget the sailboat.

The Original Sardine Boat?

Funny the things of childhood that make a deep impression and provide formative influence. More than that, something *before remembrance* may also be at work in my fishing-life story. My mother wrote in my *Baby Book* that, at two years old, "You went fishing in the rain barrel beside the wood pile at the cabin, your 'fishin' hole.'"

Author, 2, with Fishing Pole

That's something below the level of conscious recall.

What I *do* remember, however, can be told. An incident from about age ten is indelible. It is the story of my first rainbow trout.

Our family used to go up to Lake George on the South Platte River for outings. While Mom read, my brother Charlie and I found ways to get wet. Dad meanwhile fished the lake from the shore. For his fishing, he used a big red and white plastic bobber, below which he would put on a Colorado Spinner. To its treble hook he'd attach a night crawler and, sometimes, a salmon-egg cluster. Quite a juicy combination. He then worked his way around the lake, casting with a brown fiberglass Wright and McGill rod and Langley Anti-Inertia level-wide reel. After an hour or so, he would return to the car with maybe a half dozen nice rainbow trout. Seeing his luck, my brother and I would try casting his rig, to no avail. So he would set the hook on a fish and hand us the rod for landing the fish.

One bright afternoon, though, I left the lake and went down to the river all on my own. I went equipped with a bobber-less casting rod affixed with the Colorado Spinner, earthworm impaled on the hooks. In the hole just above the old Eleven Mile Ranch Bridge and below a riffle, I cast across and reeled back slowly. Well, a fish took it, took my no-help-from-Daddy cast bait. My heart was pounding as I brought this fish in. Keeping him dangling on the line, I ran back a quarter mile to the car to show off my first rainbow trout, 12 inches long.

For over seventy years—save two I can think of—I have hooked and landed rainbow trout. That day on the Platte I owned the sport for myself. I got the piscatorial bug.

Two years later, in 1949 when I was twelve, I first experienced fishing with a fly rod. It was at a pond in Cascade that once had been the catchment for the railroad water tower used by the steam engines that came up Ute Pass en route to Cripple Creek. The railroad quit running about 1947. So the reservoir was converted to a catch-and-pay fishing pond, run by a friend of mine, George Knox. I went down to see him late one afternoon, and he asked, "You wanna fish?"

"Oh, yeah, but I can't pay you."

"You don't need to. If you catch a fish, we'll let him go, and there's no one to see us, 'cause the entrance road is closed for the day. Here, try this."

He handed me a fly rod with a fly attached. "Go ahead."

I had no idea what to do, but with a few big-arm attempts and a little coaching from my encourager, I was getting line out. I didn't catch anything, but I remember the feel of the line loading and moving through the air. It was magic. I loved it and knew what I wanted for Christmas. Happily, Santa provided a split-bamboo rod, not a good one or expensive, but good enough. I still have it among twenty-three other rods acquired over the decades.

How and when I got a feel for "fishing further out" may be attributed to spending the summer of 1945 in southern California, where my father was stationed in the navy. With housing scarce, mother, Charlie, and I were staying in a boarded-up motel carport at Solano Beach. It was just a block from the ocean. When Dad got a weekend off, he'd join us, to fish the surf. As my brother and I swam, he'd cast out shrimp baits. Here again, he sometimes let me reel in a fish. The catch was of species quite different from Oklahoma crappie and Colorado brookies. I loved this California angling.

Another "venturing out" came some years later in Acapulco, Mexico. There on a chartered boat my brother and I witnessed our dad hook, fight, and boat a big sailfish. That international waters sailfish catch was special and, mounted, hangs to this very day over the family fireplace mantle in Norman, Oklahoma.

Dad went to his grave early, at age fifty-nine, but all his sons, including 1948 "trailer" Sevier, love his sport.

This, then, is an account of my early introduction to a life of fishing in general, fly-fishing in particular, fly-fishing from a boat most specifically, and doing some of this fishing in watery locales far from the Rockies.

Now a confession. Truth be told, for the first almost twenty-five years of my trout fishing life, when employing my fly rod, I used "garden hackle," that is, worms. I had no understanding whatsoever about aquatic insects, the feeding preferences of trout, or human-made imitations of insects. When I in mid adolescence went to buy my first flies, I got three:

1. A Black Gnat, size 14

2. A White Miller, size 12

3. A Yellow-Black Western Bee, size 14

I figured with a dark fly, light fly, and a two-tone I'd pretty well covered the range of what trout would go for. My fourth fly, purchased a few years later, was a Mosquito, size 12. Each fly was snelled with a 6-lb. test leader. Amazingly enough I still have all four, housed in an "H-I" round aluminum tin designed to hold gut leaders. The H-I may be found in a hinge-rusted Poloron Products tackle box located on a shelf in my garage.

Author's Original Fishing Flies

Now let me skip ahead some years.

Being born-'n'-raised in Oklahoma with summers spent in Colorado, I fished both warm-water lakes and cold mountain creeks. I grew to prefer the latter. So, when I graduated from Yale Divinity School in 1962, I hoped to land a ministerial position in the Rocky Mountain West. It happened with the First Christian Church in Fort Collins. I became assistant minister there, fully aware that the Poudre River, the Big Thompson, plus Rocky Mountain National Park streams were oh so close. My call to ministry in Colorado, I sort of believe, was—though I am no Calvinist—predestined. To friends I short-quoted Jesus, "I'll make you a fisher." (There is, of course, more to Mark 1:17 than that.) I was just happy to land in trout country.

Little could I imagine then that a guy in that congregation would become a fishing companion for nigh on to fifty-five years. What happened was that one of the members of the ministerial search committee, Gerald Kuster (and his wife Berta), thought it might be nice if their son and his wife were to get acquainted with "the new minister and his wife." So one Saturday the six of us met for lunch, and I became acquainted with Bruce Arnold Kuster. Bruce was a senior business major at Colorado State University.

At lunch I also learned the family was from Jacksonville, Illinois, having moved to Fort Collins to take over an outdoor sign business. Bruce's wife was a teacher, as was mine, as was Berta Kuster. There was, then, teaching, the Midwest, and church stuff to talk about. Conversation also revealed we twenty-somethings liked folk music, especially that of Joan Baez. (Bob Dylan was coming.) Talk went on cordially but really picked up when we recognized that all the men were into fishing. Before watermelon dessert was finished, we had planned a trip. Gerald said, "I have a flat-bottom boat and a trailer. Let's go to the Hohnholz Lakes on the Wyoming border. I hear they have some hot fish there."

Fine by me.

At 3:00 a.m. on Labor Day, September 3, 1962, Gerald, Bruce, and I went a-fishing. It was a three-hour drive up to the lakes. We got out of the truck to be hit by wind, big wind, whitecaps-on-the-water wind. Gerald said, "Well, let's go back home." So we did, three hours back.

So as not to have this day be a total bust, Gerald suggested we troll from his boat on Long's Pond near his house. We did, and on that day somehow and by some lure I caught my first walleyed pike.

Most important, though, what was caught was a friendship. I liked this father and son, and the son suggested we try another day.

I asked, "How about fishing the Poudre?"

"You're on," Bruce said.

So the first Bruce-and-Jim-together fishing trip was planned. My *Pocket Calendar 1962* says it was Saturday, September 22.

What I recall is that we parked the car at Arrowhead Lodge and, with fly rods in hand, walked across the highway to a sandy-rocky beach. Bruce had a white Shakespeare fiberglass Wonder Rod, quite thick, and an automatic reel, a Miracle Silent. I was outfitted with my Christmas of '49 bamboo rod and a Pflueger Medalist. What happened next, I'd say, was I spent a lot of time with him, stringing up his *bass* rod—he was fresh from *Illi-noise*—and instructing him on "10 to 2" casting, reading the water, etc. After my Fly-Fishing 101 instruction, I sent him upstream—giving him that advantage—while I went down. That's all I remember for sure.

Here's his version of what happened:

> We walked across the road from Arrowhead Lodge. I was ready for
> my first lesson. And you said, "All right. You go downstream and I'll
> go up." Well, I was confused and have had trouble ever since.

Through the years my friend has retold this story in imaginative ways:

Jim said, "You go down stream and I'll go up." That was the lesson. And that is why it took me so long to get into this sport. It has messed me up ever since.

And . . .

Jim said, "Just throw it upstream and let it come back and then throw it up again" For forty-five minutes I cast hundreds of times in exactly the same spot in exactly the same way. By then my right arm was spasming, I could no longer lift it. This was the beginning of my fishing career, and it set back my fishing skills for years. Thank you very much.

Anyway, it's his story, and I have had to put up with it for, lo, these many years. But the "many years" part of the sentence tells you that we have been at it together a long time—and that he is truly a really fun person to be around.

The stories all began from a child's Cascade, Colorado, "fishin' hole" rain barrel.

CHAPTER 2

Call to Ministry

OCCASIONALLY A CLIENT OR friend with whom I am fishing will inquire, "How, Jim White, did you become a minister?"

The short answer is "It was a *good fit* for me." Basic commitment in faith, connected with personal gifts, interest, and experience, made my becoming a clergyman happen.

How's that for an uninformative-enough answer?

I suspect people who ask this question anticipate hearing a "St. Paul on the Road to Damascus" or a "Martin Luther Lightning Bolt on the Road to Erfurt" story, but I have none to offer. At best I can recount only a numinous moment during my college years on a Disciples Student Fellowship retreat. Sitting on a cliff bank, Bible on my lap, I was doing a "morning watch." Looking out over the plains and aware of cloudless and endless sky, I had a convincing sense of the presence of God. It was a moment of enlightenment. Such, however, was no call to ministry, just a meaningful semi-transcendent happening. I sensed being "connected to a huge world" and "not alone in the universe."

The above being said, I can piece together a more comprehensive answer to how I became a Christian clergyman.

Theologian Horace Bushnell said, "a child should be raised in such a way that he/she never knows a time when he/she is not a Christian." I fit that prescription. I was raised by an especially faithful mother who saw to it that my brothers and I as infants were "dedicated" to Christ. She made sure that we said prayers at bedtime and attended Sunday school. We—certainly I—had a positive experience of church. As a wee child I relished eating donuts I could just reach at my parents' adult Sunday school class table. Seated beside my father during worship services, I was entertained drawing animal stick figures. There were Easter egg hunts at a sunrise breakfast to enjoy. On a church retreat to Lake Carl Blackwell there was hymn singing and preaching, but I only remember fishing for bass with a Hula-Popper. It's the faith-community *context* of all this that should be noted.

Such growing-up experiences certainly influenced my life, perhaps, creating a *tilt* toward ministry. Value shaping came from a Junior Church morning. We youngsters were shown a *Jesus and the Children* painting and told that the night before this painting was to be unveiled, the artist realized that all the boys and girls on the canvas were Caucasian. That was wrong. He then arose in the night and painted in faces and clothing for children who were black, brown, and red! To be sure, Sunday school was not a benign picnic.

My growing up in the faith story continues.

Having reached what is called "the age of accountability" (*confirmation* in other denominations) at twelve, one Palm Sunday I went down the church side aisle to make the Good Confession. I agreed that "Jesus is Lord" and that I would "try and follow him." The minster said that my decision "would make all the other decisions right." He was wrong about that, of course, but the sentiment was worthy.

Anyway, that is how I became a formal "Christian"—not, however, a minister.

During the elementary school years I was being shaped in ways, which in hindsight seem *preparatory* for preacherdom. At age nine, after I flunked out of piano, mother enrolled me in a speech class. Those "She sells seashells by the seashore" lessons led me to reciting "Ferdinand the Bull" at women's flower clubs and eventually to junior and senior high school plays, drama, oratory, and debate. I liked public speaking and, probably because of the stage and platform, was elected to student council presidencies in junior high, high school, and college. I found I liked politics and government and seemed to be successful there.

As noted, my childhood summers were spent in Colorado. Here I received *ecumenical broadening*. Some Sunday mornings, mother would ask my brother and me if, instead of going to Green Mountain Falls for Sunday school at the Congregational Church, we'd like to attend Holy Rosary Catholic Church across the highway. Invariably we chose the in-Latin Catholic mass. That service was *shorter*, over in just thirty minutes. Attending it I saw my friend, Nicky Sanborn, altar boy, privileged to be behind the "No Trespassing" altar rail. I was envious of his bell-ringing privilege. Being up front and being bedecked in special garment was "not bad duty," this low-church Protestant thought.

More important in vocational shaping was William H. "Bill" Alexander, pastor of our First Christian Church in Oklahoma City. He was a big man, red-headed (as was I, then), and a powerful preacher, moving about in the chancel in his swallowtail tuxedo, using poetry, humor, and story to make the Bible alive and relevant. He was never anti-intellectual. He had charisma and was a clergyman ahead of his time. Alexander built a youth center in which bowling, Ping-Pong, pool, and dancing (!) were allowed. Unafraid of controversy, Reverend Alexander spoke his mind regarding prohibition, then the law in dry Oklahoma. Famously he said, "When Baptist preachers shout, 'Keep Oklahoma Dry,' all the bootleggers add their strong 'Amen!'"

I guess I can state the obvious: he was a positive role model. Maybe more so because my father, however much beloved, had a lifelong drinking problem, which on many occasions made life embarrassing. If you wanted to do a Freudian analysis, you could say, Jim White was in search of a father figure and of a vocation by which to redeem the family name. That's a simple enough cause-effect explanation for something much more complex.

In my senior year of high school, Reverend Alexander called me in to his study to say I had "the spark" to be a good preacher and would be able to command a salary of $10,000! I tucked a note from this conversation into my wallet.

Mostly, though, I thought about becoming a lawyer.

At the University of Oklahoma, I was a Letters major, greatly influenced by philosophy professor J. Clayton Feaver. In my senior year, when I was planning post graduation, to fulfill my Army ROTC obligation and afterward attend law school, Dr. Feaver nominated me for a Rockefeller Brothers Theological Fellowship. If the fellowship were awarded, it would enable a year of discernment about ministry in a theological school. I received it and took it to Yale Divinity School in New Haven, Connecticut, arriving there in September 1959, with bride of three months beside me in the car—and fishing rods in the trunk.

This was to be a "trial year" of introduction to theology, no obligations beyond it.

Well, I liked YDS, its community of students and professors and divinity school disciplines. Yale was a heady place, much more so than Oklahoma University. Yet, as attractive as ministry was, I was still thinking law.

One day in early spring, however, H. Richard Niebuhr in his Christian ethics class said, "Most professions are concerned about the *quantity* of life, whereas the ministry is focused on its *quality*."

Then and there I decided to stay and become clergy. What Niebuhr said was what I wanted. Spirit and relationships ("love of God and neighbor"), I thought—and still think—trump acquisition ("getting and spending") and individualism. I opted for Christian ministry.

Two and a half years later I would be ordained at my home church in Oklahoma City and would go to my first parish in Fort Collins, Colorado—where there would be trout fishing, as noted in the previous chapter.

CHAPTER 3

Joining Fly-Fishing with Ministry

THAT SPRING OF 1960, when I made the decision for ministry, I joined it with angling in Connecticut. In the creek that runs through Sleeping Giant State Park I angled. Using a buck tail streamer, a couple of eastern brookies came to hand. As a counselor next summer at YMCA Camp Hubinger, I caught perch, bass, and my first-ever eel. Fishing from a motorboat in Long Island Sound and using grub worms, I hooked onto and, after a twenty-minute tussle, brought in an 8-pound sand shark—the capture made on my twelfth-birthday bamboo fly rod. I also took two porgy and a summer fluke. Next year in the Housatonic River, below a totally-unique-to-me covered bridge, I cast—albeit unsuccessfully—for trout. Finally, nearing graduation, a group of us weekended on Lake Winnipesaukee in New Hampshire. Here with spinning gear I boated two land-locked salmon.

(In 1964, I returned to the east coast for army chaplains' school and afterward went to Bar Harbor, Maine, and did hand-line fishing in the Atlantic . . . to bring up ling cod, haddock, and one ugly blowfish.)

In New England, then, ministry and fishing were first joined, with appreciation of fisheries away from home waters gained.

Upon graduation—at which President John F. Kennedy was commencement speaker—my wife and I traveled west. I interviewed for church positions in Arkansas and Oklahoma, at each interview really hoping Colorado. As previously noted, it happened. I was called to be assistant minister of the First Christian Church (Disciples of Christ) in Fort Collins. My starting salary was $400 a month—not the foretold $10,000 per year. That had to wait for years and years.

After First Christian, I went into an ecumenical United Campus Christian Fellowship ministry at Colorado State University, partnering up with Bob Geller, seasoned Presbyterian clergyman. Bob was a great thinker, preacher, pastoral counselor, and mentor. He got my salary bumped up by half again and turned me on to Reinhold Niebuhr's *Moral Man and Immoral*

Society, a book that radically reshaped my thinking about culture, society, politics, and theology. It turned me from Kierkegaardian individualism and toward neo-orthodox social activism.

Bob, though, was neither fisherman nor hunter. Lutheran Colorado State University campus pastor John Hallsten, however, was. He and I fell in together and on many a frosty morning tumbled into a goose blind to discuss shot loads and soteriology. In lake fishing, John had us use chicken gizzards, of all things!

Before the decade of the '60s closed, then, I had two close friends, Hallsten and Kuster, with whom to fish and, often enough, travel.

After a decade in Fort Collins, both John and I moved away, each to do doctoral studies, he in guidance and counseling at the University of Northern Colorado, I in higher education administration at the University of Denver. (I thought I wanted to be a college dean or something.). Our mutual friend, Bruce Kuster, stayed on in Fort Collins to develop travel information centers. In the early '80s, though, we three reconnected to do a hunting-become-fishing adventure beyond imagining. It was above the Arctic Circle—and is the next chapter, "Alaska Unplanned."

Segue to Alaska

AFTER WE MOVED TO Colorado in 1962, I spent most of the next nine years doing campus ministry, being spouse to Anita, and parenting daughters Cheril and Melissa, born in 1963 and 1966. The girls will become exceedingly adroit fly-fishers over the years. "*Smart* blonds" they.

With family and friends, I fished the waters of northern Colorado (e.g., the Poudre River) and the Pikes Peak region (e.g., Catamount Reservoir), where, at Cascade, my family of origin still had a cabin. One memorable venturing out—somewhat portending this book—was into Wyoming with Bruce Kuster. There, below Glendo Dam, I took a 19-inch rainbow—the largest trout I would catch in the next twenty years!

My time in campus ministry was fulfilling, even exciting. Some of the things I remember from this period include playing the guitar for contemporary worship services, leading Bible study groups, taking part in a voter registration project in Mississippi, sharing *Agape* meals with students each Wednesday evening, speaking at the first Vietnam teach-in, escorting students on work-study projects to Chicago and Ghost Ranch, participating in book discussions with faculty, establishing a coffee house called Lazarus' Tomb, receiving Joan Baez in my office, meeting Andrew Young.

One of the ways I related ministry to fishing was to take students— guys only—on weekend retreats, either to camp out in tents or stay in a faculty member's cabin. I called one such retreat by the name of "Ixthus and Ichthyology"—the same name I would label other retreats years later. The weekends were occasions to fish, break bread, talk around a campfire, and, in the great outdoors, give thanks for life. Always students pondered such questions as "Determinism vs. Free Will" and "Who wrote the Bible?"

In 1967 I received a Danforth Fellowship, enabling a year of study at the Pacific School of Religion. What an incredible year '67–'68 was: flower children in San Francisco and Stop the Draft marchers in Oakland (where I got billy clubbed). Classes and professors at PSR, the Graduate Theological

14

Union, and U Cal Berkeley made it a heady time too. By 1969 I finished the Master of Sacred Theology degree. Fishing-wise, things were also good; salmon were caught in the ocean beyond the Golden Gate Bridge.

Then in January 1971 I went with fellow campus pastors John Hallsten and Tom Laswell on a Mexican-waters fishing trip out of San Diego harbor for yellow fin tuna. En route to fishing, we three men of the cloth had a night in Tijuana where we were robbed in a bar/brothel—an embarrassing chapter in clergy stupidity. Such chapter is not included in this book, though in some ways it is the *first* international adventure.

That summer of 1971 our family of four moved to Denver for me to do doctoral work at DU. Soon we joined First Plymouth Congregational United Church of Christ of Englewood, to make new fishing friends: Fred Wuthrich, Gary Carbaugh, Dick Anderson, Stan Harwood, Jim Vandermiller, and Renner Johnson—many of them are still casting and conversing with me forty-five years later. Upon completion of the PhD, my mother provided Hawaii plane tickets for us all. On the island of Kauai we joined the Wuthrichs to troll for billfish in the Pacific. Unsuccessfully. On another adventure with Carbaugh and Anderson I fished the rivers of Yellowstone National Park, more successfully. With the Vandermillers our family traveled south to Guaymas, Mexico. There Vandy and I engaged a village fisherman to take us out in the bay in his small wooden boat. (The man was so poor he used old spark plugs for sinkers.) We caught a few reef fish and I a large ugly-toothed eel. Our guide didn't want that monster in his skiff, but I insisted we keep it. Its skin made handsome hatband Christmas presents. The eel catch was a *memorable* international fishing experience.

Another venturing out was to Ontario, Canada, with Renner Johnson. The trip included Bruce and Gerald Kuster. On Larus Lake we jigged for walleyes, and I took a few hammer-handle northern pike on the fly rod. One evening on a second-year trip to Larus, Bruce and I spotted rising fish. That night, he and I assembled dry flies out of pillow feathers glued to a shaved-down cork and, next evening, cast to the risers. We caught several 5-pound fish—whitefish, we later learned. These 1980 and '81 trips, sorry to say, are *un*-journaled.

The fishing friends I made through First Plymouth were deepened and expanded because I became copastor in that church in 1976, a position that continued until 1981. During those years I did an adult class on "Fishing Images in the Bible" and preached a sermon called "The Compleat and Incompleat Angler," hat off to Sir Izaak Walton. Such were first attempts to reflect theologically about my more-than-a-pastime passion.

Leaving First Plymouth in 1981, I went on to be executive director (fundraiser) for the CUE Seminaries, Chicago-United-Eden. This position, though, did not stop the fishing retreats I'd begun in the '60s. They continued, centered at the Hohnholz Ranch on the Laramie River; location shifted in 1994 to Arrowhead Ranch in South Park, and later to the John Wesley Ranch, near Divide.

Besides trout fishing on these retreats, the brothers, ever non pious, nevertheless shared grace at meals, songs, campfire jokes, and stories (more on this later), "wise-men" (guest) reflections, drumming together (two years running), and many spirited discussions. In latter years I introduced re-treatants, men *and now* women, to centering prayer—a.k.a. contemplative prayer.

Now, however, I am way ahead of my stories. Let me back up a couple of decades.

The friendship Bruce Kuster and I had with John Hallsten in Fort Collins brought the three of us together in Alaska. That reunion is the basis of this book's first story. Without a doubt "Alaska Unplanned" is the most daring adventure I ever had.

Buckle up.

CHAPTER 4

Alaska Unplanned

August 18–29, 1982

Why do they ride for their money?

Why do they rope for short pay?

They ain't gettin' nowhere

And they're losing their share,

And they must have gone crazy back there.

'Cause they never seen the northern lights.

—Michael Burton, "Night Rider's Lament."

"ABOVE THE ARCTIC CIRCLE?"

"Yes. Really," John Hallsten said. "That's where we'll go."

From such an exchange it all began. So I can say, *In the beginning* was the Plan: We two (Bruce Kuster and I) would fly up to Fairbanks and hook up with our old friend John. We three would then fly to Kotzebue above the Arctic Circle in northwest Alaska and connect with Mike Spellato and Bryan Rasmussen, commercial fishermen of the Chukchi Sea, which lies just north of the Bering Strait. We five in Mike's boat would then go up the Noatak River some two hundred miles to hunt. Two weeks later we would return with much caribou, moose, and bear meat, plus trophy racks, and pride of wilderness accomplishment. That was the Plan.

Kuster and Author En Route to Alaska

It started out well enough. Flight Denver-to-Seattle, check. Flight Seattle-to-Anchorage, check. The latter leg excellent, more than excellent: Bruce charmed a stewardess—a term for flight attendant now considered politically incorrect—into moving us up to first class. From these seats we saw Columbia Glacier and enjoyed filet mignon with cabernet sauvignon. Returning from the restroom, Bruce reported that a stewardess wanted to know if he'd like to do a layover with her in Anchorage.

I snorted wine out my nose.

"With *them*, I mean—the crew."

"Yeah, right, in your dreams," I said wiping up sprayed wine.

We did, of course, arrive in Anchorage to check into a near-the-airport motel and even have a Mexican dinner with the crew. They were not staying at the same place; thus Kuster's fantasy vaporized.

Next morning, he and I flew past spectacular Denali into Fairbanks, greeted there by our "back in the days" of Fort Collins friend John Hallsten, now counselor therapist for the University of Alaska and an on-call Lutheran pastor. John took us forthwith to purchase caribou, moose, and black-bear tags, as well as fishing licenses. That evening, he served up spaghetti with California rosé. After supper, cigars-by-Bruce were fired up. Then into our smoke-filled room came a call. It was from Mike Spellato in Kotzebue, captain of the boat that was to take us upriver. He said departure would have to be delayed, as he'd gotten word that commercial fishermen could fish into an extended season. "I need the days," he explained.

For sure, something about the Plan was changing. Not happy news.

Even so, the next morning we were off for Kotzebue. Not a single one of us had ever been so far north. We were going farther yet. Ours was to be the adventure of a lifetime—in ways we never dreamed.

Deprivation

We landed in Kotzebue, a spit of gravel in the middle of a sound of the same name. Right off we purchased groceries meant to last us the next several days: meat and potatoes, bread, cookies, and some fruit and drinks. Our purchase, though not large in size, was expensive. Something like 98 percent of what's available this far north has to be brought in. The other 2 percent was cheap: fresh fish and crabs from the peninsula's surrounding waters.

At ten o'clock Captain Mike, with first mate "Ras," arrived from across the bay. They came in Mike's twenty-foot fiberglass fishing boat. The pair had full beards after two months of nonstop commercial fishing. They were "rustics of the sea," hard, thin, and wizened, wearing heavy, hooded jackets over bibs and cabled sweaters.

All our camping equipment, suitcases with clothes, backpacks, guns, fishing gear, et cetera, went on board, along with the groceries purchased. Once loaded up, we went to fill the boat's almost-empty gas tanks on Hallsten's credit card. Then it was a long ride over to Sheshalik, the Inuit fishing village on a slender spit of land across the Kotzebue Sound. As we bounced along, I noticed Ras eyeing the bags of food. I asked, "Would you like a cookie or something?"

"Oh, yes, I would," he replied eagerly.

I handed him a bag of Oreos and he began popping them in—two at a time. Captain Mike at the controls said, "Pass 'em this way, Ras." He did, and before we reached Sheshalik, the pair had consumed the whole package—that, and a liter of Coke.

"Guess they're hungry for sugar," Hallsten whispered.

"Guess so," I nodded.

We landed at their rocky beach dock, greeted by barks from a big reddish Huskie-mix dog. "That's Rusty," Ras announced proudly. "My baby."

"Also known as Ranger Danger," Mike added.

The Huskie was tied to a heavy stake on the shore. As we came by with our gear, Ras threw him a saved cookie, which the dog quickly snarfed.

The boys' place was a canvas and board shack, quite weather-beaten. Inside were an oilcloth-covered table and two chairs, wood frame beds, a Coleman lantern, a Coleman cooking stove, and a small potbellied stove. Soon after unloading, Mike sat the three of us down on one bed to give a little talk about life in an Indian fishing village, the gist of which was, "Don't do anything to disturb folk." We were guests, white ones at that, ever suspect.

Fishing Shack and Tent by the Chukchi Sea

As he spoke, Kuster noticed the brightest thing in the hut's interior, a large cast-iron skillet, fluorescent orange. Interrupting and pointing, he asked, "How'd that happen?"

Turning to look, Mike explained, "Oh, that. From the use of curry in the salmon we've eaten. Salmon is all we've had for weeks now, curried salmon. We're looking forward to variety."

"Well, there may be something in the sacks you'll like," John said.

The sit-down lecture concluded, John, Bruce, and I went outside to pitch my heavy-canvas tent (which we refer to as "the Teddy Roosevelt") and inflate air mattresses. We could hear the hungry fishermen inside opening boxes and rustling cellophane.

"Hungry indeed," Kuster commented.

Mike stuck his head out the door and announced, "Lunch, soon as I get things put away."

John responded, "I'll help," and aside whispered, "To watch the food."

Bruce said, "Jimmy, let's go for a walk up the beach."

"Fine with me. I'm eager to see Inuit fishing village life."

Seeing us start out, Mike cautioned, "Watch yourselves. Remember, I'm a guest. My lot belongs to my neighbor, Herbert Forster. It was his grandfather's."

"Don't worry," I assured him.

"I'll keep my eye on him," Bruce promised.

We started along the stony shore, the sea on our left, fishing boats chugging along on the water. Mountains were to the north and east, wind from the west. The sun, here in this northern latitude, still shone high. Under its illumination I looked for jade among the pebbles, as this is a region where the semiprecious stones are found. A brown-skinned boy with hands in his pants pockets came by, stopped, and asked, "Whatcha doing?"

"Looking for jade."

He looked down at the beach to conclude, "Not here." Then we talked a bit. His name, he told us, was David. Later, he and his brother came to the hut to munch on raw carrots.

Inuit Boys Enjoying Carrots

Our stroll resumed, my eye came upon salmon fillets drying on racks, three deep. "Must have a picture," I said to Bruce. "But wait a minute."

I went over and knocked on the door of the nearby fishing shack. A white woman, perhaps Mrs. Herbert Forster, appeared, and I asked, "May I take a picture of the drying fish?"

She rubbed her hands on her apron. "Why not? Go ahead."

But before my Pentax SLR 35mm camera was adjusted, came a voice shouting, "Stop! Stop!"

I stopped. It was Mike, yelling and running toward us, coming up out of breath to stammer, "Don't do that. It'll mess things up for me."

I, putting the lens cap back on, said, "Okay. I'll cease and desist. Don't want to upset the sociological balance hereabout." Thereafter I took only seashore-'n'-boat photos.

At lunch it was peanut butter sandwiches, John going for two, Mike and Ras unembarrassed for three.

The Chukchi Sea

Mike said, "Let's go fishin."

He boarded us in his skiff, and we motored out to where his gill nets were strung. Three shackles or sections of net were suspended perpendicular to the tidal current, each shackle three hundred feet long and fifteen feet deep, and attached one to another, creating one long net. The extreme ends of the net were anchored to the bottom of this shallow sea by heavy weights. Above the weights a large fluorescent orange buoy was attached. A smaller buoy was placed where the first shackle began and where the third one ended. Two similar-size buoys floated mid-net where the shackles joined. The top rope, stretched between the buoys, was fixed with hundreds of small floats. Thus the net was held high in the water. It was held down in it by hundreds of lead weights attached to the bottom rope.

Between the buoyed rope at the surface and the weighted rope on the bottom was the net. The mesh was made of strong nylon cord tied in diamond patterns. Each diamond opening was of such size as to let a salmon's head go into the hole but not his larger body. Unable to go forward, a fish trying to back out of the mesh catches his gills in the material. Thus impaled, he struggles and in time dies of suffocation because his gill plates are stuck open, thus letting in water and drowning him. In my journal I drew a rough pencil sketch of the set.

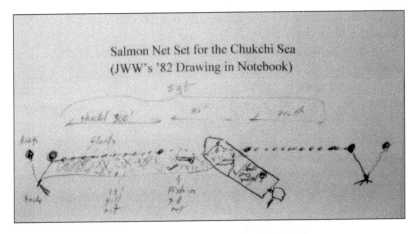

Author's Sketch of Chukchi Sea Gill Net Set

In harvesting the expected crop, Mike began by positioning the boat near the large buoy most downwind. There, Ras lifted both the floats rope and the weighted bottom rope over the bow of the boat and hoisted it to the vessel's smooth-sided middle. Then the two fishermen pulled the net from one side of the craft over to the other. The pulling moved the boat along and upwind. When a fish appeared in the net, they would pluck it out of the mesh and throw it in the hold.

Our witnessing of this work—and later helping out with it—was a plus-plus for the trip, not foreseen in the original Plan.

That afternoon, the guys netted only seven salmon (chums or dogs, they were called). All were huge in my eyes, like 15 pounds apiece. Impressed as we landlubbers were, Mike was disappointed. He'd hoped for a big catch, as they'd netted only six that morning. At the processing tender his fifteen salmon of the day brought only $55.00, hardly enough to pay for his boat's gas.

"It's been a slow summer," he admitted. "Not like last year when, in my two months on the Chukchi, I made twenty thou. My landlord, Herbert Forster, told me that between fishing and hunting he made fifty-five grand."

I thought to myself that, as much as the look of the shacks along the shore said poverty, I should have been thinking prosperity. The winter homes of these Native Americans were inland and doubtless more commodious.

Returning to camp that afternoon, Mike spoke his hopes aloud: "Maybe tomorrow—the last day I can fish—will be better. Otherwise, my summer is pretty much a bust."

That night we visitors had curried salmon, fiery hot and delicious. The boys devoured thick slices of ham. All of us together finished off the package of oatmeal raisin cookies. We drank no beer, as alcohol by tribal rule is not allowed in Sheshalik.

The gentle surf lulled us into a decent night's sleep. Bruce did not even snore.

The next morning Mike announced, "We have two slots today: this morning from eight till eleven and, this afternoon, one to four. During the second round all the nets have to come aboard. It's going to be a busy day."

That it was, busy. And the day was totally different in outcome. This time, when the nets came out of the water, there were white and silver trophies on the clothesline, caught in the mesh of the net. There were fish and more fish: heavy fish, shining fish, some stiff, most still thrashing and flashing, all fresh. The long-expected run from the sea had come. With each fish taken off the net and thrown in the hold, Mike would say, "Money, money, money!" His count for the day was

Saturday morning	294 fish
Saturday afternoon	387 fish
Saturday TOTAL	681 fish

In all, his catches were worth over $2500! Mike and Ras were happy, while their rookie deck hands were quite tired.

As the sun was still up this late summer afternoon and the weather surprisingly warm, Bruce, John, and I went for a walk. We strolled along the beach in the opposite direction from the day before, still looking for jade. After a while, I announced, "I'm going for a dip." So, I went to au naturel attire, leaving my clothes on the shore.

Bruce, taken aback, shouted, "Are you crazy? We're above the Arctic Circle, for God's sake!"

"I know. That's why I have to do it—for the Everlasting's memory."

As I "ouched" my way over the rocks and shells, John observed, "Not since Moby Dick plowed these waters has the Chukchi seen anything so ghostly white!"

"But Moby needs to be commemorated, Ishmael honored," I intoned.

"And Ahab's insanity replicated," John opined.

I got out ankle deep, then waded in above my knees. Talk about cold! This was cold. No way to go in slowly . . . had to dive . . . did . . . a belly-flop . . . took my qualifying three strokes . . . and, gasping, crash-splashed back to the shore, white skin now blue.

I thought the heads of my buds would be moving up and down in awe of manly achievement, but they went side to side in disbelief.

"My drying towel, sir," I said shivering.

John handed me my tee shirt, the one saying Lake Wobegon. It reminded me; I told them as I rubbed, that Garrison Keillor had a monologue apropos to the moment. He said that at fourteen years of age, his uncles had taken him ice fishing and, away from women, told him stories they would never let out around his aunts.

"Such as?" Bruce asked. "I'm sure you'll tell us."

"Such as, to catch fish, you sprinkle a can of peas around the ice hole . . . so, when a fish comes up to take a pea, you grab him!' That was risqué, Keillor said, adding that when he and the uncles went outside the ice hut to relieve themselves, 'It was a comfort to a fourteen-year-old boy to discover that in freezing weather all men are created equal."

Kuster's response: "Thank you, Reverend. Now, get dressed before the tribal police arrest you for indecent exposure."

At camp we were again treated to a salmon dinner. Mike and Ras consumed an eight-pack of wieners, half a loaf of white bread, most of the Fritos, a liter of root beer each, and two strawberry Pop-Tarts apiece. As we went to sleep in the tent this night, John whispered, "They'll be over their grocery deprivation in a day or two, I'm sure."

"They better," Bruce answered. "But just in case, we should buy extra food."

That we did the next morning, $350 worth.

The Noatak

With the food from Kotzebue on board, the captain looked around unhappily to say, "You're gonna have to lighten this load by half. Can't haul this much stuff."

So we repacked our gear—clothes mostly—and shoved them in our travel suitcases, which were then taken to the airport for storage. Then we were ready. I need to note, though, that there was space in the boat for seventy-pound Ranger Danger, Ras's "Baby."

The boat's gas tanks topped off, and we were ready to move upriver. Our Plan for hunting was back in play, delayed by only three days.

As we crossed the sound toward the Noatak River inlet, Bruce was standing, posed as George Washington on the Delaware, one foot on the bow. He raised his fist and shouted, "Attack the Noatak!" and, turning, asked the captain, "You taken this boat upriver many times before?"

"This is the first," Mike confessed, "but *no problemo*. It'll make it fine."

Kuster's response, "Love your confidence."

Where the Noatak River comes into the Kotzebue Sound, the delta's mouth is easily a mile wide, shallow everywhere, with many braids criss-crossing and tangled. Mike steered us up what seemed to be a main channel, though the bottom of the jade-blue river became visible at times. There were sand and mud bars on all sides. On many bars were tree trunks and root wads. Bruce continued with his questions. "What if we hit bottom?"

"We'll just lift the motor to run a little shallower," the captain explained. "Ah."

Shortly thereafter we hit the bottom, dug into a sandbar. The motor was dutifully lifted. "*No problemo*," Mike again purred, smiling through his bushy beard.

In the course of the next three hours, he had to reassure us several times more. Once we had to put on our waders, get out of the boat—the dog too—and push the craft over a long, long mud flat. My notes say it was a mile-and-a-half.

Run-amoks notwithstanding, our trip up this river was amazing. Some-times the flood plain was over a mile wide, with shallow braids. Sometimes the channel narrowed and deepened. Then you could appreciate the banks' salad sides, parsley green, spinach green, lettuce green, with bushes turned carrot orange, grass like yellow pepper slices, and tomato-red fireweed.

What a visual treat! I imagined that any minute now, rounding a curve, we'd spot a moose lifting his head from the water, moss dripping from his mouth. In such belief I kept my cased rifle between my knees. After all, for game is why we came.

Moving along, John made us all peanut butter and jelly sandwiches. "Mm-mm good, my fave," he said rather sheepishly. The Mike-Ras team consumed theirs quickly, plus a package of cheese slices, plus a sleeve of saltines, along with a quart of milk. Bruce's eyes rolled in wonder.

By late afternoon we must have been upriver some forty miles. We had seen no other boats coming or going at all and only a single barge coming down. Now the motor was seriously acting up. "Must be some sand in the works, but it'll wash out," Mike let us know.

It didn't wash out. Instead, the motor went to fits-'n'-starts-'n'-cough-ing. Even so, we went on, the engine happiest when the river was twenty or so feet deep.

Then it happened. *Clunk!* The boat bumped up from the stern. We hit a submerged floating log. After expletives, the captain said, "Okay, we'll drift to shore—onto that island we just passed—and I'll fix her there. Probably sheered a pin."

Our Noatak River Island as Seen from the Air

The boat was drifted down and tied up to logs on the bank of the island, so that Mike and Ras went to work on the motor. All the while they were eating handfuls of gorp. We three venators (hunters) left them to explore the island, Bruce and me carrying 30.06 rifles. John toted an iron-sighted, 9-millimeter Mauser. We were hunting.

But we saw no game, no tracks, and no scat on this initial reconnoitering. All we found were bright orange salmonberries, one per slender stalk, close to the ground. These we picked and ate, picked and ate, finally to collect enough into a handkerchief for evening dessert.

Upon our return to the boat, Mike told us, "The motor's broke. I'll need some new parts to fix her, which we can get in Noatak. The village is just a few miles up the way."

"Like how do we get there?" asked John.

"Oh, there'll be other boats come along. I'll hitch a ride. Not to worry."

Bruce philosophized, "The Noatak has attacked back!"

I couldn't disagree. The Plan was unraveling, even "worser."

For two hours, then three, we waited, but no boat passed. After a while, foreseeing no rescue today, we unloaded our stuff and pitched camp around a fire ring that Bruce made of gathered rocks. When the tents were finally up and air mattresses inflated, John announced, "We gotta have a meeting, guys. Get all the food and bring it to the boat." We did, and John piled it all on the center seat, then said, "Our larder has to be parceled, parceled per man. Otherwise, we'll run out."

"Like how parceled?" Ras wanted to know.

"Like in six different allotments, one for each guy, one pile for the community. I'll do the parceling."

So basic canned goods, main-meal meats and potatoes, bacon and eggs, Bisquick, coffee, and condiments went in the community stash, while fruit, cookies, crackers, bread, cheese and lunch meat slices, pickles, gorp, chips, beers, and the like went to individual piles.

"Now," said the arbitrator, "Here are baggies. You can do exchanges as you will."

So, for the next twenty minutes, bargaining went like this: "I'll trade you three saltines for two Hydrox . . . Who wants an apple? I'd like a Baby Ruth . . . My chips for half your gorp pile . . . I'll give you my eight white bread slices for six of whole wheat . . . Any bidder for my can of sardines? I'll even take carrots . . . For real money I'll sell a beer, just one dollar." And so on, till the stashes were completed and carried off to tents. No one was allowed to touch the community food, and when breakfast or dinner was prepared, according to quartermaster John's new rules, no one was allowed to eat or drink until all the evenly divided portions were served.

Supper this night was hamburgers and fried potatoes. John offered grace and all the guys bent their heads but, I'll bet, few closed their eyes. Don't want anybody snitching my grub, each thought. I shared, "My father once told me that during the Depression, when he lived in a college boarding house, the boarders would spit on their dessert, so no one else would steal it. 'It always worked,' he told me."

With this bunch I wouldn't bet on it.

Around the fire this evening we talked, told jokes, shared fishing tales, stoked the coals, and did some "roamin' in the gloamin.'" Ras took Ranger Danger for a walk. After a while Kuster said, "If we can't hunt, at least we can fish." So our rods were put together.

Before long all were snoozin' in the gloamin,' and the sun slowly, slowly sank.

Marooned

I awoke around 5:00 a.m. to the sound of a boat's motor somewhere. Everyone else was still asleep. I stepped outside our tent and rekindled the fire, to stand over it. I then began to notice what was about. I listened to the birch-kindling crackle in the fire and gazed at the just-overhead overcast sky. To the northwest, though, the air was clear. On the grass and bushes were large drops of dew. No breeze. The dog stirred and then resettled. Salmon splashed sporadically on the river, the noise competing with seagull calls overhead. There were no other sounds, not even a snore. Though my knees were toasty, I take note of a chill on my back. So I added wood to the fire and stood facing away from the burning. Meanwhile, the river moved silently with olive-silver shadows cast on its swells. More sounds: the "Owaal, Owaal" of an unseen bird, the hum of a droning boat motor from way off, the cry of distant geese, another splash of another salmon, and soft stirring in the tent behind me. The smoke of the fire impelled me to move out of its path, toward a bush, inside of which a bird twittered. On a distant mountain peak, sunlight showed itself.

Morning had arrived.

Breakfast this day took nine eggs and half a pound of bacon. As we were finishing kettle coffee, the drone of the distant boat, heard earlier, became more nearly that of a train locomotive. Two huge barges plowed by. We waved. They waved back. There was no attempt to flag them down, much less over.

Mike announced that he would find a way to the village and so left camp.

Shortly thereafter, Ras wanted to know if he could borrow my rifle.

"Certainly," I said.

He and John then went hunting. Encouraging the endeavor, Bruce spoke: "Get something. We're gonna need meat."

And off they went.

After Kuster banked the fire, he and I made our way down the river channel and, though this water was totally new to us, had success. With his spinning rod and reel, Kuster had a minislam: a chum salmon, an arctic char, and a grayling.

A grayling! How special is that?

I, with a fly rod, changed my offering from a Muddler Minnow to a mosquito pattern and also took a grayling—my first ever. Then another. How graceful they are, rising out of the water to come down on the fly.

When we returned to camp, Ras and John were there, eating bologna and peanut butter sandwiches, respectively. Kuster and I opened and shared a can of sardines with eight saltines. Just as we were finishing up, Mike came in from his four hours of scouting to announce; "I can't find a way off the island. I'm afraid we're stuck."

I considered singing the *Gilligan's Island* theme song but didn't, for I didn't believe we were stranded. After a nap, I put on my chest-high Red Ball Waders and started across the rivulets and sandbars to the west. I thought it possible to cross somewhere and find a solid bank on which to traverse upriver. About half a mile out from our island I came to a heavier flow channel. Breaking off a stout branch of a root wad to use as a wading staff, I started across the channel toward the bank beyond. The water, even before I reached the main current, got way too deep. So I came back, defeated.

"Gentlemen," I solemnly pronounced upon return to the fire ring, "we, like Robinson Crusoe, are stranded!"

John, who was reading, answered, "Well, here take my book, *Extraterrestrial Civilizations*. I'm finished with it."

"Thanks, no," I said. "Can't abide a lost-in-space narrative, so close to what I'm feeling."

Surprises

Later this evening, as we were appreciating the fire's warmth, Bruce looked in the sky above and stood to announce, "Guys, they are here, the northern lights!"

I just fell onto my back to gawk. Sure enough, there it was, the aurora borealis. Oh my, oh my! I had looked all my life for this wonder, in Connecticut, Minnesota, Wisconsin, and other northern climes, but never had had a glimpse until now. Here it was before and around us, an unanticipated gift of the trip.

The lights filled the heavens from east to west in a dance of moving waves. The ethereal spectrum grew and contracted, moved and spread, violet and emerald and orange. In crescendos and flashing-changing patterns it went. I imagined myself in the first row of an immense operatic theatre, seated in front of giant fold velvet curtains, undulating in waves, altering in hue under a slow-moving color wheel strobe. We were mouths agape for a long time. After a while I said, "You know, with this sighting I can now truthfully sing I've 'seen the northern lights,'" the memorable line from Michael Burton's ballad that opens this chapter.

I journaled, "Sight of the northern lights alone makes this trip worthwhile." Even so, I want to fill my $200-worth of big game licenses. So in the morning, "A-hunting we shall go, a-hunting we shall go," came to my lips during a breakfast of five scrambled eggs and a mountain of hash brown potatoes—but no ham of the original menu. It had already been consumed.

"Why go hunting?" Ras asked. "We've already worked the island."

"True. But something might have moved in overnight, like a caribou."

So Kuster and I went, making our way along the west side of the long island, moving in parallel paths. Having hunted together for many years, he and I normally stay in tandem pretty well. After an hour's time, though, I had lost him—or he me. So I pushed on to the top of our island, thinking he might be ahead of me. But no Bruce.

Then in the distance I heard what I thought was a motorboat. Could this be our rescuer? In hope of that, I moved to the island's east side and started the trek back. The terrain was lush. Forget the fauna, I thought, note the flora. I was *walking* on top of lichen, moss, and dead leaves; *stepping* through just-off-the-ground raspberries and salmonberries; *treading* amidst taller ferns, red leaf cluster plants, grasses and dying yellow flowers exceeded a few inches in height by purple and white flowers; *brushing* against cinquefoil and waist-high bushes; *ambling* under willows, topped by a tree with wide leaves that I called sassafras, those two exceeded by birches with bark rough gray rather than white; and *sauntering* beneath spruce trees eighty feet tall. The plants and trees, I was later told, grow in a layer of topsoil called talik. The talik, now unfrozen, lies above the permafrost.

Arriving back at camp, I found Bruce smoking his pipe and drinking coffee with John. "Where'd you disappear to, mighty venator?" I asked.

"I turned off west, to check out the water for fish."

"But what about the hunting?"

"Well, what about it? What game did you spot?"

"The animals all snuck around me—just to where you should have been."

"Right. Come on now. Anything, anything at all?"

"Yes. I saw a ground squirrel."

"Well, congratulations!"

"Thank you," I said, figuring he probably wouldn't be interested in my vegetative discoveries. "I heard a boat go by."

"You did, indeed," John put in. "Two white guys going downriver. We talked to them, and Mike got assurance they'd call back to Noatak when they reached the fish hatchery downriver. After they make the call, someone in Noatak will send down a rescue party. We'll see. In the meantime, would you like a peanut butter and jelly sandwich or peanut butter and honey sandwich?"

Quartermaster John Hallsten Enjoying PB&J Sandwich

"Perhaps a Reuben today, toasted on light rye, please, with warm sauerkraut."

"Then it's peanut butter on balloon bread for you—and half an apple."

"After you've eaten, mister," Bruce said, "we're fishin'. I spotted a couple of likely runs."

Chums

We hesitated on the fishing, thinking that rescue might soon happen. After two hours, we gave up. The guys in the boat going downriver must have forgotten to honor our SOS. So Bruce and I ventured west to where the wadeable braids were and now, by Bruce's reconnoitering, deeper pools existed.

Spinning rod affixed with a #8 Mepps spinner on 6-pound test line, Bruce headed up toward one of the pools he'd seen earlier. I went downstream with my fiberglass 8-weight fly rod loaded with a Muddler Minnow. After casting but a couple of times, I heard excited shouts: "I got one! I got one! Bring the net! Bring the net!"

I reeled in and ran up. Sure enough, Son-of-the-old-pathfinder was onto something big, so big he could not get it in. He walked fast up and down the side of this long pool, cranking on the reel handle when he could, letting the line pull out as needed. It was a powerful fish on light monofilament.

With my flimsy aluminum net in hand, I stayed right behind him, ready to use it when the fish tired.

Forty-five minutes passed.

As we moved up and down the bank, Bruce kept saying, "I love it! I dearly love it." Finally, the exhausted fish came in. It was a chum salmon, perhaps 16 pounds, as big as any we'd plucked from the Chukchi Sea gill nets. I got the net under him and dragged him to shore. A beautiful dog with vertical purple stripes.

"I love it, I love it," Bruce repeated, finally to add, "dinner."

"Good going, partner. Ya done it. Now, get another."

He resolved to do so—but only after changing spools on his spinning reel. He took off the six-pound test and put on twenty-pound. I went back downstream to the likely looking run I'd started in earlier. Third cast and *bam*! I hooked into something solid that then moved out unhesitatingly to begin an in-and-out tussle. Eventually he came in, a salmon of maybe 5 pounds. Once beached, I heard Bruce yelling, "Got another!"

"Good for you!" I shouted back. "I'm hoping for another here."

I couldn't get that other, though. My pool had gone south. So I changed both location and leader to try my luck, as the day before yesterday, on grayling. I put on a small black fly, and luck I had. Took three wonderful 10–13-inch beauties, great jumpers, gorgeous to behold in all their iridescence.

Author with Grayling

Though apart, I could hear Kuster yelling, "Another, Jimmy, another!"

In time I went back to my earlier rig and earlier run, this time adding weight to the Muddler pattern. I cast out strongly and retrieved slowly. Here is my account of what happened, written that evening:

> I got a hit. Setting the hook and not budging him, I knew he was a big fish. A few preliminary starts and suddenly WHIR-R-R, and he was off like a missile from a fighter plane. I tried to slow him by palming the reel handle, but had to yell, "He's beating my hand to death!" And he was.
>
> I glanced down. The line changed colors from yellow to white, and I hollered, "I'm into my backing!" For the first time ever I had on a fish big enough to strip out all ninety feet of my fly line and take me deep into a hundred yards of backing. The reel racketed like a machine gun. It was unbelievably neat. I looked downstream and saw my line in the water. But twenty yards in front of where the line went in, this submarine was charging on the surface back toward me. After thirty minutes, Bruce getting my camera, I got a chum salmon in the net. He weighed about 12 pounds and had big hooked jaws.
>
> A thrill nonpareil.

The arctic sun was ever so slowly setting as I set up the camera on time-delay to take a picture of the two of us holding our kept catch. It's a most prized photo.

Author and BAK with Chum Salmon Catch

Once we were back in camp, Mike filleted the salmon; setting aside strips for dinner and strips for preserving. As he grilled our dinner, I dug a hole down two feet to the permafrost and there laid in the extra fillets, covering them with fir boughs.

Green beans from a can were taken with the salmon that night. Each strandee also got three soda crackers and twelve salmon berries on top of two chocolate chip cookies. Four ounces of beer went into each man's cup. We toasted our Gilligan's Island, and literate John announced, "We are Swiss Family Robinson. Better that," Hallsten added, "than upriver with Kurtz and 'the horror, the horror' in *Heart of Darkness*."

Ras responded, "Huh?"

John said, "Don't ask."

A second bottle of beer was split five ways as we squatted round the fire bemoaning our plight.

Chukchi Warriors

About eleven o'clock, just after the gloamin' ended, we heard a motorboat coming up the river. With flashlights at the bank we signaled the night travelers to come in. Two Eskimo men—dark, disheveled, and quite intoxicated—made their way to the fire ring.

"Hey, what you name?" the motor-handler asked John in a too loud voice. "Call me Bob. Me go Noatak. This is my bro." He gestured to the man beside him.

John replied, "Hi, I'm John."

The man nodded blankly and turned to Mike. "What you name? Call me Bob. Me go Noatak. This is my bro." And so he went around the circle, introducing himself and bro. The pair managed to free a beer from our store. More than the beer, we needed rescue help.

In Q&A we learned the two had been in Kotzebue and were returning to Noatak, their village. I thought to myself, they, though intoxicated, managed to count curves and in the dark come up the navigable channels—no mean feat!

Unfortunately, Bruce let slip that both Hallsten and I were preachers. That information upset Call-Me-Bob. He began to apologize. "I never drink beer, just this once, with you. What you name? Jim? Reverend Jim, call me Bob. Me go Noatak. This is my bro."

On and on.

Then they were off, promising to send a rescue boat for us "first thing in the morning."

That didn't happen. Most of the next day they were probably sleeping it off, totally forgetting their promise. Still, hoping for rescue, we five hung around camp all morning. Bruce worked some with Mike on the outboard. Ras and Ranger played throw-stick-in-the-water-retrieve-stick-from-the-water. John read and smoked his pipe. I made journal notes and shortly before noon decided to go for a swim. Taking a bar of soap and a towel to the riverbank, I lathered up in the shallow water. Then, to rinse off, I did my customary dive and three qualifying strokes.

John told me later that Ras asked if this was what "the horror" meant.

Not to his credit, Dr. Hallsten replied, "Indeed."

It was not until midafternoon that reliable rescue help appeared, in a boat with a half dozen people aboard. It was a Quaker/Society of Friends pastor, an Inuit, going up to his Noatak parish with his wife and children. In a pastors-to-pastor way, John and I explained our plight. The reverend invited Captain Mike to ride with them up to the village.

Less than an hour later Roland Ashby, tribal elder in Noatak, and Victor Onalik, a part-time river guide, showed up in the pastor's boat. There on the banks of the Noatak we struck a deal: for $300—money to be held by Roland—Victor would take John, Bruce, and me upriver hunting.

"I'll be here first thing in the morning," Victor assured us.

Next morning, long after first light, affable Victor showed up. "Chukchi Warrior ready for the Chukchi Warriors," he called out. Victor's boat was a fourteen-foot aluminum with a 10-horse outboard motor. Once loaded, it moved us upriver only slowly. By the time we reached Noatak Village he'd concluded, "Warriors, must lighten load or not make it." So we left my heavy tent, all fishing equipment, most of our camping gear, any change of clothing, and gun cases with Roland.

Purchasing $50 worth of gas and $50 worth of groceries from the Noatak Native Store, we were ready to go. John mumbled, "More expensive than in Kotzebue."

During these preparations, Roland brought Mike, Ras, and Ranger Danger upriver. I am happy to report that, as we pulled away from the dock, these three seemed fuller of face than when we had met them six days earlier. Their work of motor repair—or finding a replacement outboard—was just beginning.

Then we of the remnant party went upriver some forty miles and many bends to where the River Kugururok joins the Noatak. Here's my description of our passage:

> Three of us huddled in the bow
> Light blue sides to this boat
> Constant rrrr-rr-rrrr of the motor
> River is jade-colored more than blue
> Its edges are cobblestone sand beaches
> Its banks dirt 'n' cobblestones then trees
> Beyond the banks . . . just wide expanse
> Distant bare mountains, Brooks Range
> Clouds broken and streaked in the sky
> That sky on the far horizon is light blue
> Deepening overhead to dark blue
>
> Rrrr-rr-rrrr-rr-rrrr

So we went. Victor kept the skiff midriver to avoid tree boughs called "sweepers," hanging over the river. After a couple of hours, we reached the Kugururok and there made camp. To our surprise, another party was settled in across the river, albeit more fully outfitted with canvas tent, folding chairs, and a table made of cut branches. The occupants were not there.

Our sparse camp readied, we were eager to hunt, to claim what remained of the Plan. Victor motored us up the main channel of the Noatak several miles to where the river narrowed and there was a steep bluff. "Go up, Warriors," Victor said, "maybe see a *deniigi*, the moose." So we climbed to the promontory. There wasn't game to be seen, only a promising-looking valley a half-mile inland. Toward that valley we started to troop.

Now the discovery: you can't walk on tundra. No way. Tundra looks like it's solid soil, smooth grass. It isn't. It's a wildly uneven bog with clumps of thick grass, tussocks of vegetation. You can neither walk on top of these nor slog through the hollows to their sides. There was no way to progress across. In winter when snow fills and packs the depressions, then one might. But not now. Defeated, we went back to the promontory, straining to walk.

Returning to the Kugururok, John suggested we pull into the campsite opposite ours and meet the occupants. They were Jürgen Zimmerman and Manfred Sauer, pharmacist and doctor, respectively, from Germany. We learned they'd been helicoptered into the Gates of the Arctic National Park and Preserve, several hundred miles upriver. For the last month they had hunted their way down using a pontoon boat with a 4-horse motor. Six huge caribou racks on their craft testified success. Serious hunters, hardcore outdoorsmen they. Jürgen had been in the German Green Berets.

"Stay for dinner," Manfred offered. "It'll be caribou tenderloin steaks."

"Gladly!" we chorused.

Into the long evening we talked. The two were from Heidelberg but did not know the music about their town from *The Student Prince*. I gave them a few bars of it:

> *Drink! Drink! Drink! Lift your steins and drink your beer.*
>
> *Drink! Drink! Drink! To eyes that are bright as stars when they're shining on me!*
>
> *Drink! Drink! Drink! Let every true lover salute his sweetheart! Let's drink!*

That we did—coffee made from the dehydrated crystals they'd brought on their trip.

Upon return to our camp, Victor entertained us with Eskimo humor stories. one was about a herpes queen who went on a GH, Good Hunt, and gave the hunters *anymuch*, that is, unlimited food, favors, and medical bills. Victor let us know that a Chukchi Warrior does not *anak* near camp.

"*Anak*?" Bruce asked.

"Shit," he replied.

"Oh."

We all laughed about What-you-name?-Call-me-Bob, whom Victor knew well.

Then it was try-to-sleep-on-the-ground time. We white guys managed without air mattresses. Victor used a *pokrak*, or caribou-hide sleeping bag, with the hair on the inside to keep the cold away. Our tent was Visqueen, noisy but dew resistant.

The next day's hunt was up the Kugururok, its surrounding terrain marked by pine forests with both solid soil and rock—not tundra —underneath.

Game

For a successful hunt on this, our three-thousand-mile odyssey, this day seemed our best chance. Victor dropped us off on the east side of this coming-from-the-north river. I wanted to go high and see what could be seen. John and Bruce went low. I began to work my way up a steep hill, part of 1,350-foot Mount Misheguk.

Russet sumac—or something like it—was on the sides of the hill. As I picked my way across a particularly steep and rough spot, I thought, "Likely no white man has ever walked here before." So I strode ten bold steps: one . . . two . . . three . . . to ten. "There! Done." Coming to a gentler slope, I went into song from *The Student Prince*, inspired by meeting the Germans the night before.

> Golden days, in the sunshine of our happy youth
> Golden days, full of happiness and full of truth.

For sure, this day was golden. Then, from the same musical, I offered up,

> I'll walk with God from this day on,
> His helping hand I'll lean upon.

A squirrel chattered to me, "Off key!"

After three hours, I finally came to the top of a ridge and found an outcrop with good field of vision. I called it "far enough" and sat down with the thought: This is the point farthest north that you'll ever be in your life. Decades later, I know it was. I set the timer on my camera to capture me in this incredible location.

Author at Farthest Point North, Overlook of Kugururok Valley

To the east was a section of what I surmised to be the Brooks Range, probably the Mayumerak Mountains, or perhaps the Bairds. To the west was the Kugururok Valley and to the north an expanse over which game might move. Beyond the valley were lower-lying mountains. Long and hard I looked on that valley floor. I looked as I ate lunch. I looked as I prayed open-eyed thanks scribbled down:

O Lord God,
Creator of all that is—

the majesty of the distant mountains,

the springy moss soil under my feet—

You have blessed me greatly with

body and strength to carry here,

resources to pay for it,

friends to enjoy it with.

Your wonders are before me, marvel to behold.

They bring me into your presence.

I hope

that I can be something of a blessing to you,

as you have me—greatly.

Amen.

It also occurred to me that God spent a lot of time—five billion years—to get me this visual treat. So an extra, *"Thanks, God!"*

I then looked through the scope of my rifle for movement in the valley. I looked and waited, looked and waited. Then game appeared. Less than a hundred yards below, an arctic fox, the size of a healthy coyote, materialized. Beautiful and brown, long bushy tail swishing, I put him in my scope, but decided, No. I have no license, need, or inclination. He explored until he disappeared into some low green bushes.

That was it. No moose. No caribou. No bear. The hunt was over, though I didn't know it.

In return to camp we had a "what-now?" conversation. The answer: return to Noatak. Not one of us had found any sign of game. It seemed unlikely we would, unless we went way upriver. Victor let out that going farther was out of the question: "Gas almost out. Maybe enough to get us back to Noatak. Maybe, maybe not."

So, reloading the boat, downriver we went.

We did not, however, run out of gas. Not yet. Rather, Victor's outboard motor overheated and cracked the block. "Not to worry," he assured us. "I have back-up engine." It was a one-cylinder job, and it soon had us putt-putting along slowly, down the river. Before long *this* motor ran out of gas.

Now we were drifting to Noatak, loose in the current, upriver without a paddle. We made it to shore and there cut poles from some birch trees. With them we floated and poled down. Especially we learned sweepers, sweepers in spades, sweepers up close and personal. We poled around them, under them, sometimes through them. We worked our way out of eddies, pushed off sandbars, and used our poles as rudders. We did twenty miles of poling.

The Village

By late afternoon we made Noatak, a five-thousand-year-old village of around three hundred souls. At the dock we said good-bye to Victor and made our way up the steep bank into town. Village headman Roland Ashby welcomed us back, directed us to the shed where our upriver gear had been stored, then preceded with pride to show off his village. The newer houses, built above the permafrost, were wooden modular. Some had skirts, others no. Some had plumbing connected, others no. The older homes were wood frame and quite simple.

I wrote down a one-word descriptor for so much of what we saw: squalor. Empty oilcans and trash everywhere, broken down snowmobiles in almost every yard. Many villagers seemed listless. I wondered about their inner state. When we later met up with Victor, he was quite drunk. Call-me-Bob had supplied him with Kotzebue booze.

Roland introduced us to two Anglos, twenty-something teachers named Nick and Amy. They'd come to Alaska to pay off student loans. Nick told us, "It's a challenge to teach here. For one thing, I'm sad to report, interest in the tribe's native language is minimal." The couple said that about eighth grade kids start dropping out. Some move to Anchorage or other larger towns. Young men often go to work in the oil fields. And, as Amy put it, "There is little opportunity for women."

John, Bruce, and I would have stayed longer and talked with these two, but we wanted to clean up and get some sleep.

Roland's brother, Herbert, offered us his old pre-modular home for the night. The house was essentially a shack with half a roof. While thinking over this offer, one of Herbert's daughters brought out a washbowl and a bucket of warm water. Using a line from *Cinderella*, I said, "Thank you kindly."

Amazingly enough, she replied, "You're kindly welcome." Then she blushed.

Finally, Herbert spoke. "If you want, you can sleep in my living room. It's heated."

We chose warmth over the smell of motor oil. So began the most bizarre night I ever had.

Helen

Our backpacks were placed by the front door, our cased rifles stacked in the washing machine. John, having spread his sleeping bag right behind the couch, was soon snoring. Thus, he missed what was to come.

Bruce and I took a seat on the home's overstuffed couch. Herbert left, just disappeared, leaving us with his wife, Helen. She offered us a bowl into which a big dollop of chocolate ice cream was plopped, topped by salmonberries, which, she told us, she and her five children had picked. These hard-frozen berries were extracted from her six-foot-long, three-foot-high freezer. "This is different," Bruce commented.

When the children went off to bed, Helen moved her copies of *The National Enquirer* from the middle section of the couch and took a seat there, all two hundred and fifty pounds of her. She'd come to watch television. What a threesome we were watching big-screen TV live from Los Angeles in full color. Salmonberries and satellite TV, the ultimate contrast of cultures!

Above the TV set was Leonardo da Vinci's *Last Supper* in velvet. Elvis was festooned on a sidewall. When Helen went to the kitchen, I whispered to Bruce, "Where's Herbert?"

"I don't know. Maybe he lives elsewhere. I hope he's not observing the traditional Eskimo custom."

"You mean the share-wife tradition?"

"That be the one."

"You go," I conceded. "Me, I'll watch—television, that is."

We three, though, just continued with the set. First was a made-for-TV movie called *Mr. Horn*. When it went to credits, I was hoping that would end the evening and that I, having won the coin toss, would get the couch. No, there was another western to watch. It featured a young John Wayne. Halfway through the saga, neither Kuster nor I could take it any longer. We bid Helen good night. She nodded and continued with her viewing, the volume quite loud.

We two spread our sleeping bags behind the couch, beside John's, but we didn't get in them, just laid on top, clad in our sweaty, many-days-worn clothes. I was way too hot in the room, which must have been over eighty degrees!

Sometime, maybe around 3:00 a.m., I got up to relieve myself and was aware of silence. The set was off, Helen gone. I went into the bathroom. It was an unconnected commode with a white plastic honeypot in the bowl. The backyard, I believe, was the septic system. Duty done, I went back to bed and noticed that Bruce wasn't snoring. He wasn't sleeping.

It was, to be sure, a long night.

Next morning Kuster got up with the words, "We're outta here! I'm paying for it."

So his time that morning went to arranging for a wing-away plane.

Kuster Makes Trip-ending Phone Call

Meanwhile, John and I walked the village. As it was a Saturday, out-of-school children were riding about on four-wheel ATVs. Teenagers walking along had earplug stereos on and were drinking canned sodas, obliviously dropping the containers on the ground. We ran across the Anglo teachers, Nick and Amy, and they took us to see a Native woodcarver, Ralph Downey. His craft was constructing berry pickers, that is, wooden scoops, from bent wood.

"Quite handsome," John said.

"Indeed," I added.

Woodcarver Ralph directed us to meet his brother, Walter Downey, an older man who from used saw blades made *ulus*—ivory-handled, crescent-blade knives. Traditionally, the ulu was employed to cut whale blubber. John and I purchased two of the unique tools for $35 apiece. John also bought a small whalebone oil lamp with a wick hole and pedestal legs carved from walrus ivory.

Interestingly enough, the then-governor of Alaska, Jay Hammond, came to visit the village that day, and I shook his hand. While he walked the village, his wife Bella, herself a Native American, went out with the Noatak women to gather salmonberries.

At eleven o'clock Bruce informed us that he had made connections with Shallaburger Air for a special flight to come here from Kotzebue. "The Plan" to depart from here tomorrow by boat was changed to this day by air.

"We'll get out today," Bruce asserted. "God owes us one!"

"Since when did you get to be a theologian?" I wanted to know.

"Since you reverend doctors seem not to have any connection with the Almighty."

A single-engine plane came in. The pilot took a photo of John, Bruce, and me about to board, while Roland Ashby and Captain Mike looked on with smiles. It did not include Ras, who had hitched a ride downriver two days earlier.

Flying down the Noatak River, we saw our island in the sun with its lonely beached boat. In less than thirty minutes we were in Kotzebue. I'm sure Bruce paid the pilot handsomely. As John and I went to reclaim luggage, Kuster walked to the Wien Air ticket counter to bargain. He returned smiling, "God is still good. At no extra charge, I've exchanged our day-after-tomorrow tickets for a flight out today."

At this point we made a beeline to the airport restroom, there to take a major sponge bath. Good-bye to a week's worth of smoke and sweat. Good-bye dirty clothes. Would that we could have taken a real shower. Someone might have thought we *had* showered, so much water was on the floor. To the point, a guy came in, saw our mess, and did a one-eighty back out. Eventually we emerged decent in travel clothes.

I said to Bruce, "Please watch my stuff. I have a Daddy-errand to run."

And run I did, some five blocks, to the jade factory. I have to take something nice home to the wife and daughters, I thought. True to form with my luck on this trip, the place closed at noon. Sorry, girls. I hoped I would be able to make an Anchorage airport purchase. I ran back to board our plane.

Exodus

A few hours later, we three hunters—game licenses unfilled—stood awkwardly on the tarmac of the Anchorage airport, John's plane home to Fairbanks about to take off. We were trying to think of appropriate departing words.

John finally offered this benediction: "Yep, now we know what we were going to find out." I have no idea what that meant, but it sounded profound.

Bruce offered, "We attacked the Noatak, got hit back, and survived."

I philosophized: "Your plane's ready, John," hugged him, and said, "Go!"

Flying over the mountains of British Columbia the next morning, as we sped toward Calgary, I tried to evaluate our trip into the wild. Without question, the best part of the ten days was the company. Bruce and John were great companions: adventurous, flexible, fun guys, given to wonderful banter. Mike, Ras, and Rusty made our first four days exceedingly educational regarding commercial salmon fishing and the consumptive capacity of humans. Victor was just a hoot and, as long as I live, there will be Call-Me-Bob. And Helen, of course! Colorful, unforgettable company.

On the other hand, in terms of what we intended to do, the trip was a disaster. Almost everything went wrong, was delayed, cost too much, was hard, or sent us scrambling to come out whole. Robert Burns had it right about "the best-laid plans of mice and men" going awry.

We arrived home at the old Stapleton Airport in Denver, coming through the plane ramp doors to be greeted warmly by family members. After hugs all around, I dug into my backpack and offered up a wild-game, return-home present: a three-ounce package of vacuum-sealed smoked salmon, purchased in the Anchorage airport souvenir shop for $1.60.

The hot shower I took this night was the best I ever had.

Then to sleep with one last thought: If you want to make God laugh, tell *her* your plans.

Segue to New Zealand

THE SPRING BEFORE THE just-recounted Alaska adventure of 1982, Kuster and I made a fishing trip to the Bighorn River in Montana, the first of fifty-some to be taken here over the next quarter century. On our third trip in 1984 we met Ron Granneman, a lanky, most competent fishing guide, an earlier-career bow hunter holding Pope and Young elk-trophy records. He became our go-to ghillie on the Bighorn and, after a few seasons, a close friend—so much so that he invited Bruce and me to join him "down under" in New Zealand, where he repaired each fall when Montana guiding ended.

Kuster and I were able to accept Granneman's invitation in 1987. So the next story, of our adventure on the northwest coast of NZ's South Island. While in New Zealand, Bruce, Ron, and I fished half a dozen rivers. Into two of them we were "wop-wop" helicoptered.

On the NZ trip we exchanged the northern lights of Alaska for the Southern Cross stars, right-side driving for the left lane, Inuit humor for Kiwi tongue-in-cheek, motorboat travel for the helicopter, upriver salmon for sea-run browns, and more—much more—that, I believe, you will find fascinating.

A pause in this segue, however, is in order.

After the Alaska adventure and leading up to the New Zealand trip, a number of professional and writing things happened: I did fund raising for three United Church of Christ theological schools, ran a phone bank for the Denver Democratic party, briefly followed a western artist around Montana, started a hospital capital campaign in North Dakota, served as interim minister at Christ Congregational Church in Denver, and in 1985 accepted a call to be senior minister of a large-membership UCC church in Moline, Illinois. This ministry, however, turned out to be an *unintended* interim position.

"Unintended" means I was fired.

You may now ask, "Why fired?" The answer is an almost-funny story in itself. That the church and I were not a good fit is as close as I can come to understanding the requested resignation that came about. I was "too liberal," several said. "Your rusty fishing station wagon in the church parking lot doesn't look proper," a woman told me. "Your wife's not coming with you here isn't right." And so on. When I was being interviewed by a local newspaper reporter about my pastorate and the leaving of it, I asked her what she had heard. She said, "The whispers are that you are a womanizer and gay."

I told her, "I just thought I was being celibate!"

I shared this conversation with a ministerial colleague. He looked at me, smiled broadly, and said, "Ah, Jim, you must remember the words of St. Paul: we are called to be 'all things to all people.'"

That was priceless! His consolation one of the funniest things I think I've ever heard. But it was *gallows humor*, for the ministry's ending sure felt like an execution!

Happily, the church leadership felt so guilty about asking me to leave that they gave me a year's severance salary. So, in the year of unemployment, I was able to complete a book called *Intergenerational Religious Education,* the most significant contribution to scholarly thought I ever made. This book, I should mention, grew out of inter-age summer programming done at First Plymouth Church, Englewood, the church I served during the 1970s. In it I argued that, in this by-age-separated culture, the church is uniquely positioned to bring young and old together to share wisdom and hope. Lots of good social science and educational theory is offered in the book. *IGRE* shows the influence of process theologians Alfred North Whitehead, Norman Pittenger, and Teilhard *de Chardin.* Process thought, to be sure, emphasizes dynamism and change, as opposed to a static understanding of God, humanity, and the world. Readings here introduced me to the pre-Socratic philosopher Heraclitus, who offered a truth about the world—and about trout fishing: "One cannot stand in the same river twice."

The other positive thing to come out of Moline's unhappy ending is that the words Joseph (of the Hebrew Bible) spoke to his betraying brothers now rang true for me: "What you intended for evil, God intended for good" (Genesis 50:20). The New Zealand trip is part of that good.

Through all the moving about in the '80s, I continued fishing with friends and doing fishing retreats in Colorado—*and* one thing more: I started writing articles that appeared in *Fly-Fisherman* magazine, *Colorado Outdoors,* and *Southwest Art.*

The above paragraphs are to say that ministry and fly-fishing were still commingling in the '80s.

So, now, to the New Zealand adventure.

CHAPTER 5

'Coptering into the Wop-Wops

New Zealand South Island
February 1987

IT WAS A SIMPLE cloth patch on the fisherman's vest: "South Island." We were on Armstrong Spring Creek in Montana. I thought I knew what it meant. To confirm, I pointed to it and asked the wearer, "New Zealand?"

"Yes, he said, "been there several times."

I was filled with patch envy.

Two years later a Kiwi was saying to me, "So you want to go to fuck-out Egypt, do you?"

"Pardon?" I replied.

"To the wop-wops?"

"Eh?"

"To the bush—the outback?"

"If that's what you call it, yes. To fish for sea-run browns."

"All right, then, mate, at bird's fart."

I fumbled at the language. "Say what?"

"The crack-a-dawn," he said. "Be here."

Early next morning Ivan Wilson, helicopter pilot, dropped Bruce Kuster, Ron Granneman, and me off on a riverbed deep in the northwest wilderness of the South Island, New Zealand.

Ready to Board Helicopter

Our gear and four days' worth of food unloaded, Ivan and his chopper took off, and we trekked up a path to a one-room hut hidden in the woods above a small stream. An hour later, we were looking at the gin-clear water of the Waitaha River, ready to fish.

"But *fish* we don't do here in New Zealand," said Ron, veteran South Island angler. "Like I told you the first day you guys got here, we *hunt* fish here, we stalk 'em. It's not like the Bighorn in Montana with five thousand trout per mile. Not at all. There may be only a half dozen per mile—but big—and we've got to find them."

Bruce interrupted the instructions. "Are there eels here, as in the Grey?"

Ron looked up and down the river, to say, "Not right now."

On arrival in Westport three days earlier, Ron had taken us through a farmer friend's pasture to fish the River Grey. On that stretch Bruce went downriver, Ron and I upstream. Down there alone, Bruce had a "close en-counter" he could not forget. We heard him shouting, "Got one, got one!"

Ron and I sloshed back down to witness the action. By the time we arrived, Kuster was holding his rod in one hand, fish attached, and throw-ing rocks in the water with the other hand. In that water was a long black something—an eel! Apparently the creature had seen the trout flashing in the stream and come to investigate for his dinner. Bruce was desperately attempting to scare him off. Ron and I added rocks.

Finally the serpent—three feet long—slid back downstream.

"I hate that damn thing," Bruce said.

That was on the Grey. Now on the Waitaha, in fear and loathing, he repeated himself: "I hate those damn things."

I said, "Don't be such a wimp. All he might do is take a chunk out of your leg."

Ron intervened with understanding. "Not to worry. They mostly like brown trout, not white meat."

"How reassuring."

"So," Ron continued, "let's cross this river here and eyeball our way down."

In his short pants and rubber sole hiking boots, Ron splashed forward. Bruce, in felt-sole fishing boots and drip-dry long trousers, followed, as did I, my boots outfitted with strap-on aluminum cleats.

"Better leave those here," Ron suggested. "They'll be dangerous when boulder hopping."

I removed them, for boulder hopping aplenty was just what we did.

Author Rock Hopping on NZ River

That, and fording and refording the river as we went down, all the time looking for fishy game. Sometimes we went through lush vegetative areas with lots of exotic ferns. Finally Ron stopped on a bank to say, "There's one." Now he instructed, "You guys go down below and come up slowly. I'll tell you what to do."

So Bruce with a 6-weight rod and I with a clunky 8-weight did as instructed. We were using floating lines fixed with twelve-foot leaders. He had on a bushy Irresistible—a.k.a. the Rat-faced McDougal—size ten, and I was armed with a lightly weighted Pheasant Tail Nymph, size twelve.

Standing on the bank, Ron directed Bruce: "Get over to 90 degrees from the eye of this hole. The fish is in the bottom."

Kuster cast.

"Go again," Granneman said, "but don't line him."

Bruce cast again.

"Oops! Too much. He's gone. Took off downriver. Let's go find another."

And we went on, boulder hopping, stream crossing, and pool watching. At the next sighting, I went in with the nymph, but according to Bruce, then spotting for me, the fish simply moved off as the Pheasant Tail came near. Two pools later I had a touch, then nothing. At sighting six, Ron deftly placed a Royal Wulff into a seam and a nice 18-inch river brown came up and took it. I expected Ron to hit it, but he didn't. Instead he hesitated with the words, "God save the queen," then set the hook. Happily, this fish didn't freight train downriver and ere long was beached. Releasing the fish and standing to see him swim away, Ron said, "Well, that's about how it goes down here. Ratios on typical day are ten sightings, five takes, and one fish landed. Let's go find another."

On we went. We found two in a pool's tail who saw us and fled. Bruce hooked up with a big boy who ran him downstream and, running between boulders, broke his 3x leader. I switched over to a Gray Wulff and—lucky first cast, Granneman directing—had it swallowed by a silver brown fresh from the ocean. The fish tried to return there, but Bruce's splashing the water turned it back upriver, and we finally got it in. A 23-inch female!

Author with NZ Searun Brown

At four o'clock, Ron said, "Time to head back, guys. Down here we fish ten till four, for best sighting. Before or after it's too hard. Besides," he continued, head nodding up, "these clouds coming in will make it impossible to see fish—and rain's a-coming. Not a bad day, though. Five fish-to-hand, a 23-incher, a 20, Bruce's 16, and two that were a foot long."

As we started the long trek back, fording, boulder hopping, tree skirting, it began to rain. A drizzle at first, becoming serious by the time we reached the cabin. A fire in the potbellied stove felt good, and the pork chops fried over it tasted great. I ate my portion of Ron's steamed veggies, cauliflower, broccoli, and brussels sprouts. Little did I know that such would be our every-night fare. Bruce acted as if he enjoyed it.

"You're both weird," I said aloud.

"Man up," Kuster advised.

"Get used to it," Ron warned.

As we bed-rolled, rolling up our jeans as pillows, the rain pounded on the tin roof. Long and hard it pounded.

Then came morning. The sun was up—and so was the river. Like fifteen feet up. And chocolate brown. The tiny creek running behind the hut was full too, its water happily at least clear enough to drink.

"This upsurge is what they call a *fresh*," Ron said. "No chance to fish today. In fact, it may be a couple of days before it goes down and even more before Ivan can come get us."

"Oh, joy," I managed to say.

Offering faint solace, Bruce said, "Deal with it. After breakfast I have a treat for you: Jane Fonda's exercise program. I've got her on my portable recorder."

Sure enough, he did. So, at ten o'clock we began big stretches, body twists, toe touches, on the floor sit-ups, push-ups, and—hardest of all—touching-the-toes-behind-your-head contortion.

Ron sat on the edge of his bunk amazed. "You guys have lost it. Never in my life would I expect to see anything like this. Just don't let any Kiwis see you. They deport the mentally defective."

Ron's amazement standing, we "did it with Jane" two more times that long day. Our routine started over, Ron would go out to see if the river was dropping. Midafternoon there was a sign. The fresh was getting a little stale, down three inches. By supper it had dropped three feet.

Next morning it was almost back to its former flow of—I'm guessing—300 thirty cubic feet per second. Its former gin-like color, however, was now root beer. Going down the path to check it out sent me back up it to retrieve my fly rod. There was a fish holding in the pool just beyond the landing pad. Kneeling down I cast above him. Up he ascended, took the fly, and went back down. I "God save the queened" it and he skyed, then ran his pool in circles. Three rounds done, he came flopping onto the bank, a beautiful and dark 18-incher. Three hours later I came back and caught him again. A most cooperative fish. The fish upriver were not as accommodating, though Ron and I went there to hunt. Bruce went down.

Ivan and helicopter appeared at noon to lift us out. As we flew back to the home pad, I asked about the glass bubble underneath the plane's cockpit.

Ivan explained. "At one time the deer population in this country was so great the protective vegetation on the hills was almost eaten off. So the government paid us to shoot as many deer as possible."

"Oh, my. How many do you think you killed? A couple hundred?"

"No, no. Many more."

"Like . . . ?"

"Like, I don't know. I think I turned in ear-evidence for, maybe, thirty thousand. Today we only capture 'em with nets. I've got half a dozen penned up at my place now."

"As pets?"

"No. I sell 'em to a guy who has a deer farm. He keeps 'em, fattens 'em, and sells the meat to the Germans. It once was marketed as 'Black Forest venison,' but since Chernobyl and the fallout over Europe, they now say, "New Zealand venison, guaranteed not to be from Black Forest deer.'"

"Tell him who the other market is, Ivan," Ron prompted.

"It's the Chinese, especially. In our deer farms, the antlers are shorn off while in velvet, then ground up and sold as an herbal medicine. Antler powder is thought to be a powerful aphrodisiac."

With that, the helicopter set down. We unpacked and headed back to Reefton.

"Tomorrow," Ron advised, "we'll go south to the Ahaura River. It's car-accessible."

In Ron's two-passenger car, me squeezed in the middle over the console, we drove thirty miles down to the Ahaura, only to find it blown out, fresh with cocoa water. Back to Reefton then. There we spent most of the afternoon in a local pub drinking DBs, a "fair dunkin" (pretty good) beer, also called a Brown. The small telly in the place carried a cricket match, boring and interminable in my estimation, but two guys in the place sat watching, mesmerized. I was drawn to the dartboard, where I first let Bruce, then Ron, beat me. After a while, we wandered the town and found a most unusual evergreen in a churchyard. Its branches had long bristles like a dust broom.

Lots of things down under are different. Driving is reversed, on the left side of the road. Water swirls down the drain right to left. And the stars are totally unrecognizable. Guess I should spell that *unrecognisable*. A tire shop down here is a *tyre* shop. And so on.

In the pub-café I seemed to upset the waitress by asking for ice in my water, to further insult her by leaving a tip. Though English—that is, British English—is the spoken language here, it is a different country and culture, quite wonderful. When Bruce lost his thyroid medicine, for example, Ron took him to the hospital and he got his prescription filled there for free. Socialized medicine exists quite comfortably with the Kiwis. They are strongly anti-nuclear in politics, made so with remembrance of nuclear bombs dropped on Pacific islands, whose fallout came New Zealand's way. For their politics alone, I think I could live there most happily. The fishing, however, would be reason enough.

On the start of our South Island second week, Ron announced that he had arranged for another trip into the wop-wops, to the Karamea River. We drove north past Westport, toward the uppermost peninsula. There we met our second helicopter pilot, Terry Belcher. First he loaded our gear for camping in the wilds: backpacks, tarps, sleeping bags, cooking equipment, food, along with our fishing gear.

"It's a fairly quick trip over the mountain," Terry explained, "only about twenty minutes in my plane. But it would be more than a hard day's walk to get there otherwise. I'll drop this load off and come back for you."

So up and over he went, returning shortly for his passengers. Part of the flight was through a steep-walled canyon to a riverbed wide spot to land us on a sandy shore, our gear nearby.

Unloaded, Terry said, "I'll be back for you in three days."

With the sound of the helicopter receding, we made our way down the riverbank to where we found a suitable open space in a riverside glen. We stretched tarps, placed our sleeping bags underneath, and gathered wood for a fire. Dinner that night was more cauliflower-broccoli-brussels sprouts and, mercifully, sausages roasted over the fire. After dinner, we sat around sipping scotch from tin cups and conversing about growing up in the '40s with the Lone Ranger, Superman, and other afternoon radio heroes.

We were sitting there conversing as the fire died down. Then a phenomenon occurred that none of us had ever experienced.

"What's that?" I said, pointing.

"What?" Bruce asked.

Ron said, "Where?"

"There. Those little lights on the root base of the upturned tree."

"Must be fireflies, like back in Illinois," Bruce offered.

"Except, they're not flying. They're just there."

I put my flashlight on the root clump, and the flickers disappeared. I drew up close to look and could see nothing.

"Ah, I think I know," said Ron. "Up on the North Island there's a famous cave visitors go to where there are glowworms. That's what must be here."

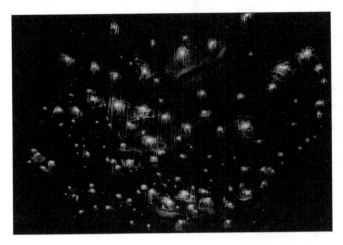

Glowworms of the North Island Waitomo Cave.

"It's like the Milky Way rounded," Bruce suggested, "a kind of filled-up Christmas tree wreath."

Amazing. I've never seen anything like it before or since.

Talk of the Milky Way suggested stargazing, so we walked out to the river's sand bank to check out the night sky. The Milky Way was not there, only the heard-of Southern Cross. I thought Scorpio might be visible, but it wasn't.

Night well on, we bid the stars and our glowworms good night and retired to sleeping bags atop inflated air mattresses. Mine had a slow leak, making for a little-sleep night.

The next day we fished hard—or, I should say, we hiked long to fish hard. Ron remembered from a previous trip to this river that there was a wide, braided area way downstream. "Last year," he said, "I caught a 12-pound sea-run brown there. Are you up for a trek?"

Sure.

So we went. As we started out I asked, "Will I need my poncho?"

Ron answered, "Likely. The Kiwis put it this way: 'If it's raining, take a raincoat. If it isn't, take your chances.'" So I took it in the backpack along with sunblock, lunch sandwiches, no water, camera, and flies.

We went, went, and went, through thickets, around cliffs, over boulder fields and blown-down trees, crossing the river several times, hunting while traversing. Spotting quarry, we'd stop to present a fly. A couple of big resident browns took our bushy offerings. Already it felt as if we were in a better river.

A better river, indeed, when we finally made the braided area sometime after noon, still in the 10:00–4:00 sun-at-high-angle-for-sighting-fish window. Here the river flattened out but still had good holding water. There were a number of large washed-down trees to get around, yet stand on, that we might spot fish. Positioned on one, Ron exclaimed, "There's a big boy in the eye of the pool in front of me. I'm going for him. Watch for me, Jim."

I stood on his log while he false cast out a likely amount of line—but not over the pool. Then at the pool he let the fly drop in.

"You're short," I called out.

He let out more line and threw again.

"Too far right. Try again."

This time his cast was spot-on. The fly floated in perfectly. So the fish came up from the bottom of the eye to eat Ron's fly. I thought, "God save the queen," then strongly instructed, "Hit Him!"

Ron lifted his rod, and I knew he'd stuck the fish by the slight twist the fish made. The trout, though, just settled down to the bottom of the pool unperturbed—miffed, I thought, by the metal in his mouth. Slowly Ron backed out of the river keeping a taut line, and the fish under mysterious pressure drifted toward Ron. For the first time the piscine realized the source for lip aggravation and his head being pulled: a humanoid, his nemesis! The fish jetted up to explode into the air, then madly circled the pool. Ron splashed in, thinking to drive his quarry upstream. It worked momentarily. The trout went upriver, only to reverse direction downstream, seaward.

Keeping his rod high, angler moved with angled. Ron ran when he could, navigated around root wads, stayed upright over slippery boulders, went back midriver to take his line out where it was stuck between rocks, fearing he might be buggered. But he wasn't. Ron was resolved not to let this fish get away.

Next the fish came to another deep pool well over a hundred yards downriver. Here the fish stopped and sulked on the bottom. Applying gentle pressure, Ron eased him up and toward shore. Though the big boy pulled back out, he was tired and let himself be drawn back in. Finally the trout entered the shallows and was aground. We measured him at 26 inches and thought his weight to be about 7 pounds. Ron was a happy, tried, and tired fellow. He had just taken the biggest fish of the trip.

Meanwhile, Bruce discovered that, in these waters, you don't have to pre-sight every fish. He told me about it. Doing blind casting, he'd had three takes and landed two fish. As Ron and I came over to him beside a long run, he was battling a third. Suddenly he let out a huge "Auggh" and levitated right out of the river onto a boulder. Certainly it was as fast an exodus from a stream as I've ever seen. A big black eel had come up from behind. I don't remember what happened to the fish. Perhaps the eel got him, but Bruce stayed on his boulder shivering.

"You're a wuss," I told him.

"Yah, maybe, but I still have all my body parts."

The wuss was a long time coming down. So I went a-hunting by Bruce's blind cast technique, to discover it could be done. Fish often are there, though not seen. I had five takes and beached two resident browns, both just short of 20 inches, weighing 3 pounds. Nice fish.

As the clouds rolled in, Ron said we'd better go. So we did. It was a difficult slog back to our campsite, made harder because rain came during the last several miles of the return. It did not, however, dampen our satisfaction for this day.

The glowworms gave us good go-to-sleep light.

Author Resting after Long Day

Next morning, though it was raining lightly, we fished in it, all the while hoping against a fresh. The fresh didn't come, but Terry did, in his chopper, about noon, to do the take-outs.

By late afternoon we were back in Reefton, ready for the trailer park's semi-warm shower and an in-town lamb dinner. DB's were downed before, during, and after the meal.

The next day, Ron drove Kuster and me to the airport in Westport. We then flew Westport to Christchurch, Christchurch to Auckland on the North Island, and home via Honolulu and Los Angeles—almost 8,000 miles all told.

I now wear my "New Zealand" patch with unfeigned satisfaction, invoking invitation to tell others about tight lines on 24-inch browns in the beautiful wop-wops.

Fishing Vest Patch

Segue to British Columbia

MUCH GOOD FLY-FISHING, PASTORING, and a melding of the two—with considerable reflection—went on in the years between the above-recounted 1987 adventure in New Zealand and the soon-to-be-told trip to British Columbia in 2005. Let me insert a word about doings and developments in the eighteen-year hiatus between trips—*and* some of the years before and after.

Two years after the NZ "Wop-Wops" trip, I was called from an interim assignment at Hilltop United Church in Parker, Colorado, to be senior minister of First Congregational Church in Colorado Springs. (I came without Anita, as we were separated, legally divorcing in 1990.) In this new parish setting, I continued leading fly-fishing retreats for men.

Such retreats, you may recall, began in the 1960s when I was in campus ministry at Colorado State University. These retreats continued with colleagues with whom I worked doing doctoral study at the University of Denver and then, especially, with friends I made through First Plymouth Church in Englewood, where I became co-pastor in 1975. Most of the time I took these town-and-gown friends to the Hohnholz Ranch on the Laramie River in northern Colorado.

Accommodation at Hohnholz was in the "Tiltin' Hiltons," rustic cabins with cracks in the log chinks through which hungry mice and mosquitos made entry. What made this hostelry attractive—besides its low cost—was the Laramie River, which, for several miles, ran through the property. In early summer, when the green drake hatch came on, the Laramie made for some of the fastest fishing I ever experienced. In one twenty-minute thunderstorm, for instance, I took six great browns on a #10 Royal Wulff!

At Hohnholz, meals were mostly communal with lots of banter, stories, and sharing around a campfire. One evening I invited response to a thanks based on Psalm 100—to "make a joyful noise to the Lord." The brothers offered these ejaculations: "Fish on!" "Here We Go!" "It's a Double!" This may be the best call-and-response ever. One particularly joyful grace was offered by Jack Poynter of Christ Congregational Church, Denver, a church where in 1984–85 I'd been interim minister. Here it is:

> *Thank you, Lord, for*
> *Breakfast lunch and dinner*
> *If it weren't for these*
> *We'd be much thinner.*

To his prayer came an all-round hearty "Amen, brother!"

Late evenings at Hohnholz included stargazing with attendant awe under the Milky Way. Rightly then, Jim Vandermiller, playing his guitar, sang this verse from "Home on the Range":

> *While I stood there amazed*
> *I asked as I gazed*
> *If this glory exceeds that above?*

Rightly too came Stan Harwood's interpretation of transcendent meaning. "Heaven," he opined, "must be, at least, something like this."

"Plus good company and rising trout," Dick Anderson added.

My take was—really *is*—that we were fumbling after the Mystery of the Trinity: God Above (Father/the heavens), God Beside (Son/Jesus/friends,) and God Within (Holy Spirit/peace).

Al Almanza from Moline, Illinois, who'd come west to fish with us, credited my interpretation as being "right on."

Close, anyway, to Christian orthodoxy, theologian Paul Tillich's perhaps.

Jokes and stories were on the menu most campfires, some leading to theological consideration. Here's one heuristic-apocryphal tale I told:

> *Once upon a time a faith-full Lutheran pastor died and found —to his utter amazement—that he had landed in hell. Beyond that, he discovered fellow Lutheran pastors and seminary professors there too. So, they formed a Lutherans-in-Hell Club and wandered around together. E'er long, whom should they come on but Martin Luther? Martin joined their band? After some years, of all people, they found the apostle Paul in hell.*
>
> *"St. Paul," Martin Luther exclaimed, "what are you doing here?"*
>
> *St. Paul hung his head and ruefully confessed, "I was wrong. It's works."*

Well, most of the brothers—basically low-church Congregationalists—didn't get the joke. The telling of it, though, led to a great fireside discussion on justification *sola fide,* "by faith alone."

Serious theological conversations notwithstanding, mostly we shared stories and jokes about "issues ever unsettling"—that is, women, sex, death, and human stupidity. Here's an example: Sven and Ollie marked an X in the bottom of their rental boat so as not to forget the spot where they caught walleyes. "But then," Sven asked, "what if, Ollie, next time we don't get the same boat?"

Remembering Hohnholz stories, I could—time and space allowing—retell those told in other locales—a Scottish loch (1996), a Kodiak Island river (2009), and a Venezuelan beach (2011). In a Tasmanian *shack* (2012) with an *exaggeration* of fisher*men,* a *bloke* from Melbourne asked, "Do you *cabbers* know the animal that grows after it is dead?"

Looking around, we all shook our head.

His answer: "A fish."

We all laughed—albeit, nervously, knowing ourselves to be contributors to such postmortem growths.

The *meaning* of jokes and humor, I have come to believe, is that they constitute what sociologist of religion Peter Berger calls a "signal of transcendence," that is, a turn of thought with words, a turn that helps bridge uncertainties in our life. Such humor, aided by good conversation around the campfire—along with casting together over rising fish—is invariably positive, "making and keeping life human," or creating what Yale Divinity School theologian Miroslav Volf calls "human flourishing," making one's life a *good* life.

My first retreats happened on the Cache la Poudre River. Then for years they were beside the Laramie River on the above-mentioned Hohnholz Ranch. Eventually my guys and I did our retreats at the High Country Center on Lake Dillon and at Arrowhead Ranch on the South Platte River, near Fairplay. For these weekends I often invited fishing-knowledgeable Christians like Richard Bondi (theologian from Atlanta), Mark Miller (UCC Conference Minister in Texas), Rich Tosches (Catholic humorist and journalist), or Dave Leinweber (Evangelical fly shop outfitter) to be guest reflectors and conversation starters. Often the conversation was about the faith-fishing relationship. This subject was one I myself spoke about on a contemplative retreat, using Sir Izaak Walton's book *The Compleat Angler,* subtitled *The Contemplative Man's Recreation.* That same evening, retreatants enjoyed my caught-that-day cutthroat trout for dinner. The next day we did a "morning watch," meditating on Psalms 104 and 105.

O Lord, how manifold are thy works!
In wisdom thou hast made them all

. . .

Yonder is the sea, great and wide,
Which teems with things innumerable.

While in this segue, I want to insert a few lines about ministry, 1989 to 2005, in Colorado Springs. I preached about forty sermons a year, and I think a content analysis of them would disclose focus on the sovereignty of God over culture, the centrality of Jesus Christ as exemplar, life in the mystical Spirit, inclusive community, social justice, and peace (wars against Iraq were happening). In addition, of course, there was administration to do, meetings to attend, counseling, hospital and home calling, Bible studies, confirmation, membership classes, baptisms, weddings, and funerals. We went from one Sunday service to two, the earlier always observing Holy Communion. While I was at the church, we did two capital campaigns, one for $775,000 and one for $1.4 million, these for additions to and restoration of our 125-year-old Richardsonian Romanesque building. Through these years I was accompanied and blessed by excellent ministerial colleagues Paul Tatter, Frank Jopp, Gene Yelken, and Benjamin Broadbent.

During my sixteen-year tenure, the church became the first mainline Protestant church in the Springs to declare itself "open and affirming" of gay and lesbian persons—a whole other story not without controversy, to be sure. Controversies weathered, we grew from being a congregation of 350 to having a membership of more than 700.

It was a "flourishing" time for ministry—and never bad for fly-fishing either, the South Platte so close.

My years at Primo Cong included two sabbaticals, one to Europe and one to Columbia Theological Seminary in Atlanta. These enabled me to study, write, *and* fish in some farther out locations (Scotland's Isle of Butte and the Smoky Mountains of Georgia). My Christian histories book, *Basic Christianity 101: Tracing Basic Beliefs,* was born of these sabbaticals, plus church-allowed study weeks, and my customary early-in-the-a.m. reading and writing.

Upon retirement the congregation established the "JWW Lectures," to include a plaque that reads, *James W. White, Fisher of Men and Women*. A miniature casting rod and reel are attached to the plaque. The lectureship is a humbling honor. The speaker scholars through the years have been John Shelby Spong, Walter Brueggemann, Amy-Jill Levine, Bernard McGinn, Joan Chittister, Robin Myers, Brian McLaren, John Dominic Crossan, Nadia Bolz-Weber, Yvette Flounder, Peter Rollins, and in 2018 Miroslav Volf. I have personally grown by the excellent biblical, theological, and cultural "stuff" these folk offered, increasing honesty to God and neighbor in thinking, speech, and writing, even for this book. So I pray.

Now and finally, preparatory to the coming adventure story, three setup pieces.

After the New Zealand trip of 1987, most of my next twenty years of fly-fishing was regional, done in Colorado and nearby states. Many of these regional fishing trips were written up and shared with compatriots, family, and friends. Some of those write-ups appeared in my 2010 fishing book, *Round Boys Great Adventures: Fish-a-logues through Rocky Mountain Trout Waters*. The shorter stories were from fishing in Arizona ("Jaws and the Rubber Duckie"), New Mexico ("The Gendarme of Stone Lake"), Utah ("On the Green, Worst Trip Ever"), and Colorado ("The Donut Hole"). The longer *RBGA* adventures in the book were "Big City Turn Me Loose," "Ichthyologic Pursuits/Gastronomical Concerns," "Round Chauncey Yellowstone Adventure" ("written" by Patti and my golden retriever), and "Pre-Millennium Tour, Consort Included." The longer adventures took place mostly in Wyoming and Montana and included fishing such rivers as the Madison, Missouri, and Big Hole and lakes like Monster, Hebgen, and Clark Canyon. The book also has some arty photos, e.g., *Wicker Creel on Old Cabin*.

Secondly, for most of the late '90s and early 2000s, my main angling colleagues were Bruce Kuster and Gary Carbaugh. We *tres amigos* fished most often out of Water Otter pontoon boats—boats I christened with the names *Fish Hawk* (mine), *The Predator* (BAK's), and *Little Sunbeam* (Gary's, he eschewing the name). The boats figure in the next story.

New Water Otters on the Green River,
Tres Amigos on Spinney Mountain Reservoir

Thirdly, regarding the British Columbia trip to come, I want to say I loved the BC trip. Its telling makes it the longest in this book but the fullest presentation of what is in almost all the accounts: fishing information, lively banter, interesting characters, tongue-in-cheek humor, remembrance of folk past, landscape sketches, observations of things botanical, zoological, and geologic, expression of feelings, talk about food and more food, plus a smattering of religion, politics, with a hint of sex, considerable mishap . . . and all ending happily, mostly. In this travelogue is revelation of the depth of friendship that two stiffs have developed over half a century of angling together. Moreover, you will rediscover the oft-noted truth that it is in the journey, not in arrival at destination, where the joy and meaning of life resides.

So, to "Kamloops with Honey."

CHAPTER 6

Kamloops with Honey

British Columbia, Canada
May 24–June 8, 2005

IT WAS MONDAY, THE day after the final Sunday of festivities surrounding my retirement from sixteen years of ministry in Colorado Springs. In exhaustive glow I went a-fishing with my many-journeys friend Bruce Kuster. We loaded his Tahoe with our personal luggage, fishing gear, deflated pontoon boats, and fly-tying cases (two), and headed toward British Columbia.

Tahoe and Trailer Readied for Travel

There we planned to hook up with Gordon Honey, well-known Kamloops guide. Many joys, learnings, and trials were before us.

Toward BC

Beginning this road trip, I had this sense that I was traveling alone, for as I looked over to the driver's seat, there seemed to be no one—that is, no mass—there. After months and months of exercise and dieting, Bruce was a ghost of his former portly self. I wondered if the winds of Wyoming would carry him away. As for myself, I had no fear that my well-padded frame could be blustered.

Pulling away from my house, Patti and Chauncey the Golden were at the stone wall waving goodbye, Patti offering her enigmatic "Take care of your hands"—whatever that means. She would be leaving in a few days for Cordova, Illinois, to spend time with her dear friend Sunny Moorhusen. Good weather allowing, she and Sunny might fish the Rock River, perhaps the Mississippi.

Colorado to Wyoming

Getting onto I-25 for the ride north, Bruce played Alison Krauss's song "The Lucky One." He had put this song into a five-minute video as part of my retirement roast the previous Saturday. The video had old photographs of "Jimmy with Fish." Photos went back to 1962, the year Kuster and I first met. The pictures revealed that, back then, I had a full crop of hair and a red beard. The progression of slides, however, made clear that I'd lost hair and the beard went two-tone, then white. One year along the way, my urologist said, "Jim, you have what it takes to be an ideal pastor: silver sideburns for the look of distinction and hemorrhoids for the look of concern."

In Longmont we had a full breakfast at McDonald's.

Travel Coffees and Indicators Dangling

The meal's fullness, I suspect, was Bruce misleading me. My too-skinny friend would soon put the hammer down with a low-cal diet. He was being supercilious for the moment, as I had been running a fever with night sweats and an upset stomach, all brought on by retirement doings. So he was humoring his ole bud. Through Wyoming, for example, he indulged me by actually counting antelope—a thing he's adamantly refused to do for years. But now, what a guy! The count was eighty-seven.

When I wasn't nodding off in the car, I read to Bruce from *Roadside Geology of Wyoming*. The reading lead us to turn off in mid-Wyoming to see Ayres Natural Bridge, one of only three natural bridges in the United

States through which a stream flows. Mayflies were hatching in the water there, but no fish rose.

Late in the afternoon, we arrived at Monster Lake and checked in with Steve Bassett, lake manager. He gave us a commodious room with spread-out space. There, from my big aquamarine fly-tying suitcase, I set up operation for later vise-work. Then it was a quick trip into Cody for a walnut-and-fruit salad at McDonald's. That was all. Back at the room Bruce allowed for three—only three—ginger snap cookies. The hammer had come down.

"What's it going to be tomorrow," I asked, "celery on toothpicks? You're gonna starve me."

His retort: "Get used to it."

This night Shakespeare's "to sleep, perchance to dream," did not happen. Rather, it was "to sweat, toss, and turn." Getting healthy, it seems, may take a few days.

Monster and East Newton Lakes

Next morning in our pontoon boats, we fished Monster Lake, guided by Steve. Most of the time I went with a Callibaetis dry fly and a Hare's Ear dropper, to have but modest success, four fish netted. BAK, using his bobber technique, "went down" with chironomid patterns. His luck was greater: nine good fish, one of which was 18 inches—but hardly a monster. We concluded that fishing here was not worth the $200 a day charge.

The most fascinating thing learned was about pelicans. Steve hated them, and though the birds are federally protected, he had permission to shoot any that came onto his lake, the birds being "a lethal threat" to his livelihood. He'd shot thirty-five this year.

"Good for you," Bruce commented. "We've seen pelican devastations on Lake Hebgen in Montana and Ice Lake in Colorado."

Steve added, "A single bird will eat six or seven hundred pounds of fish a year. Last summer I cut one open that had two 18-inch trout in its gullet. But the worst thing about them is how they stink. Pick a dead one up with your hands, and the stench will stay on for days—no matter what you do." When he shoots one on the lake, Steve informed us, he lassoes its foot or wing with a wire, pulls it to shore behind his boat, then ties it onto the bumper hitch of his truck and drags it to the dump, where he covers it with a backhoe.

Quite the ritual procedure, I must say.

In the afternoon Steve left us, and Johnny Stafford, a wiry cowboy from Kaycee, Wyoming, became our ghillie. Though short in height, Johnny was tall with stories. Such as, once he went into a biker bar with his even more diminutive godfather, George. While George was standing at the bar, a hulk of a truck driver bumped into him. Defiantly little George pushed back, saying, "Hey, fella, you wanna fight? If you do, let me tell you, it'll take one big, mean son of a bitch to whip me . . . but it won't take long!"

Johnny was a songwriter, so he said, who gave Jerry Jeff Walker inspiration for the C&W hit, "I Like My Women a Little Bit on the Trashy Side." Johnny also thought that Willie Nelson's album *The Electric Horseman* was the best ever.

"Which song on it?" Bruce inquired.

"The one with the line, 'She could suck the chrome off my trailer hitch, and it would come out shining'!"

At one point that afternoon, a couple of red-eyed grebes swam by. I said I wished I could see one up close. "Well, hook one," Johnny suggested. "But, mister, getting it off the hook will leave your hands so peckered they'll look like you've been sorting bobcats."

Johnny would be a good candidate for a *Reader's Digest* "Most Colorful Character I've Ever Met" story. Still, he was a knowledgeable guide, pointing out that fish circle in the lake. "So wait for them to come back by."

We did. They did. And we hooked up.

For dinner this evening we each had a tin of sardines in mustard sauce. Such food, I was told, was good for me. "It provides your body with much needed omega-3 fatty acids."

Whatever they are.

At meal's end I was allowed only three ginger snaps. So this night my sleep-sweats were accompanied by hunger pangs.

Breakfast, however, provided hope. We had scrambled eggs, bacon, toast with preserves, juice, and milk. It seems that our friend Jon Thomas, lawyer and fisherman, told Kuster that human beings need protein to survive. Bruce acquiesced, as he did not want us to flag while fishing East Newton Lake today.

While driving to the lake, Bruce recounted that on Memorial Day weekend two years ago he and Ron Granneman had a banner day with many 5- and 6-pound trout. We hoped to repeat that story. Though we fished long and hard, such success was not repeated. I netted but three, one being a skinny 19-inch brook trout with a head large enough to support a 10-pound body. Bruce caught six healthier bows of up to 18 inches.

East Newton was a disappointment, but good news was on the way. For Bruce announced, "Tonight we go to Bubba's Barbecue."

I knew that meant heavy eats, but why Bubba's? Then I remembered. Last year we'd taken dinner there. Upon leaving that evening, Bruce, ever gathering facts, asked the attractive cashier, "What time do you get off work?"

"Why?" she replied. "Do you want to go out?"

Undoubtedly this was the highlight moment of his whole last year, for as we'd left the restaurant a year ago, I swear, Bruce's feet did not touch the pavement! So now I think that he must be hoping for a repeat . . . and perhaps a better follow through?

Going into Bubba's, nothing like *Auld Lang Syne* recognition happened. Still, the now-cashier was friendly enough. She smiled at us. I, anyway, smiled back. At table Kuster and I ordered a rack of ribs apiece, full salad bar, baked potatoes with all the trimmings, vegetables, beers, and pecan pie à la mode. This was nourishment!

During the meal I excused myself. "Be back in a minute," I told him.

Eventually the waitress took our credit cards at the table. After paying, we headed for the door. Almost to the exit, the cashier looked up at Bruce and said, in the sweetest way, "Hi! Remember me? I still get off work at 10:30."

Well, he blanched, then flushed red. Mouth agape, he looked at her, then at me, to stammer, "White, you . . ." Turning to the hostess, he asked, "How much did he pay you?"

I tell you, it was worth every penny of my $10.

For the first time in several weeks, I slept peacefully through the entire night. Anxiety surrounding retirement seemed to be falling off.

Yellowstone

En route to Montana through the north corridor of Yellowstone, we passed spectacular country, the very route Chief Joseph traveled a century and a quarter ago when he escaped the US cavalry. Below us, perhaps a thousand vertical feet, was the Clark Fork River. "To go down there would be quite a trek," I suggested. "Wanna try it?"

"Why not? No problem," came my compatriot's reply. "All I would need is your seven-piece pack rod, a tin of sardines, and one Rat-Faced MacDougal fly. That's all I'd need . . . and maybe a back-up Royal Wulff, a Gold Ribbed Hare's ear, a Bead Head Pheasant Tail—or a Bird's Nest. That's all I'd need."

"What about water?"

"Right. Water, because of giardia . . . and two allergy pills . . . and sun block. That's all. And my polarized sun glasses with Croakies. Period. For extra, I think I'd take along a very small bag of Tostitos Scoops! And salsa, mild. That's all I'd need."

"No more?"

"Well, four folds of toilet paper, just in case . . . and three low-fat ginger snaps. That's all . . . No, I want to take my loon flute, the one Jon Thomas's wife Jan gave me. That'd be all I'd need."

"You will certainly travel light."

"And my camera."

"And a beast of burden?"

"Yes. You can come."

But we drove on.

Then it was Cooke City and into Yellowstone Park via my Golden Age pass. Traveling through the park we saw buffalo, elk, deer, and antelope. At the travertine mound, identified by *Roadside Geology*, we fell into conversation with a young fellow holding up what looked like an old TV antenna.

"It's for tracking coyotes," he explained. "We're trying to ascertain how coyotes affect antelope population."

"Not a bad summer job," Kuster opined.

When asked about wolves in the park, the fellow said that, in the Montana-Wyoming-Idaho area, there now were six hundred, but that their protected status might soon be removed. "Ranchers hate 'em," he said. "They don't like coyotes much either."

Outdoor lunch, taken at Mammoth Hot Springs, was leftover barbecue from Bubba's. As we ate, a huge buffalo nonchalantly walked by our table. Happily, he didn't even smell, just plodded on.

So then on to Bozeman, where the road turned north. Here I started singing an old song loved by my father:

> *So, git along, mule,*
> *Don't you roll them eyes.*
> *You can change a fool,*
> *But a doggone mule*
> *Is a mule until he dies.*

Bruce had never heard this song, but my offering sparked remembrance of one of his father's.

Way down upon the Suwannee River,

Far, far away,

That's where my heart is turning ever,

That's where the old folks stay.

Songs shared, I told him my dad spit chewing tobacco on worms for good luck. He said his dad talked to the fish, saying, "Take a holt. Take a holt."

We remember these things, though my father has been gone for thirty-five years and Bruce's for ten.

The Missouri

Arriving in Wolf Creek late in the afternoon, I was excited, for Wolf Creek is the town where, in *A River Runs through It*, Paul Maclean got in over his head gambling. Paul, I am sure, walked these very streets in the 1920s.

Right away we checked into the Montana River Outfitter's Motel. The proprietor informed us, "The fish are taking midges these days." So we each bought a varietal dozen in the #20 size range. A quick trip down to "the wide Missouri"—medium wide here—revealed nothing was up. Fishing then was postponed until tomorrow.

Our motel lodge neighbors were Jim Shrive and Maureen O'Donnell. Longtime fisher on the Missouri, Jim told us the fish here are heavy and hard fighting. "Most of the time you can't follow them downstream and you can't horse them in either. So what you have to do is go for the rodeo ride.'"

"Meaning?"

"Meaning, if you can hold on to the fish for eight seconds, it counts as a catch!"

Bruce said, "I think we're going to need more flies."

That night's dinner was at the Frenchy (and Me) Restaurant, mostly a bar offering Moose Drool Beer as its specialty. Though tempted for such, we opted for Coronas and pork tenderloin sandwiches. Quite good. With such meals, I'm beginning to see my too-slim compatriot again, his once-emaciated frame filling in.

(Next morning—this belongs in the "for what it's worth" department—Bruce reported he'd had a good BM. I asked him for details, but he said he was not into descriptive prose. Too bad. Not.)

So, on to fishing on what should be called "the day of the upriver wind," for we fought *Mariah* all seven miles of the float from Holter Dam down. Beaching our pontoon boats where we could, Bruce netted two browns in the 17-inch category, and I had one 16-inch brown and one rodeo ride. That was all.

Even so, the canyon float was impressive, with dramatic red rock wall outcroppings, mountain goats on one side hill, and Canada geese bobbing along on the water, yellow goslings between the ever-protective parents. The temperature in the sixties was most pleasant, but fighting the upriver wind all day made for sore stomach and shoulder muscles.

That evening I talked with Patti, now in Illinois. She said that she and Sunny were going to fish the Rock River the next day. "Folks here," she noted, "go after catfish."

"Well, good luck," I offered. "Just don't go noodling."

"What's that?"

"When you dive down and feel under the banks for a fish, stick your hand in its mouth and pull him out."

"Are you kidding me?"

"Scout's honor."

"Well, I won't do that—for sure."

She said she was sleeping a lot, having been deprived of it by the retirement activities. "How are *you* doing?" she asked.

I began to cry, then stammered, "I miss you." Which brought on *her* tears. Followed by mutual I love you's and "Good night, my Pattigirl."

"And to you, my Jimik."

She and I are yet tender.

After a supper of sardines in the room, it was still light outside. Bruce asked if I wanted to go back to the river.

I said, "I'd rather go to the bar."

"I never thought I'd live so long to hear you say such a thing."

"Well, now you have."

We went for Miller Lite longnecks and took them to the billiards table. Bruce and I are poor shots. It took forever to clear the table. Then we threw some dollars into the Keno slot machines, which a local cowboy had to 'splain us. We staggered out of the bar late, at 9:45. Back at the room, I fell into a solid night's sleep.

I awoke the next morning to have a pre-breakfast snack of half a bagel, cream cheese, and marmalade. These constituted 135 plus 50 plus 50 calories, Bruce informed me, totaling 235.

I complimented him, "Good adding, Einstein. What a brain you have!"

"Yes, but just how great do you think it is?"

"Oh, vast—or, half that, anyway."

"Thank you."

Later we had a true breakfast at an eatery down the road. We agreed that after yesterday's wind-ravaged fiasco, we'd wade-fish today. Starting in at the Bull Pen area, we walked to the west side of the island there. Yesterday we'd seen two guides with clients here. Here today Bruce caught six bows and browns, one of which was 21 inches. I caught four such, along with a big sucker, the only sucker of our trip. What worked for BK was a Zebra midge and, for me, a Pheasant Tail.

While streamside casting, my friend started talking *brunch*. "I'd like," he said, "Belgian waffles with whipped cream, brown sugar and pecans, patty sausages, an egg omelet with onions and peppers, churros added. That's all I need. And juice and milk."

Where, I was about to ask him, had his resolve not to think and talk about food gone? Then I realized what was happening. He had been deprived of nourishment for so many months that finally, with a little priming of the food pump, his true self had kicked back in.

So off we went to an early lunch at the Holter Dam Café, there to split a "Posterburger" (three Big Macs made one). It was gross, its poor quality made worse by Bruce insisting that grilled onions be added. The mound of cold french fries put on each plate did not help. The waitress told us if we came back tonight, we could have their advertised "Buckets of Chicken and Boxes of Beer."

Our eyes agreed, "Pass."

Instead that evening it was return to Frenchy (and Me)'s. Here we shared a table with Jim and Maureen. Jim assured me that Paul Maclean and Old Rawhide, the whore in *A River Runs through It*, sat at these very tables. He then asked Maureen, a newbie to fly-fishing, to share her special names for flies. She did. He translated.

Chickadee—Caddis

Tripod—Trico

Little white-haired guy with green body—BWO

Little pink-haired guy with gray body—Adams

Little red wire guy—Red Midge

Little copper wire guy with copper head—Brassie

Little haystack guy—Elk Hair Caddis

Little French guy—Prince Nymph

Pretty creative, Bruce and I agreed.

Our fried chicken dinner was topped off with apple pie à la mode, leading me to think, E'er this trip is over, it will be round boys plural once again.

Let the reader rest assured: we are still headed toward Canada.

Kalispell

The next morning, with me driving, Wolf Creek went into the car's rearview mirror. Our highway pointed north and west. Bruce read aloud from *Roadside Geology of Montana*. We saw elk, a coyote, antelope, and a number of deer, including three roadside carcasses. Once over the pass, our highway paralleled the Big Blackfoot River, made famous in Maclean's novella. Aloud and from memory I recited the story's closing passage, ending with "I am haunted by waters."

"Good job," Bruce affirmed.

A road sign said we were on the edge of the Bob Marshall Wilderness Area, the second-largest wilderness in the lower forty-eight states, a wilderness of 5.5 million acres. This is the area into which our friend Ron Granneman had packed to get his Pope-and-Young trophy elk.

We wended our way around Flathead Lake's northeast shore. Sight of the lake brought me back to the mid-'80s and being there with Hank Lawshe and his two wild buddies, RJ and Carl (last names lost). We'd raced Carl's speedboat on the lake, much too fast. That night I was offered cocaine. "Thank you, no," I responded. "This funny cigarette passing around is quite sufficient."

Reaching Big Fork, I flashed back to the evening Hank took me down to an art show there and afterward, per his custom, to a biker bar. I fell into conversation with a girl on crutches. She'd broken her foot skiing. After a while, she said she needed to go out to her car to check on her dog. She did. Before she returned, Hank asked, "Why didn't you go out with her? It'd been a great blow job." (What can I say? "They never covered this pastoral situation in divinity school"?)

Hank, western artist, auto mechanic par excellence, mountain man, consummate storyteller, and alcoholic, is perhaps the most colorful person I've ever known. Sad to report, he died in 1993, but his wife, Pat, still lived in Kalispell. I called and left a message for her that we were forty miles north, staying in a recently built motel in Whitefish. The proprietors here were John and Laurie Maruster Bowers. Laurie was from North Olmsted, Ohio, I learned, the very town in which Patti and the Limpert siblings grew up. Laurie thought she remembered Patti, class of '70, and confirmed it by checking an old yearbook.

"Small world," I later reported.

"Indeed. Just wouldn't want to paint it!"

Bruce and I fished two small lakes of the area, Frank and Theater. Frank had two loon pairs with babies the size of your thumb. Theater had nothing but newly built houses around it. Neither had fish, at least for us.

The second night back at the motel we found a note on our door: "Call Pat Lawshe." I did. So later we rendezvoused in Kalispell with her, the three Lawshe daughters (all now grown), their spouses, and their kids.

Author, Pat Lawshe, and BAK

Cigarette smoke notwithstanding, it was a joyous reunion. I had done Hank and Pat's outdoor wedding in 1976.

At the motel that night, I phoned Patti, who had just returned from Illinois by train. "In the Mississippi River, right off Jim and Sunny's dock," she said, "I caught a 21-inch walleye. It weighed 4 pounds. Not only that, in the Rock River, a 45-pound flathead catfish!"

"Way to go, Pattigirl!"

"Yes, and Sunny, using grocery-sack brown paper, did *tracers* of both my fish. She says the tracers will be fiduciary evidence to you of my victory."

To Kamloops

After more than a week's travel, we entered Canada. The border guards were cordial enough and, when asked, pointed me to the men's room. Here, though, I discovered what I wasn't going to love: they hide TP in giant un-roll-able rolls, behind opaque, plastic coverings, usually inaccessible. "Canadian toilet paper companies," I told Bruce, "will have to be included in my class-action lawsuit against those in the United States. This withholding-of-wipes, as you know, is cause of widespread mental anguish. Every year millions of discomforted people are traumatized by the conspiracy. I just hope Jon Thomas gets on things soon and stops giving me the excuse that he is waiting on a retainer fee before taking the bastards to court. I say Jon should be satisfied with 10 percent of court winnings. But no. He's strange, even implied that my case wasn't worth a crap."

Lawyers! Go figure.

Now into Canada.

En route to Golden in British Columbia, Bruce said he needed to take a nap. "I do not, though, want you to become mentally bored while I sleep. So you are required to think about and report back on the following: wild game you spotted, questions for Gordon Honey (our guide to be), better management of the car's temperature control, and something else really interesting."

"Okay. Will do," I promised. But I thought only about *something else*, namely, Napoleon in Russia looking at his pocket watch and saying to his aide, "At this moment all the school children in France are saying *amo, amas, amat, amamus*." But I, Jim White, got stopped on the plural for "you love." Is it *amaeus, amtatus, amatus*, what? I could get *amant*, they love, but not the plural you. What is it?

I put the question to Bruce when he awoke, but he just sunk his face back in the pillow and mumbled, "Hopeless."

At the Apostles Café in Golden, the waitress Lynette, when asked, did not know the Latin plural either, nor did any of the people at the other tables, though I inquired. On the street there also was ignorance. "Give the poor loony a loony," one sympathetic woman instructed her husband. But he just hustled her off.

Bruce seemed glad to get out of that town.

Driving along, we listened to Garrison Keillor's cassette tape, *WLT* (*With Lettuce and Tomato*), learning from him, to our comfort, that

> *The beauty of retirement is the way it raises your reputation. You keep plugging ahead, you'll soon become a ridiculous relic and a*

board member. But if you quit soon enough and live long enough, you'll soon be regarded as a genius and pioneer. The key is to know when to quit.

Listening, I silently wondered, did I quit soon enough?

Over Rogers Pass of the Canadian Rockies, thousand-foot ribbons of white water streamed down the canyon valleys, abutted on either side by hills of bright green. Then too we were in rain, the most we had on the trip. Dropping down, we crossed the Columbia River, went over another mountain pass, and then in Revelstock met the Columbia, by then monstrous in size. Lake Shuswap was next, a tarantula-like impoundment with arms so long it took us an hour to drive around just one arm. The Thompson River, bigger than the Missouri, went out of Shuswap on the west, headed toward Kamloops, where it joins the equal-size North Thompson River. What water!

We made Kamloops late in the afternoon, and Debbie Honey, wife of our guide-to-be Gordon, met us in town. She led us north to the Sun Rivers development, where our residence would be in a B&B run by Sandra Wiseman. Hers is a home catering to golfers and fishermen, quite posh. Graciously she let us open our fly-tying suitcases and tie on a basement table. As we worked she asked, "When did you two meet?"

"After Jim got out of jail," Bruce said.

Sandra did not know what to say.

"He meant 'after Yale,'" I corrected.

"Oh," she offered suspiciously.

Phone calls to the States indicated all was well, but a few days previous a scorpion had stung my Phoenix daughter, Melissa. Oh my!

Lac Le Jeune

Gordon Honey picked us up the next morning. He came in a big rig pulling a seventeen-foot custom-fitted boat with a 35-horsepower Evinrude motor. Turns out he is one knowledgeable guy about stillwater fishing. Brian Chan, whose magazine articles first drew Bruce to consider coming to BC, had recommended Gordon to us as a guide. We drove south from Kamloops, elevation 1200 feet, to Lac Le Jeune, elevation 4200. Gordon said that for a time he and his wife Debbie lived on the lake, that he'd fished it often and knew it well.

Like us, Gordon fishes with a floating line and hard bobbers, asserting they are less susceptible to the vagaries of the wind. Bruce was overjoyed to discover that Gordon was a chironomid devotee. Thus he started us fishing with a Black Midge having a white bead head, ribbed by red thread. "It's my exploration fly," Gordon said. "Size twelve. I sometimes tie on one a size smaller."

Once on the water with anchors out fore and aft, Gordon put his version of the electric Fishing Buddy into action: hemostats. What he did was clamp his hemos onto the bend of a fly, then drop the hemos into the water till it hit the bottom. Knowing the depth, he could set baits a foot off the bottom, suspended there by the bobber. Through the day his hemos guided us into angling depths of three feet down to twenty-five.

Also, to locate fish, Gordon kept an eye out for rises, especially for fish jumping out of the water. The latter do so to break loose parasites on their bodies, he said. Their jumps are high and splashy. A rise of either type indicates where the fish are gathering.

Here then is how we fished: throw the rig out as far as possible, let the flies sink, retrieve the line by a figure-eight finger twist, then let the flies sink again, and repeat the twitching.

Our luck on Lac Le Jeune was fair, each of us taking six to eight Kamloops rainbows. These are hot fish, quite acrobatic, sometimes jumping five or six times. One jumped seven. But these fish were not particularly large; none among those we netted was more than 16 inches.

Kamloops rainbows are descendants of land-locked steelheads, we learned. That is why they are such excellent fighters, perhaps the scrappiest of several varieties of rainbows. In this lake the fish want to spawn, Gordon said, but can't, as it is a spring-fed impoundment with no in-flowing streams in which to reproduce. So simulated creeks have been created. They pump water uphill and let it run down the creek bed. In spawning season, the fish swim up the created waterways, lay and fertilize eggs, then return to the lake emptied, their innate desires completed. If they don't do this, it takes a month longer for them to get healthy. In one faux stream we saw the biggest bows of the trip, some 19 inches. (Bigger ones to 40 inches and 30-plus pounds, I later read, are found in some BC and US waters.)

Unlike Colorado, British Columbia has a fishing season. It is April 1 through the end of November. During the year a wide variety of fly patterns is employed.[1]

1. To wit: (1) beginning in April with ice-out—leeches and the black-red midges (Gordon's "go to" pattern), (2) May— the basic chironomids adding more greens and browns, some flies with red butts/tags, and Chromies, (3) June as the callibaetis begin to come off—such patterns, (4) later June—caddis, including big sedges and damsel flies (5) July—bomber hatches occur for which the biggest midge patterns are used; dragonflies too, (6) then there's the mid-summer doldrums when little works, (7) late August/ September ff.—return to leeches, smaller midges and water boatmen; dry flies, such as The Tom Thumb, which works best late in the season but periodically throughout. (I

I observed the lake fauna and found the yellow marl, dark green chard weed, and other plants quite different from other bottom vegetation I've been over.[2]

About 4:00 p.m. we loaded the boat back onto Gordon's trailer and returned to town. Once Bruce and I got cleaned up, we went for dinner in downtown Kamloops. Afterward in a bookstore Bruce tried to interest me in the magazine *Furniture Refinishing,* saying, "After thirty-five years of preaching, this can be your new career . . . and your new sport will be bowling, for which there also is a magazine."

"Thank you, no," I responded. "Mostly I'm considering a post-career and pastime of rodeo steer wrestling."

"There are no magazines for that. Sorry."

Lakes Horseshoe and Bleaker

On our second day of being guided, Gordon took us to Horseshoe Lake, a tannic-colored impoundment much smaller than Lac Le Jeune. Bigger fish would be found here, Gordon said, because they are all triploids, that is, sterile females. Triploids do not spawn and so use their energy to grow big. For them we used the same patterns and techniques as the day before. The fems, however, didn't cooperate. We got zero fish.

What we got one of, however, was a call on my cell phone from Jon Thomas. He mostly wanted to know how the trip was going. Chatting along, we lost the connection.

Gordon asked, "Who was that?"

"Good friend," Bruce answered.

"Oh," Gordon responded. Then he was silent for a spell, to assert, "I once had a friend of whom it was said, 'He was so homely as a child his mother tied a pork chop around his neck so that, when he went out, the dogs would play with him.'"

I thought I'd never stop laughing.

Gordon's line inspired Bruce to let out a great truth from Mark Twain: "The older I get, the more clearly I remember things that never happened." As Bruce had found other aphorisms for my retirement video, he let out

---

think I got all this right.)

2. *Marl* (calcified vegetation, muck that is light green, almost yellow), *chara weed* (flat, dark green growth that is brittle), and *potomageden* (long-tendriled plants with pink flowers and willow-like leaves that hold a kind of mushroom seedpod on their underside).

with two more: "Life is easier when you plow around the stumps" and "Never drink downstream of the herd."

Gordon guffawed, to add, "We're downstream now. Time to go."

We moved to a new site, Lake Bleaker, to try spots usually hot for Gordon. Today, though, the lake was cold. One other boat was on the water. As it motored past, Gordon inquired about results. The driver reported a great day trolling with leech patterns, having taken a dozen fish. Without reverting to trolling itself, we started throwing leeches.

Again we were blanked.

Later, loading up the boat to leave, Gordon summed up his frustration: "In fourteen years of guiding, only once have I been all-day skunked."

Bruce consoled him, "To improve your skunked count, fish more with Jimmy."

"Thanks," I countered.

Back in town, we stopped in at the Kamloops Fly Shop and there met Brian Chan *hissef,* chief fish biologist for the region. He's the author of many publications on stillwater fishing. Told of our zero results this day, Chan offered this advice, "Keep at it, fellas."

Later, glad that "food can be counted on when the fish let you down," we dined on halibut and chips in Harold's Diner. Our winsome waitress, Michael, told us she was named after an angel in a movie. When I asked her if she knew about the biblical and legendary archangel Michael, she indicated no familiarity. So I shared that that heavenly being slew dragons.

"I just slay men," she said.

Bruce nodded, "I can believe that."

To be sure, Michael won a good tip.

Hefley Lake

Third day of being guided, we were off to Hefley Lake, north of Kamloops. Its size was similar to Lac Le Jeune's but with more finger channels. We motored to a wide shoal of marl and soon were into fish up to 17 inches, all Kamloops rainbows but, perhaps due to a lack of parasites, not as acrobatic as Le Jeune's trout. In the morning we took fish at nine feet of water and in the afternoon at twenty. As the hours went by, all three of us backed away from the twitching technique and began to use the still-bobber style. Either way, all told, we netted about thirty-five fish this day.

So, whereas, the night before, Kuster had been thinking about an early bailout from BC—and I confess to the same—this day's catching success made us forgo that idea.

Later, with cocktails at Debbie and Gordon's, Bruce showed *The Lucky One* video, which he'd made for my retirement. Gordon was impressed by the size of the fish we had taken from Colorado's Spinney and Antero reservoirs; his very words were "very impressive."

"Beautiful integration of music with slides," Debbie added.

Eventually we fell into conversation about the *meaning* of fishing, Gordon saying he once guided a Canadian theologian who asked rhetorically, "Is it better to be out fishing thinking about God or to be in church thinking about fishing?"

I thought this a right-on question.

Before leaving that evening we each gave Gordon a tip of $150—that on top of our basic $900 contract for guiding and lodging.

Driving back to the River Lodge Motel—into which we had earlier moved—Bruce spoke aloud what he'd been whispering to himself: "I can't believe the small size of the fish up here." On the other hand, he affirmed, "I can believe in the Canucks. Any man—Gordon Honey, Brian Chan, or another—who has such respect for chironomids warms the cockles of my heart."

Conversation at our motel went to *what we've learned up here.* I made notes: use hemos to determine depth of water, employ the double anchor system, and "move, move, move" to find feeding fish.

Then too we learned a surprising thing about BC fishermen: they hate loons. They hate 'em! Loons are amazingly large and powerful underwater swimmers and like pelicans consume enormous quantities of fish. Often one will dive under a boat in hopes of getting a just-released, disoriented fish. Gordon told us he'd hit several loons with his oar. Sharing that on Le Jeune, he had encouraged me to put a hook in one. I cast and missed. The bird just stared back in contempt.

After polishing lines this evening, it was lights out. Tomorrow we were on our own.

Hefley and Le Jeune Again

From the Hefley Lake Lodge next day, we rented a fourteen-foot Lund aluminum boat with a Mercury 4-horsepower motor, cost of $30. Our first angling stop was the marl flat where yesterday we'd had our best fishing.

And?

And, *nada,* to speak of—there or any other location. During this whole day I lucked into only three fish, and Bruce's tally was a big goose egg. Maybe, I told him, he was just too busy being James Audubon. For, as we motored the lake, he'd spotted a blue heron rookery and, at the top of a topped-off tree, a nest for osprey. So he had us go by those nests twice. Most of all, while I was bent over, busy trying to net a fish, he yelled out, "Look! An eagle!"

I jerked about, got off balance, rocked the boat, and fell hard against the gunwale, never to see the eagle. A huge purple bruise on my hip long reminded me of Kuster's bird-watching.

One word describes our thoughts on fishing for the day, the word used by the double-crossed thief in the movie *A Fish Called Wanda*: "Disappointed!"

We were not, however, disappointed with dinner. Michael, again our waitress at Harold's, recommended the house specialty: the Monster Burger served with onion rings and french fried potatoes. We topped it all off with banana cream pie. Michael, thirty-seven-years-old, revealed she was "never married because I've had no luck with men."

"Really? How's that?" Bruce inquired.

"'Cause I always liked the bad boys."

"One day, Michael," I prophesied, "you're going to be a bestselling author."

"I've made notes," she allowed.

As Michael went to serve another table, Bruce and I discussed bad boys and decided they were alpha males exuding raw strength to females. Thus my friend wondered aloud, "Is that what we are?"

"That, or impotent old geezers," I suggested, "ludicrous and good for a better-than-average tip, geezers who need to be in bed by 9:30. Let's go."

Resigned, we did.

The next day it was Lac Le Jeune with breakfast at the Grand Lodge. Outside the lodge was a huge stone hung by a rope affixed to a tall wood tripod. This so-called "Weather Stone" came with instructions on how to read the rock:

If warm, the weather is Sunny

If shadowed—Cloudy

White on top—Snow

Wet on top—Rain

Wet on bottom—Flood

Swinging—Windy

Bouncing—Earthquake

Missing—Tornado

I told Bruce this gauge was more reliable than his assiduously watched TV forecasts, but he thought this stone was a bit heavy to carry around.

We were fishing by 9:00, going to the spots Gordon had taken us three days earlier. Our results, takes-to-capture, were zero for zero. Toward noon, a small callibaetis hatch came on, and I went to the bushy Tom Thumb dry fly pattern. With it I experienced a couple of refusals, and then a take and a serious fight . . . until, way out there, the fish did a LDR, that is, a long distance release.

After lunch I did catch one on the Tom Thumb, as did Bruce with a Chromie. It was his only fish in two days, but the biggest on our trip, 18 inches. He repeated himself: "I can't believe how small these fish are up here."

At 2:38 we were back at the motel. In no time we were z-z-zing. Afterward, knowing Michael did not work Wednesdays, we had dinner at Fogg and Suds. At table we made basic appraisal of our trip: for fish-catching it was mostly a bust, but for learning about stillwater tactics, there was surplus. Our bobber technique, we agreed, is as good as—maybe better than—the twitch method practiced around here.

Much of our gear this evening was taken inside the motel room to clean and pack for the next day's travel. Doing so, we went car-to-room and room-to-car many times.

Homeward Bound

In the morning we awoke to gently falling rain and a harsh discovery: we'd been robbed! Overnight our vehicle had been entered, probably because I'd left it unlocked on my last trip in the dark. Like other times when I've been ripped off, there was that sick, sinking feeling in the stomach. That feeling returned with lots of self-blame. How could you be so careless, White? Stupid, stupid!

After my self-flagellation, Bruce suggested we inventory what had been taken. We did: Bruce's camera (with the only pictures of this trip), my cell phone, my laptop computer (crashed earlier), and—most significantly—our fly-tying suitcases.

With assist of the motel manager, we got in touch with the local gendarmes. Twenty minutes later Constable Laurie Hewitt of the Royal Canadian Mounted Police came to take our report. She arrived in a squad car, not on horseback. Mountie Hewitt efficiently made notes and got our identification information. Then we began a search around the motel grounds . . . and found nothing. I kept wondering what a thief could possibly do with fur, feathers, threads, hackle pliers, hooks, et cetera, which he'd find in Bruce's twenty-pound suitcase and my forty-pounder. It would be difficult to sell such, and hardly any buyer would know what to do with the stuff in the cases. But it wasn't just "stuff" to me. It was beloved, widely gathered, an often-used collection of thirty-five years—replacement value of, probably, a couple thousand. My jungle cock neck alone (contraband from China) was worth $300.

Bruce waxed philosophical. "Now we get to practice letting go."

Of course, he was right.

Detach, oh man.

Still, while we drove south, I made an alphabetical list of items that would be in our cases, entries like bodkins, beads, BBs, buckskin, and brassie wire, for the letter B alone.

The robbery's effect and the rain through which we drove certainly dampened our spirits. Where we stopped for lunch, for instance, the waitress seemed not the least bit interesting—or interested in two morose old guys. "Where's Michael when you need her?" Bruce lamented.

At the town of Sumas on the border, we got $37 back for lodging taxes overpaid in Canada. Traveling along an all-but-deserted road in north central Washington, Bruce purchased fresh strawberries at a fruit stand. "For my daughter Shelly," he said.

We did, you can believe, sample a few.

Heading toward Seattle on I-5, earlier uncrowdedness of road became parking-lot crawl. On arrival at Shelley's home in Bellevue, happy to say, single malt scotch—Glenlivet, no less—was a-waiting. Later there was Mexican food in a local restaurant and, later still, strawberry shortcake. I told Michelle that her father and I had enjoyed other excellent desserts and cuisine on this trip, so that he was now plumped up.

"Obviously," she responded.

"Solid muscle now from much casting," Bruce insisted.

"Assuredly. Right. Me too." I said.

Next morning, June 8, I awoke early, fixed a pot of coffee, and read some. Breakfast by Shelley was pancakes topped with strawberries. Delicious. During the meal we called my daughter Melissa in Phoenix to wish her happy birthday. We learned she was recovering well from the scorpion sting.

Thank you, Yahweh!

We visited Kauffman's Fly Shop following breakfast. Looking around in the shop let us know what else, not on yesterday's long list, had been stolen. A lot. Cost to replace was going to be way up there.

Bruce took me to SeaTac Airport for a 2:30 p.m. flight out. In the terminal I bought dark chocolates by Godiva for Patti, her fave. Thinking about "things and her," I realized that the walleye she'd taken one morning while fishing in the Mississippi River was bigger than any single trout we'd netted in fifteen days, and her 45-pound flathead catfish from the Rock River weighed more than all the trout we'd caught in Wyoming, Montana, and British Columbia put together! The capricious fish gods clearly had exercised "a preferential option for the distaff." So it was that Bruce and I were "laid low" (as said in Job 41:9) when comparing our modest catching record with hers.

Even so, I was ever so glad to see that fisher gal who met me at DIA. Once home, I saw on the refrigerator door the brown-paper-sack tracers of her Illinois trophy fish.

Impressive. Also humbling.

Six days after my return, I received an email from Gordon Honey: "I've got good news for you."

The hurried phone call that I made to Canada revealed some story. It was this: Years ago, when Gordon and Debbie lived up at Lac Le Jeune, they had a next-door neighbor with whom Gordon sometimes fished. This neighbor, it happens, has a ninety-year-old mother living in Kamloops. Every week or so, the man goes to town to mow her lawn or in winter to shovel her walks. Now here's the incredible coincidence. Her home is next door to the restaurant that is next door to the River Lodge Motel. As the man mowed yesterday morning, Gordon said, he spotted something strange under her front yard bushes: two suitcases. Opening the smaller of the two, he discovered a fly-fishing book written by his old neighbor, Gordon. The inscription on the book's flyleaf said, "To Bruce Kuster." In the larger suitcase was a "recipe book" for fly tying—mine, my journal with how-to notes and drawings going back to 1964. The man called Gordon, who came and picked up the cases, notified the Mounties, and then emailed me.

By the time the cases came back to us by UPS, I was still in wondrous disbelief.

Postscript

In February 2016, after I'd emailed a version of this story to Gordon, Debbie Honey emailed back saying, "Gordon passed away June 19, 2013, after a six month battle with cancer."

So sad to receive such news.

Requiem aeternam, Kamloops guide most excellent.

Segue to Ontario

FOLLOWING MY RETIREMENT AND the just described fishing trip to British Columbia, I spent the rest of the summer of 2005 getting ready for a 600-mile trek on the *Camino de Santiago* in Spain. Later in this book I will come back to this pilgrimage that created international friendships, subsequent fishing opportunities, and remarkable stories. But first, some fill-in before the next-to-be-recounted major adventure in Canada.

During the years of mid-2005 to late 2007, Patti and I were in a state that she called "banishment," meaning that, by denominational polity and ministerial ethic, a clergy person who retires from a church yet living in the community is not to be involved in the life of that congregation until a year after the new clergy person is settled. It's a healthy rule. In the interim, Patti and I did a lot of church hopping, quite enjoyable, and I had more time to fish sundry waters.

I also worked up a number of short stories,[1] some which appeared in *High Country Angler* and all of which are available from me on request. Not to forget the short stories that went into *Round Boys*.

As noted in the segue leading to the BC adventure, my church history book, *Christianity* 101, came out in 2006. So, in the post-publication years I spent considerable time and energy promoting that volume.

I also continued doing men's fishing retreats, often at Arrowhead Ranch on the South Platte.

---

1. "Wrapped on the Arkansas" (from 1987), "The King and I" (1987), "Nymphs of the Tarryall" (1989), "Extreme Fly-fishing" (1992), "Blair's Behemoth" (1993), "Anthony in the Hog Trough" (1996), "Mousing for Moby" (2002), "Butt Naked on the Bighorn" (2003), and "How Else Might Flies Be Arranged?" (2006).

Music and Drumming at Arrowhead Lodge Fishing Retreat

With Kuster and other friends I fished the Bighorn River in Montana, staying at the Old Hookers (!) Guest House. He and I together also wet-a-line several times on the San Juan River in New Mexico and the Blue River and Spinney Mountain Reservoir in Colorado.

Now, toward August 2006 . . .

On invitation, I went into the woods—and onto a lake—of western Ontario. The invitation came from friends made in 1985–86 when I did the *unintended interim* ministry in Illinois.

As hard as was the ending of that pastorate, I made wonderful friends while there. One couple, Sunny and Jim Moorhusen, stayed particularly close. We had fished together on the Mississippi River, and shortly after Patti and I married in 1991, the Moorhusens took us on an "accompanied honeymoon" to Mazatlan, Mexico. While there we all fished in the bay and surf-cast from the beach and later grilled our catch on the sand using drift-wood as fire fuel.

Well, twenty years after my departure from Moline and fifteen years after the accompanied honeymoon in Mexico, Jim invited me to go with him and seven other Quad City fellows on an Ontario fly-in fishing trip. The story to come is that trip. I do believe you will enjoy the account. What guys do and say *sans* feminine restraint can't be *totally* revealed, of course, but this report lets out considerable "inside information." So, cabin tomfoolery *and* piscatorial success are reported in this story—the latter about walleyes and northern pike, northerns taken on a fly rod. Still, it's the camaraderie that makes this story live, aided by description of nature's extravagance.

CHAPTER 7

With the Boys of Illinois

Keeper Lake, Ontario, Canada
August 11–20, 2006

IT ALL BEGAN AT a funeral, the funeral for Scott Blair, outdoorsman and friend to many in Moline, Illinois. George Jamieson said, "We ought to do a fishing trip in Scott's honor."

"It ought to be to Keeper Lake in Ontario," Bob Schluter added. "That's where Scott took us in 1974."

"Keeper Lake? Isn't that where you and your family go each summer?" Bruce Peterson asked, looking at Jim Moorhusen.

"Yeah, and, if you're serious—I never know with you guys—I'll make arrangements for a fly-in week."

"Make 'em," encouraged Jeff Campagna, Scott Blair's son-in-law. Seconded by Scott's other son-in-law, Mike Brandt.

A year later, the trip came to be.

Rounding out the Quad City Six (named just above) were Gary Young from Clearwater, Florida, who'd also known Scott earlier, and I, Scott's pastor some years back.[1]

On Thursday night before the trip north, there was a loading of the van and dinner with wives. By then the eleven-passenger Ford Transit was "loaded to the gunwales" with all our gear, food, and beer—especially beer, as a case is $15 in the United States but $35 in Canada.

---

1. In thumbnail sketch, here are the eight of us: Mike Brandt, contractor/builder, a Hawkeye pheasant hunter now living in Atlanta; Jeff Campagna, crate business magnate, trophy bow hunter, photographer; George Jamieson, print business executive, Monmouth College grad, golfer; Jim Moorhusen, general contractor, Mississippi River boater, trip organizer; Bruce Peterson, dentist, Iowa U grad, canoe portage, and pyrotechnician; Bob Schluter, stockbroker, Monmouth College grad, and stand-up comic; Jim White, minister (ret.), writer, fly-fishing guide, Coloradan; and Gary Young, airline pilot (ret.), scuba diver (ret.), and deer hunter (not ret.)

Shortly after 5:00 a.m. Friday, August 11, we were headed north 600 miles through Iowa-Wisconsin-Minnesota to International Falls. En route we picnicked both breakfast and lunch and managed stops for cheese, gas, fishing lures, and rest rooms—for which Schluter regularly flashed his IBBC (Itty Bitty Bladder Club) card.

At one stop en route Moorhusen (responsible for inviting me on this trip) whispered, "The brethren are a little apprehensive about a minister in their midst. Suppose you could tell a disarming story?"

No problem.

"Fellas, listen up," I said as we neared Duluth. "There was this guy who one year wrote a dirty limerick and sent it in to the National Dirty Limerick Contest. To his satisfaction, he won. So the next year he wrote another. It too was a winner. The third year he composed his dirtiest ever and sent it in, only to learn in the *Dirty Limerick News* that he'd come in second. Disappointed, he called the national office to find out what the winner's entry was. The secretary there said she could not read it over the phone, it was so filthy. So the guy asked, 'Could you just say *de dah* when you come to the offending words?'

"'Okay,' she replied. 'I'll try. *De dah de dah de dah, De dah, de dah, de dah, De dah de dah, de dah de dah, De dah, de dah . . .* fuck.'"

That seemed to clear my credentials.

We checked into the Day's Inn at International Falls and went for prime rib dinner at the Thunderbird Inn on Rainy Lake. I realized then that this was going to be a fun trip, as Schluter persuaded the waitress to give him a grandfatherly hug—and she obliged. Later he said, "She pinched my butt too."

Jameson, Schuler's friend since childhood, said, "We have to watch him all the time."

The wake-up calls came in early, and soon we were on our way, crossing into Canada and enjoying sight of beautiful lakes, lush woodlands, and road cuts revealing complicated granite. For fishing licenses we stopped at Bobby's Corner, where "Loud Al" presided. He was, to say the least, directive. "No, no, you don't want that piece-of-crap lure," he said to me. "You need this one—and three of 'em!"

I asked him about fly-fishing for northerns, which flies to use. His judgment was, "Don't bother. Forget it. They never work. Stick with spoons and spinners."

I was cowed but not convinced.

At the end of our shopping, Loud Al complained, "Moorhusen, you told me when you were last here you'd be coming back with a lot of big spenders. But these guys, they're all cheapskates!"

Moorhusen explained, "They settle only for quality goods, if any can be found."

After five hours of driving north from Bobby's, we arrived at Red Lake, deep in western Ontario. Just outside the town a cow moose and her calf were casually grazing. Quite charming. In Red Lake itself were the Chimo Air fly-in office and docks. The owner, Peter Hagedorn, had his guys weigh and load our gear, groceries, and beer onto his de Havilland Otter. We boarded and soon were off another fifty miles north.

Ready for the Fly-in to Keeper Lake

United Airlines pilot Gary went to copilot in the cockpit. Jameson went to the rear and in the turbulence took sick. Schluter's lunch sack was added to. After thirty minutes the plane set down north of Woodland Provincial Park on Keeper Lake. We chain-ganged our stuff out of the plane, up the plank walkway, and into our four-bedroom "little cabin in the woods."

The cabin had rustic amenities, including lighting by Coleman and heated indoor lake water for showers. Out back were two privies, pungency reduced by lime.

By 2:30 we were ready to fish. Then the rains came—happily the only significant downpour for the next seven days. Before it ended, I was boated up in a fourteen-foot Lund motorboat with Moorhusen.

So off we went. Right away at the Vagina Hole—I'm not making this name up—we were into walleyes. They were taken by spin-casting marabou-skirted jigs. We'd let a jig sink and retrieve it in short jerks. Thinking others might not catch enough for supper, Moorhusen and I held on to fourteen. We had more than enough for supper.

The fish were filleted, dipped in milk, breaded, and then deep fried. The best tasting of all prepared fish, I do believe—and just as tasty Friday as this first night.

After supper's cleanup, a card game known as euchre began, Peterson and Campagna versus Moorhusen and Brandt. I tried to follow the game. Couldn't. More complicated, to be sure, than slapjack. So I went to bed, finding a single sheet more than warmth enough. Strange, there were no mosquitoes.

There were, however, mice. The next morning our bag of trail mix was gnawed open and the bread nibbled into. We set snap traps.

Then breakfast and to the boats.

Boats Ready for Keeper Lake Fishing

As Moorhusen and I pushed off he said, "Today I'm taking you on an adventure, up a little creek, to Hidden Lake."

It was more than an adventure. It was an ordeal. Since the water in Keeper was low this year, it also was low in the creek. Our task became getting over four beaver dams that blocked the shallow entry channel. We'd run full throttle onto a dam, get stuck, have to unload boat weight—the tackle boxes and gasoline tank—rock the boat over the dam top, reload our gear, and power forward to the next blockage, there to repeat the procedure.

Eventually we made it. My shoes were wet and muddy. Barefooted Jim was soaked to the waist.

Once on the lake, he said, "I want to start us in the lily pond area, where we've taken our biggest northerns."

Fishing for northerns I soon learned, is done here with a Johnson Silver Spoon, three inches long and weedless. To the lure's single barbed hook a rind of walleye stomach meat is attached for wiggle. With this spoon one can throw into weeds and not get snagged. The lure flashes like a small bait fish. Right away Jim and I each caught a couple of hammer-handle northerns.

Jim assured me, "There are bigger ones here."

I threw my spoon out into a little open spot and saw a swirl where my lure should have been, but felt nothing. Again I threw into the same place. A strike on the metal this time, but I didn't set the hook.

"You gotta really stick it to 'em," Moorhusen instructed.

Third cast, same place, and a swirl-touch again. "Wonder how big he is," I asked aloud.

Fourth cast. Nothing. "Guess I've scared him off."

"Go again," Moorhusen encouraged.

I did. Big hit this time. Huge swirl. I set the hook hard. For a second, maybe two, the fish floundered in the weeds, then made a V-line for our boat. I cranked as fast as I could. He dove under us. My rod tip followed him down, almost doubling the pole. "This is a big fish!"

With the drag of the reel preset too tight, not allowing play-out, I realized I was in trouble. I had to forcibly move the down-in-the-water rod toward the prow and around it to get a direct line to the fish again. I was afraid he would break off in the process. Fortunately, the fifteen-pound monofilament and connections held. The fish, still there, headed out.

Moorhusen reengaged the motor, saying, "We want to get him out of the weeds and into that deeper water for this fight."

Cleared from the lily pads, this big boy now was in the greater depth cabbage weeds. Now he'd head toward the open lake and then back toward the boat. Each in-and-out pass, as I'd see him in length and breadth, I'd cry, "Oh, what a fish! What a fish!"

In ten minutes he began to tire and could be brought alongside the boat. I held his head up by the lure. Jim reached under his belly with both hands and jerked him up and into the boat. There the fish flopped, and I repeated myself, "Oh, what a fish!" We then measured him on the gunwale's Gander Mountain tape: 39 inches. Approximately 18 pounds! The no-take slot limit in Canada is 29–35 inches, so this one was four inches over. We could keep him. But we didn't. I released him to the water, and quietly he swam away as if nothing had happened.

Happy/lucky fish. Happier/luckier fisherman. I sat down on the boat seat shaking. "39 inches. The longest fish of my life."

39-inch Northern Taken on a Spoon

Spooning through the weeds continued for a while, and then we went after walleyes. We had only a little luck on them but nothing like the 158 fish Jim said he and Sunny had taken here a month and a half earlier.

In the early afternoon we negotiated our way out, over the beaver dams to Keeper.

Going back out later in the afternoon, Moorhusen let me drive the boat. We motored north and east around islands, through various channels, across bays, on and on. By late afternoon we were looking at some beautiful high granite cliffs way back in somewhere. At this locale Jim asked, "Can you find your way home?"

I replied with bravado, "Of course."

Only twice on our return was I totally lost.

Offering grace at supper this evening I made a point to give thanks for "this day, this company, the beauty here, our food, and my 39-inch northern. Amen." Campagna gave addendum thanks for a 19-inch walleye he'd boated.

That evening Peterson made a lakeshore bonfire for us all to sit around. Schluter then held forth, telling of pranks that he had pulled over the years on his friend George. Like when in the second grade at recess, he told the kids in their class to look at George when the substitute teacher turned to the blackboard. When she did and the kids on cue turned to stare at George, Schluter made a farting noise with his hands. Shortly thereafter George was in the principal's office.

Schluter recounted putting a Band-Aid in George's wife's bean casserole at a formal dinner one evening. Instantly she knew where it came from and simply said, "Schluter, you son of a bitch!"

One time Schluter got Moorhusen to wire in the Playboy Channel at George's house of an evening when guests were coming. The guests, they knew, were sure to flip on the set for an Iowa basketball game. Sure enough, the Hawkeye fans, male and female, went to the TV room, and up came the porno. The women, Schluter said, forgetting basketball, loved watching the X-rated programs.

Schluter told tales of getting another friend to pretend he was a doctor, call George, and direct him to bring a full stool sample in a fruit jar for his medical exam. Not able to sit and deliver on the toilet, he created in the bathtub. Then, jar in hand; George presented it at the clinic. The nurse did not know what to do. So Jamieson said, "The doctor ordered it."

"Okay," the nurse said, "if you insist, we'll test it." They did and of course charged George for the test.

For forty-five minutes the stories went on, many ending with the tricked person also exclaiming, "Schluter, you son of a bitch!"

I wish I had a tape recorder. Such would make a great comedy CD. We laughed and laughed, though some of the guys knew the stories by heart.

Moorhusen, again at the outboard motor controls the next day, took us farther out, way up to the Deliverance Channel—sounds of banjo music, please. We hooked only three walleyes but boated eight to ten northerns apiece, one of which was 27 inches. It was here I decided to try my fly rod. I tied on a Deer Hair Mouse pattern and began to cast into the lily pads. The wind made it hard to place the fly accurately. When I had a successful cast and got a no-snag retrieve, no takes came. I cast and cast and cast. Maybe Loud Al was right: forget fly-fishing for northerns.

The silver spoon with walleye belly rind, however, worked and, sad to say, in the very water I'd cast in the mouse moments earlier.

While I napped that afternoon, Jim went about the business of building a better mousetrap. He ran a clothes-hanger wire through the high side of a five-gallon plastic bucket. The wire was then run through holes punched through the top and bottom of a Budweiser Lite beer can. Then the wire was secured to the opposite sides of the bucket. The beer can spun on the wire and was next smeared with peanut butter. We would try the trap tonight.

Mice in the cabin were not all the critters we saw. That very day Moorhusen and I spotted five black otters playing along a shore. Young and Peterson watched a sow bear and her two cubs on a ridge. Everybody saw ducks, loons, kingfishers, crows, cormorants, ravens, and many unnamable smaller birds. Birds also provided entertainment. Each evening we'd dump fish guts on the shore of the island opposite our campsite, back our boat off, and then watch seagulls dig in, only to be sent packing by big brown vultures. Finally eagles swooped in to finish off the goodies.

After supper that evening, Campagna and I stood on the boat dock to cast fly rods, his an eight-weight, mine a five. His rod had more power and would be better, I told him, using big ties for big fish. I wanted to try streamer patterns for northern tomorrow.

"Let me know how it goes," he said.

The four card players got into euchre again this evening. Peterson and Campagna won. Later in the week, it was Brandt and Moorhusen. Their games were always loud—heard clear to the campfire circle—with lots of moanin', bitchin', and accusation. Seeing as how I was making journal entries, Bruce asked me to record for posterity, "Jim and Mike were doing ethically questionable card playing."

So noted.

Shortly after the gas light over the dining room table was turned off, we went to quarters. Ere long, though, in the darkness we heard a plop. Then came the sound of scratching on plastic. All of us getting up saw that the Moorhusen-made better mousetrap worked. A mouse had climbed to the first level of the food shelf, smelled the peanut butter, jumped onto the can, and was spun to the bottom of the bucket. There he was not quite drowned. So we added water. Later in the night I heard another plop. Later still, in getting up for a trip to the bathroom, I put my flashlight on the beer can and saw three drowned mice below it. By morning the number reached six; with three others taken in conventional snap traps, our total catch was nine. Some kind of record, I'm sure.

There was talk at breakfast of selling the invention to Budweiser for use in a Super Bowl commercial. It sure will be well remembered, though women viewers might eschew Bud Lite forever.

La "Super Bowl" Mouse Trap

Our wives, though, we were convinced, would have been proud of our domestic acumen—more likely, amazed. We did well in the kitchen this morning, fixing omelets and frying bacon. The cooking, table setting, clearing, and cleaning for all the meals seemed to be shared without direction. After breakfasts, we packed individual lunches.

Peterson and Young headed into Hidden Lake this third day, and the rest of us started wending our way north, five miles as the crow flies, ten-plus by water, toward McCusker Falls.

En route we fished and explored, revisiting the granite wall outcropping on Cairns River. The wall was topped today by a half-moon. We found a beautiful spot to picnic beside a run-in creek.

Satisfied by success in conventional spin-fishing ways, I again got out the fly rod and, forsaking the top-water mouse pattern, went to a white and chartreuse streamer of about three inches. It had lead eyes and sank quickly. I'd cast it out and retrieve it by varying speeds but usually by stop-and-start action. Well, it worked. I hooked into and boated a 20-inch northern. Continuing with the streamer, I found that in the bays of wild rice, water lilies, or cabbage grass, my fly regularly hung up. Even so, when an opening appeared, the fly rod was in action. My line was a five-weight forward, and I used a tapered leader cut down to about 1X strength. That leader, though, was scissored by a northern, and I lost another streamer. So, out came a steel leader. It prevented loss of lure but prohibited the best action of the fly. Ultimately I returned to the spinning rod with silver spoon and thin rind.

Midafternoon we reached McCusker. What a special place. A fish-rich moving impoundment heads the spillway. Then there is the spillway itself; walking alongside it was a Rocky Mountain white-water river. I loved it. Below that was McCusker Lake. We took fish in the impoundment above, holes of the falls, and the lake below.

Too soon we had to leave. It was a long ride back to the cabin, two hours' worth of travel.

No walleyes were kept today, as it was "steak night"—filet mignons provided by Campagna. Dishes done, some of us went out to enjoy pyrotech Bruce's fire, while the insane-four, plus kibitzing Gary, resumed euchre by gaslight. George, Bob, and I stayed with the coals and watched the sky go bluish gray to black. The planet Venus soon arrived and stars popped. Without a moon, the Milky Way came into full display. The summer triangle stars of Aquila the Eagle, Cygnus the Swan, and Lyra shone straight above us, the Big Dipper, Little Dipper, and North Star strong behind. I stayed on alone for a while to find Pegasus in the east, Scorpio in the south, and La Corona in the west. There were satellites moving along, quite easy to follow. Occasionally shooting stars streaked through. Then it was back to the cabin for what turned out to be Schluter's second greatest tomfoolery.

With the euchre game winding down, kibitzers Jamieson and Schluter retired to their room. This time, though, George closed the door. "Too much light," he explained.

Bob added, "We need privacy."

The cabin now fell quiet except for the card players' shuffling, bidding, and occasional protest.

Then a sound from the next room: *Twhack, twhack, twhack.*

What?

Twhack, twhack, twhack, Schluter hitting the back of one hand against the palm of the other?

Well, the guys at the table simply came apart laughing. Too funny.

Then silence.

Then more *twhack, twhack, twhack.*

More laughter. Campagna shouted out, "Ride him, George!"

George cursed, "Schluter, you son of a bitch!"

The next morning, Schluter saw me journaling and came near to say, "Nothing about last night's joking goes in there, right?"

"Right," I assured him. "But how do you spell *twhack*?"

As to other things, the mice were on the run. Overnight only two were caught in the Budweiser trap and one in a snap.

To fish this day, Moorhusen and I went to several "usual hot spots." But all were cold. Only around Three Sisters Islands did we finally find action, taking a number of various-length walleyes, keeping four 14-inchers on a stringer. Dinner catch secured, Jim and I motored to a south-facing shoreline. I was positioned in the prow, to cast my fly over underwater rocks and fallen trees. Moorhusen trolled us along slowly.

My weighted, chartreuse streamer with steel leader worked. I put the lure over a yellowish boulder a foot below the surface when, swoosh, the fly was attacked. I pulled back and knew when he dove that I had a nice northern. Stripping line, I brought him toward the boat and lifted him out for my ghillie to remove the hook. Before returning the fish to the water, Moorhusen measured him against the gunwale tape. "It's 22 inches. Now go get another."

That I did, another 22-incher. When we did the same shore later in the day, two more of similar length were boated.

I credit it all to my guide's boat-handling prowess and told him then and there that I would not just double his usual tip but triple it.

"Right. How much was the first tip to be?" he asked.

"You just can't imagine how big."

"I'll bet I can."

"You know me that well?"

"I do."

"Okay, so I'll just double it."

"Right."

At supper this evening Moorhusen asked the voyageurs who had struggle-portaged into Hidden Lake how they had done.

Guys Pushing Through to Hidden Lake

Campagna reported that, in the same bay of water lilies where I'd taken the 39-incher on Monday, he had landed one 34.

"Well, all right!" Jim affirmed.

Schluter and Jameson, also fishing Hidden Lake, took walleyes in double-digit number. George boated a perch, the only one taken the whole week. Peterson and Young on Keeper, instead of 14-inchers, brought in two that went 19.

At the campfire this night, Campagna offered up his satellite phone for calls home. It was nice to hear the voices of Sunny and Patti; Patti letting me know that peace had *not* broken out in the Middle East. So the world was same ol', same ol'.

Interestingly enough—to me, anyway—no one on this trip has spoken about the war in Iraq or about anything political. I wonder if we're all agreed on such matters and it's a settled topic or, more likely, we aren't agreed and guys are being careful to avoid controversy. I know I'm working to hold my tongue about Bush and his neo-cons' preemptive, illegal, immoral, and shameful war on Iraq. So we don't broach social, political, or cultural things.

Religion is not quite so off-limits, but nothing controversial. Golf is safe and interesting: Who will win, Tiger or Mickelson? We can talk eas-ily about other sports (notably football), places visited (Hawaii), people known (the curmudgeon who always counted fish), wives (whose weighs the most—just kidding, dear), medical matters (prostates), and food (good-better-best restaurants). Daily we offer jokes, such as, "Why is drinking lite beer like making love in a canoe?" Answer: "Both are fucking too close to water." We laugh a lot. Overall, I am reminded of a truth: "Do not judge. We have all walked in different gardens and knelt at different graves."

End of discourse.

As the bonfire became coals, Bob, George, Gary, and I talked. I shared a little about Patti's and my walk across northern Spain on the *Camino de Santiago* last year. On that pilgrimage I had a personal revelation of "*Shema*, O Israel" or "Hear, O Man." To hear, to listen well, is something Patti says I seldom do. Interestingly, each of my fire mates reported his wife says much the same thing: "You never listen!"

George allowed, "Maybe you didn't need to walk all those miles, Jim, to learn that."

George is right, of course. But, again, have I learned it? The jury re-mains out.

As the stars this night spoke "the silence of eternity," we fell into silence too. A sweet, quiet reverie. I tried to deliver a line by Thoreau: "The music goes on, interrupted only by occasional listening"—or something like that. Finally Gary arose, got the water bucket, and dowsed the fire. We retired to quarters in the now-still cabin, card playing long since ended.

The brothers slept a little later the next morning, four of them ex-hausted by the pull-the-boat-over-the-beaver-dam ordeals of yesterday. Everybody now having done it, no one felt the need to try it again, even though that was where the largest northerns had been caught.

Still, it was northerns on the fly that Campagna and I wanted today. We boated together, and Brandt went with Moorhusen. In the shallows just before the S-Curve into Trapper Bay, I had our first take, a nice 18-incher. Then we entered the bay. Right away I hooked up and landed a hammer handle. And another. Then Jeff took his first. After that fish's release, we reached to do a high five. A few minutes later, we doubled. By the time we finished the curve around the bay, we'd boated six northerns each, having our best luck not in the water lilies but in the cabbage grass on the outside edge, nearer the deeper water. The fish were 18–22 inches long, and when they came on, they attacked. One fish tore up my chartreuse streamer when it went deep in his throat. I then put on a red streamer. It did not provoke any takes. Jeff, though, got action on a chartreuse Bunny Leech with a seven-inch tail. So I put on one similar, and the takes began again.

For every fish actually hooked, we had three or four hits. The amazing thing to me was how persistent these northerns are. With a trout, you get a strike, miss him, and that's it. These fish, uniquely, will follow your lure to hit it again, sometimes yet again. On occasion they'll come right to the boat, and if you do a figure eight with your lure in the water, they may attack it.

We concluded that our flies worked well enough, but probably not quite as effectively as weedless spoons. We wished we had weedless sinking flies.

When we came in for late lunch, all the boats had their prescribed walleyes for supper. Young's included a 22-incher, the largest walleye caught all week. Jeff and I needed to get ours; so at 4:30 he and I went back out. It was a slow go, but by 6:15 we headed home with our four for dinner but stopped off at the Indian Camp to explore and take our pictures beside the massive moose rack there.

Moose Antlers at Indian Camp

Though thoroughly bleached white and dry, the rack must have weighed thirty pounds.

Upon arrival at camp, Brandt commented, "Well, that took long enough."

Campagna and I just ignored him, as visions of northerns on the fly still danced in our heads.

Breaded fried fish were on the plate this night, thirty-two fillets consumed.

As on previous nights, Peterson built up a fire for us all, big, bright, and warm. Talk went to "other fires shared," streamside and mountaintop, with friends—Scott Blair especially being remembered. We hung there for a time in the twilight.

Keeper Lake Silhouettes

In time the gamesters went indoors for euchre, leaving Gary and me to see the fire go to coals. Eventually, Gary went in to read. Sitting there alone, I took in the stars and looked for satellites. My eyes soon went to the northeast and . . . whoa, stopped! I beheld three up-shooting shafts of light. They were like sunset beams coming through evening clouds—what I've called "Jesus rays"—but these came from the ground. The shafts shimmered as silver fibers blown upward. I stared in amazement. The shafts then began to spread and move.

Finally, it hit me: northern lights! I yelled out their name: "Aurora borealis, guys!"

With that, the troops came pouring out of the cabin, to take in beautiful, shifting curtains of purple and green filling the horizon. Before long the waving curtains gave way to a luminous haze, and the haze took over half the sky. Lovely. Magnificent.

To me, this was the highlight of the trip. The aurora borealis was something I thought I might never experience again. I had seen it in 1984 in Alaska and once in North Dakota in 1985 but never since. I tell you, if I had died then and there, I would have gone with heaven in my eyes. After the trip I found a poem by the ancient Ptolemy, which says better what I experienced:

> *I know that I am mortal, ephemeral,*
>
> *Yet when I track the*
>
> *Clustering spiral orbits of the stars,*
>
> *My feet touch earth no longer: a heavenly nursling,*
>
> *Ambrosia- filled, I company with God.*

Yes, yes, yes!

Now, from the sublime to the ridiculous, the funniest, totally most outrageous, ribaldest happening of the trip.

It began quietly, just as euchre ended. Guys straightened up the cabin, brushed their teeth, etc., en route to quarters. I myself was all but asleep when my roommate, Moorhusen, turned in. He stopped, though. Something was on his pillow, a piece of paper, a note. He took it back to the main room to read, then began to laugh out loud at its contents:

> *Jim, I can't tell you how much being invited on this trip means to me! I'd like to show you my true feelings! Please meet me tonight at 1 a.m. in the Gas House! I can 'HARD'ly wait! You're the best! Much love. Your Friend, Bob.*

Moorhusen came unglued, hooting, showing it to others who returned to the table, and everyone given to laughing—*almost* loud enough to wake up George and Bob.

"I oughta put a note in the Gas House," Moorhusen said. "'I wuz here. Where wuz you?'"

When the then-sleepers arose the next morning, we showed the note to George and commiserated with him for having been jilted. Schluter then confessed that, sad to say, he had been betrayed too. There had been a note on Jamieson's pillow: "George, meet me @ midnight down at the dock! I'll bring the fish oil! Love, Mike. XOXO."

Mike demanded, "Who did this?"

So detective work began. Both notes seemed to have been written by the same hand. Moorhusen checked the script against some that he had from Campagna. They matched. "Did you write this, Jeff?"

"Yes," Jeff confessed. "I cannot tell a lie. I wrote them just as Bob and Mike dictated."

The verbal exchanges and quips with innuendos went on for some time. Finally Schluter took control. "Tell you what. Let's just all take our clothes off, jump in the lake, and get this over with once and for all!"

More laughter, but the water was too cold for entry.

Next morning as I was journaling, Jamieson proclaimed, "Of course, gentlemen, what happens at Keeper Lake, stays at Keeper Lake."

"Right, George," we all agreed.

(So, dear reader, please disregard or tear from this book the pages above.)

On this last full day on the lake, Moorhusen and I stayed in the bays close to the cabin. In the weed bed by the Indian Camp, he took a 26-inch northern. In the Vagina Hole we soon were able to stringer four walleyes for supper.

Late morning we made our way to a run in front of the first of the Three Sisters Islands. It was noon when we got there. Right away Jim had one, then I. Then we doubled. A count then began: five . . . six . . . a walleye, a northern . . . two more . . . count now to ten . . . doubles . . . scissoring here . . . missed take there . . . fifteen . . . fresh rind put on . . . twenty-two . . . stuck on the bottom, break off, rejig . . . how many now? . . . twenty-nine . . . can we catch thirty? . . . yes, thirty . . . and on to thirty-four and thirty-five! Stop.

The result: in sixty minutes, thirty-five fish.

Moorhusen said, "This is the way it's supposed to be, the way it usually is when Sunny and I fish up here, like I told you when we caught 158 one afternoon in Hidden Bay. It's the kind of fast fishing I thought we'd have all week. I'm glad you got a taste of how good it can be."

Turns out it was the fastest action anybody had on the trip. Even so, at lunch all the guys reported that they too had done more than well. The barometer, the water temperature, the moon, the effect of the northern lights—something was different about the day to make catching, not just fishing, excellent.

After my power nap, Moorhusen and I went out again, this time to nearby Eagle Lake. In a wild rice bed between two small islands, I decided to flex my fly rod one last time and did, to take a nice 19-inch hammer handle. It was a good note on which to end our fishing day—essentially our trip.

Our fight out the next morning was on time and smooth, the $766.20 each paid to Chimo Air in Red Lake painless, and the ride back into

Minnesota uneventful, except that Moorhusen got caught in a speed trap of a "town with no buildings," his $200 fine shared by all. We spent the night in Duluth and at dinner recalled highlights of the week: mouse trapping, 34- and 39-inch northerns, the northern lights, euchre by gaslight—Brand and Moorhusen "Champeens," McCusker Falls, Loud Al, Peterson's bonfires, Schluter stories, the Hidden Lake ordeals, no bugs, and no rain.

Next day Schluter and Jamieson were dropped off at Stone Lake, Wisconsin, where their wives, Jo and Pat, were waiting. As their men stepped out of the van and the women saw serious whisker growth, each screamed, "Don't come near me!" They screamed again, even louder, when shown Jeff's digital photo of *la mousetrap*.

It was quite a trip, Scott Blair honored by the incredible camaraderie.

Segue to Mexico

THE YEAR AFTER THE just-recounted "Boys of Illinois" adventure, I returned to Ontario's Keeper Lake. This time it was with my wife Patti, the Moorhusens, and another couple. As in the previous year, we took many excellent walleyes, the world's most delicious fish when battered and put to the oil. *The* memorable thing about that trip, however, was that Patti and Sunny, using an 18-inch walleye as bait, captured a monstrous 39-inch northern! That's a whole other story, "Great Northern and *les Femmes.*"

Tracers of Patti's Giant Northern, Walleye Too

That second trip to Keeper Lake came in the middle of a four-month interim ministry at University Congregational Church in Wichita, Kansas.

A longer interim position happened a year after my Kansas stint. This one was at University Congregational United Church of Christ in Seattle, Washington. It ran from July 2008 until June 2009. Ministry at U Cong Seattle was quite different for me. After my years at the churches in Denver, Moline, Westfield (NJ), Parker, Colorado Springs, and Wichita, I was accustomed to being senior pastor, head of the staff. Here, though, there were *three* clergy equally sharing duties (worship leadership, calling, administration, etc.). I preached once a month. It was a challenge to adapt but, overall, a most satisfying charge. A quite memorable thing that happened while I was there was that our social justice church welcomed homeless folk to pitch their tents in our parking lot for the month of December. When a freak snowstorm blew in one Saturday night, packing the streets and stopping city traffic (Seattle has no snow plows), there were more homeless in the pews Sunday morning than members—and this church had a roster of 1500!

Fishing-wise, I went with conference minister Mark Miller for steelhead on the Olympic Peninsula. We fished out of Forks, Washington, "the wettest and darkest place in the United States," epicenter for the *Twilight* books and movie. A Bob Ball guided us. Mark took seven—something of a record—and I *finally* took one. But, hey, a steelhead!

University UCC was a fulfilling ministry, enabling me to meet New Testament theologian Marcus Borg and make new friends, like Mike Emerson, who, in that year, began to join me and others fishing the Bighorn. Opportunity to fish "further out"—that is, internationally—happened when Patti and I joined her sister and her husband for a week at Cabo San Lucas on the Baja peninsula. There brother-in-law Sid Shelton and I fished for sierra mackerel. We had some time of it negotiating price with "the sharks of the wharf," but eventually struck a deal that got us to the blue Pacific. Below is a *piece* from the story, which probably should be shown with dollar signs, thus: "$ierra$ on the Fly."

CHAPTER 8

Sierras on the Fly

Cabo San Lucas, Pacific Ocean
March 5, 2009

REVVED UP, THE *SANTI II's* Suzuki motor powered us around Cabo's iconic Land's End Spires and onto the Pacific Ocean.

Spires at Land's End of Cabo San Lucas

Captain Victor Salazar headed the panga north, past the beachfront hotels and high-on-the-cliff luxury homes—one reputedly belonging to John Travolta. Miles ahead was a lighthouse. The *Santi* purred and plowed toward it. Just before reaching it, Victor shut off the motor and announced, "We'll start here."

I looked shoreward. Beyond the nearby sand beach, so clean and white, were low, gray sand hills. In the distance, white limestone mountains in this desert clime, quite sparse of vegetation. The Baja range was, I believe, lifted up as the Pacific tectonic plate subducted under the North American. The only sign of human tread was an Italian villa, abandoned; its Roman arches weathering well.

Captain Salazar put us to drift-fishing the swells just before they became breakers. He kept the motor running and in gear to make drift adjustments. Level-wind rods were set out armed with caballitos—or big-eyed shad—about ten inches long. Though we were fishing by trolling, the captain was mostly looking, looking for surface disturbance. Finally spotting nervous water, he promptly moved the boat beside the swarm, put the motor in neutral, and rushed to the live well to seine up a good scoop of lizas (small sardines) and pitch them overboard. Then a second scoop of them went in. Suddenly the surf was alive with sierras—a.k.a. Spanish mackerel—slash-feeding. I was handed the fly rod and told to cast beyond the swirling. I did a double haul and then, in strong, quick-quick pulls, ripped the streamer through the maelstrom. But nothing. So I cast again. Voila! One of the mackerel "took a-holt" and went screaming off, putting me into the reel's backing. When he turned I started cranking frantically. Then had to give line as he powered out again. Only to have the line suddenly go slack.

"Ah, he scissored us," Victor lamented. "We'll put on heavier mono."

That he quickly did, adding a new Clouser Minnow, this one green and white. "All right, Señor Blanco, once again."

He threw out another dipper of lizas. I then cast, had a hit, but didn't connect. So cast again. On the third heave, a slam-bam followed by an in-and-out tug of war. After a full five minutes, this mackerel tired and came boat-side.

Victor grabbed my line and lifted the fish into the boat. This silver beauty, torpedo-shaped with a blue racing stripe along his side, was 31 inches long and sharp toothed. He weighed 6 pounds.

Sierra Mackerel

This fish was one of two I took this day on the fly. Sid boated four, casting live bait via conventional level-wind tackle. We went in this evening with fish to show the wives and take to a restaurant on the dock for culinary treat. On the dock was a sculpture of a giant marlin.

Wharf Sculpture of Giant Marlin

(A little addendum: In 2016, on a return trip to Cabo, I brought along a twelve-foot spey rod, purchased while living in Seattle. I tried it with the macks. Unsuccessfully.)

Segue to Kodiak Island

IN JUNE 2009 I completed interim ministry in Seattle. So Patti and I left for our Colorado home. Just before leaving, however, I had my eyes checked, and the optometrist discovered the beginnings of AMD, age-related macular degeneration! Not happy news. It would change—yea, *has* changed—my life. More about this when we come to the Europe trip.

Returning to Colorado, eyes still functioning well, I did much of "the usual": fishing on the Arkansas, Spinney, Eleven Mile, etc., and guiding for Anglers Covey. Such guiding I had done since 1996 when a parishioner and fishing guide, Anthony Surage, set it up with Dave Leinweber, Covey outfitter. At the first guides' meeting I looked around and instantly knew I was the *Senior* Guide—all others were well under fifty! That said, I was immensely pleased to be in the Covey's "stable." I became a C or "Corporate"/large group ghillie. B guides were "*Better*," full-time employed elsewhere but guides on weekends, and A guides were "Awesome," doing so professionally—as did A-for-Anthony. More on him later.

Anthony Surage Giving Fishing Instruction

118

In the summer all guides helped with the Boy Scout fly-fishing merit badge program at Camp Alexander. That involved teaching knots Monday, casting Tuesday, fly-tying Wednesday, and, on Thursday, we put the Scouts in the river. Sometimes they caught a fish for their badge. One written story came of the days with the boys while also volunteer-guiding a woman friend learning Spanish, "*La Pescadora* and the Boy Scouts."

Quite *unusual* for me this summer was travel I did *within* the state. It started from Josh and John's Ice Cream Parlor. The parlor had a "trivia question," which, if you could answer it, would gain points for a free ice cream cone. The question was, "What state has no rivers or water that flow in, only out?" Most people guessed Colorado, but I knew it wasn't so, as I'd fished the Green River coming in *from* Utah.

(The right answer, of course, is Hawaii.)

The ice cream parlor question sent me to examining topographical maps, which indicated every state around Colorado pumps in some water. To verify what appeared on paper, I went motoring to each corner to investigate and take photographs. I discovered, for example, how rain that fell in Arizona could carry down a Utah gully into the Colorado's San Juan River, which river enters Colorado from New Mexico. A high spot in Kansas sends water back into Colorado, to quickly flow into the eastward-bound Arkansas River.

The travels enabled some fishing, as on the Little Snake River on the border with Wyoming. I also discovered a trout-bearing impoundment in northeast Colorado, the impoundment receiving water from Nebraska. The last verification trip was to the southeast to photograph the dry riverbed of the Cimarron River coming in and across from Oklahoma. Oklahoma!

(Findings and photographs eventually went into an article for the *Colorado Outdoors* magazine.)

Right after the southeast Colorado corner visit, the Kodiak Island fishing trip began. I here share only seven pages from the longer, thirty-three-page write-up. The full story is called "Seeking Silver with Brown Bears." Silver salmon (a.k.a. coho) is what we went there after, and we caught them, along with Dolly Varden, in several rivers of the island. My longer account of the trip includes the afternoon when we shared the river with a brown bear (a.k.a. a grizzly).

Kodiak Bear Fishes with Us

The episode with the bear notwithstanding, the most memorable day of the six spent on Kodiak was the *first*. This is the story about to be told, "The Miracle of the Seeds and the Kings." The title sounds biblical, the story apocryphal, and the events unbelievable. You can decide.

CHAPTER 9

Miracle of the Seeds and the Kings

September 19, 2009

Kodiak Adventure Shirt

"Hustle it up, guys. Captain Rick's waiting," J. D. Parker, our host and scheduler at Chiniak Lodge on Kodiak Island, urged.

So, with Blair Kuster driving the lodge's Suburban, we were off to the ocean side of the peninsula. As we came into Captain Rick Baker's compound on the Pasgashak River, Blair asked, "Does anybody have bananas on them?"

"Didn't have time to pack any," Jon Thomas answered. "Do you want one?"

"No, no," Blair replied. "Just checking, 'cause if we had even one, it would have to be thrown out. Captain Rick says they're forbidden fruit—bad luck on a fishing boat."

I wondered if dried banana slices were in my trail mix.

"Driftwoods" in Captain Baker's Compound

Soon after the above photo was taken, we five *pescadores* —Blair and Bruce Kuster, Steffan Knapp, Jon Thomas, and I, called "Blair's Bunch"—were inside the boat, *C-Grace,* being trailered down the road toward the put-in beach. *FISHKODIAK.COM* was stenciled on the inside of the stern, obviously there so that the name would show up in angler-catch photos. Captain Baker, a Michael Moore look-alike, backed the boat into the water, and soon we were cruising out to the fishing grounds. The sun was shining, the water almost calm.

Two of our bunch, Blair and his father Bruce, had fished Kodiak before. Steffan, Jon, and I, however, were newbies with hardly a clue of what to expect. For sure I watched intently as the captain set up the downriggers.

Rick attached a flashy, fish-shaped lure, six inches long, to a heavy monofilament line, joining them by a swivel. The line was from a level-wind reel on a stout but flexible six-foot, extended-handle rod, the handle able to fit in a gunwale pocket. Line was then paid out some twenty feet, then snapped shut in the jaws of a strong yellow-plastic clip. The clip was anchored to a three-pound cannon ball, and the ball on a cable threaded through a metal pulley at the end of an eight-foot boom. Cable and ball moved up and down via an electric winder on board the boat. The boom, when dropped to the side, lowered the weight, line, and lure into position well out and away from the boat. When the winder let it fall, it went down forty or fifty feet, there to ride along above the ocean floor.

In addition to the port and starboard side downriggers, three additional trolling rods were put into action from the stern. For these unweighted set ups, line went out twenty-plus pulls, a "pull" being from reel to first eye of the rod, getting line out twenty to thirty yards. So the three baits from the stern rods were fished shallower than those of the downriggers.

All set, we now trolled for thirty minutes in Rick's "first-choice, always productive, hot spot" in the bay. Alas, there was no action.

"Let's move," the skipper finally said.

All lines were brought in, and we went to a location just out from some protruding rocks that looked like Stonehenge of the sea.

Rock Pillars—"Stonehenge of the Sea"

Back and forth we went, with the same nil harvest. In a completely serious tone, the captain asked, "Has somebody brought bananas on board?"

We all looked about, searching for a trace of the forbidden fruit. Though we found none, I still wondered if some yellow menace might be around. While then moving to a third location, I sat down to check out the trail mix in my backpack. Sure enough, there were dehydrated banana slices among the raisins, nuts, and M&Ms. Self-shamed, I moved surreptitiously to the stern, there to feed my snack to the waters. "Enjoy, O gulls," I whispered.

Now no bananas were on board.

The *C-Grace* was brought to a third location, and this time, instead of trolling, the motor was idled and we started jig fishing, our weighted lures being lifted half-dozen cranks from the bottom, then pumped up and down. Bruce had a hit and brought up a fish new to me, a rock bass.

"They're great eating," Captain Rick said, "but that one's a little small. He's only about 5 pounds."

Bruce let him go.

"How about this baby?" Jon, reeling in, asked.

"Better," the captain answered, "but not enough." He twisted the hook with his needle-nose pliers and let the fish fall back into the ocean.

Then I felt a pull. "Must be stuck to the bottom," I said. But no. The bottom moved when I lifted the rod and I felt a pullback, the pullback of a good fish. "Perhaps a halibut," I hoped aloud.

"Doubt it," Rick said, "but maybe. Just keep lifting your rod up and then reel fast as you let the rod come down."

I did that for a while and, finally, saw the fish.

"That's a keeper!" Rick exclaimed.

Indeed, my fish was such a keeper that the skipper, with his camera, made a point of taking a picture. "A 15-pound sea bass is welcome any day. Get another," he then directed.

Rock Bass

I didn't. But Jon did, and so did Blair. Both of their fish were good enough for the hold. A few other, smaller rock bass were caught and released, and then it was time to try farther south.

We drifted below a high cliff bank where bunkers from World War II gun emplacements were still visible, eerie reminders of a war-filled period. Farther up the island, we had encountered a huge nuclear missile silo, now decommissioned. Both sites made me shiver.

The *C-Grace* moved back and forth on that water for almost an hour, jigging and trolling simultaneously, the downriggers set at a shallower level. No further success was had.

"Okay," Rick said, "let's go back where we began. Maybe the tide has changed in our favor."

With the boat churning back north, all of us gathered out of the wind in the open cabin, or cuddy. After a while, Blair reached into his coat pocket and pulled out a packet of sunflower seeds. "Here," he offered, "seeds to chew. They might change our luck."

"Hope so," I said, "but no thanks. I could never figure out how to crack 'em in my mouth and still get the kernel."

"You should try."

"Another life, maybe."

Jon shook his head no, but Bruce put away his cigar to try a few. Steffan took a complete handful and popped some in. He and Blair then moved to the stern rail to mouth multiple seeds, crack individual shells, find the meat, chew up the same, and spit the husks.

"Mm good," Blair said over his shoulder at me.

I responded by turning a thumb down.

Once we were returned to the first-tried fishing location, the downriggers were set at depth and we were back to dedicated trolling. This time, however, the bait was wired-on mackerel. Almost immediately Steffan at the stern announced, "I got one," and, sure enough, there was a flashy splash out a couple hundred feet.

"It's a silver," the captain said; and we watched as Steffan brought it toward the boat. Halfway in, Bruce shouted, "I got one too—on the downrigger!" Triumphantly he lifted the affected rod from its holder on the portside.

"I'll be," Jon let out, "a double!"

Rick netted Steffan's bright, 12-pound silver and turned to the second fish, Bruce's.

"I think it's a king, a chinook," Bruce guessed.

"Doubtful. Think it's a silver, just like Steffan's," Rick asserted.

It was, however, a king—a 25-pound king—and Bruce couldn't have been happier. With elation he pronounced, "This, my friends, is Alaska!"

Then Blair, spitting a sunflower seed husk, lunged toward a pulsing stern rod, "Hold on! This rig's going!" He lifted it up and started cranking furiously, then stopped. "Nope. He's off. Spit the hook." Disappointed, Blair reeled in slowly. Then his face relit. "Wrong. I was wrong. He's still there!" Ere long, another king salmon was flopping on the deck, this one coming in at about 20 pounds.

I looked at Blair. "Good going!" and added, "Have you any more sunflower seeds? I might try a chew."

I picked out three from his bag and began the mastication process. I cracked the first with my molars. Shell and kernel separated. There was a strong taste of salt. With my tongue I tried to find the kernel, isolate it, and, at the same time, spit the husk. Okay. Done. Now, go for another. Crack!

But a different crack—more of a *whang*, the downrigger boom being jerked. I pulled the rod out of its pocket holder and put the butt of it in my stomach, then tried to reel. The fish, however, just pulled line out, and then turned hard left. His directional change sent me scrambling with my rod over the transom to the port side of the boat. (All other rods, happily, were reeled in.) Standing there I tried to spit the husks from the second sunflower seed and still hold the third one in my mouth. That, for some reason, I remember clearly. Now my fish dived under the boat, and half my rod went hard in the water, thus to keep him from getting the line tangled in the propeller. Rod tip staying down deep, I stumbled back across the transom with it, only to have my fish power away. Finally he tired, settled down, and came to the net.

"A 28-pounder," Rick announced at fight's end. In the picture that was taken, to be sure, I was beaming.

Author with King Salmon

"Let me try some of those seeds," Jon asked.

"They're magic," I suggested.

Jon began the cracking-positioning-spitting-ingesting process. In a minute, he announced proudly, "One seed down."

"Be ready, then," I alerted him.

"I'm ready," he replied, spitting husk number two. Just like that, Jon was on to one. Without hesitation, this fish went screaming away, far out, and then jumped.

"It's a toad!" the captain shouted, "a toad!"

Such toad did not want to come in. He would approach the boat and then flair back out time and time again. The captain, with his long-handled black net, stood beside Jon and advised, "Take your time. You have a big boy."

Jon stayed with the action and finally the toad, also called a "hawg" by Rick, was in the black net and boated.

"Forty-five, maybe 50 pounds, this one will go," Rick estimated. "Well done, ole salt of the sea . . . and now you, Steff," the captain indicating Steffan with nod of the head, "now it's your turn."

"I can be had," Steffan answered from the starboard side, twanging the downrigger rod's taut line. "I'm easy."

On the boat's second pass through the fish-producing alley, the clip holding the line deep down snapped loose. As Steffan jumped to grab the rod, the water behind the boat suddenly was split, split by a big king flying into it. Steff, of necessity, let out line, and the fish jumped a second time— jumped out well over five feet high. Following that jump, he powered even farther out, and then made a third airborne appearance.

What a show.

"You got Old Fighter," Bruce shouted.

Indeed.

When Old Fighter at last came *near* the boat, he went down, way down, down to Davy Jones's locker. There he sulked. Steffan, though, worked him back up by slow lift-and-reel, lift-and-reel. Ultimately the fish succumbed to Rick's net and took a place on the boat floor.

The fish, by the captain's estimate, was 37 pounds. Not our heaviest chinook but certainly the scrappiest.

After that, it went quiet. No action. But we all felt wonderful. Five kings for five fishermen!

Bruce mused, "If you but have the faith of a sunflower seed . . ."

For sure, we'll never leave shore without them.

On the island Blair may have continued chewing sunflower seeds. See picture below.

Blair Kuster with River Run Silver Salmon

Segue to Tasmania

THE PERIOD BETWEEN THE Kodiak Island week and the next major outing is short, October 2009 to January 2010, just four months. Happenings between the times can be quickly told. I fished a bit, guided some, and on-call served my church, which church, had by this time, made me a minister emeritus. Emeritus status meant I "covered" for the regular clergy when requested and preached once a year. That was about all.

Except during the fall of 2009. Then I, with my electrical engineer brother-in-law, Sid Shelton, did a series of adult classes on science and spirituality. We began with a statement of mathematician/nuclear physicist Albert Einstein:

> *The most beautiful and most profound emotion we can experience is the sensation of the mystical. It is the power of all true science. He to whom this emotion is a stranger, who can no longer stand, rapt in awe, is as good as dead. That deeply emotional conviction of the presence of a superior reasoning power, which is revealed in the incomprehensible Universe, forms my idea of God.*

Much of what I offered in the class I drew from "The Holy Spirit," part 4 of my book *Christianity 101: Tracing Basic Beliefs*. Sid and I dealt especially with the spirituality of science and also of American culture and pastimes. Touching on the latter rekindled my reflecting on what kind of spirituality is connected to—or *can* be involved with—fly-fishing. Most certainly I want to consider this subject. I will do so specifically in the "Ixthus and Ichthyology" chapter. For the moment, though, let us go to the Tasmanian tale.

Patti and I flew to Australia, where the next—and singularly unique—fishing adventure happened. To explain how it came about needs a minute. Six years earlier, in the fall of '05, after my retirement and the "Kamloops with Honey" trip to British Columbia, Patti and I found ourselves walking the *Camino de Santiago* in Spain. It turned out to be a five-week, 600-mile trek, quite wonderful. Early in the pilgrimage, just after we crossed the

Pyrenees, we met up with a young couple from Australia, Toby and Deanne Eccles. They were Waldorf/Steiner School teachers on earned leave. Despite our age differences, we hit it off, started walking together, laughed a lot, shared meals, sang, and took in the art-music-and-worship services of *The Way's* cathedrals and shrines *with viga*, good ole St. James's arrows leading our way. Whenever we crossed a bridge, Toby joined me in spotting trout in the pools below —trout like those Ernest Hemingway spoke of in his writings. After reaching Santiago, we four traveled on by train and rental car to Madrid and other places. In Seville we four hooked up with an audacious and most gracious couple from England, Audrey and Terry White (whom I'll introduce fully in the "Europe on the Fly" account). We six went on to enjoy the Mediterranean sun and sand of Spain's southern shore. When it came time for all of us to part, the Eccleses and we specifically promised to visit one another "sometime."

That time proved to be January 2010.

So the story to come, with serendipitous happenstance to land me in the Central Highlands of Tasmania going after brown trout and Australia-ese ("down under" language).

CHAPTER 10

On the Piss and the Fish with the Aussies in Tassie

February 2–6, 2010

"The hardest-fighting trout in the world is a Tasmanian brown—heard that since I was a kid," I said.

"Yah. They'll bend the sage [rod] and pump the bluud, mate," he replied.

"And you're going there, to Tasmania?"

"Yah. To Tassie. Me cousin Donny is a Tasweegian and every year I go over to Donny's shack, sharking, polaroiding, and getting on the piss."

I was stopped, could not comprehend.

My wife Patti and I were in Australia vacationing with Aussie friends Deanne and Toby Eccles, whom we'd met in Spain on the *Camino de Santiago*. Traveling about Victoria with the Eccleses included an overnight with Deanne's family in Echuca on the Murray River.

Seeing my Anglers Covey ball cap with its trout logo, Deanne's mother said, "You ought to meet my next door neighbor. He's a fisherman, ties his own flies."

So I was introduced to Glenn Ogden, a bespectacled, well-tanned, chain-smoking, stories-filled, yogurt maker by trade. "Oggie" was seated under a corrugated vinyl back porch shelter, tying flies on a vise attached to the arm of a deck chair. Beside him was the largest fly box I'd ever seen in my life: two hinged wood panels 18"x24", lined with foam. I introduced myself, and he said, "Nice to meet ya, Yank. Where ya frum?"

I told him Colorado Springs, where I was a sometimes trout fishing guide. "Could I look at what you're tying?"

"Yah," he said. "It's a battle."

"Beetle?"

"Yah, a battle."

And that it was, a beetle, a beautiful iridescent green beetle. "Do you fish this around here?"

"Nay, mate, in Tassie."

"Tasmania?"

"Yah. Tasmania."

My eyes widened. "The hardest-fighting trout in the world is a Tasmanian brown—heard that since I was a kid," I said—to repeat how I began this story.

So ten days later I was with Oggie and his mate Stuart, "Stuie" Rundenell, in Tassie. Stuie is a close-cropped, quick-to-laugh, fortyish union electrician from Melbourne. The two were in Tasmania at the town of Meina, come to fish the Great Lake and other waters of the Central Highlands. Their residence was with Oggie's cousin, Donny Ogden, a native Tasweegian with a salt-and-pepper full beard and to-the-shoulders head of hair. Donny was a fifteen-year policeman on the island, now voluntarily retired. "Saw too many bluudy traffic deaths," he said. Over the years he'd built up this great "shack" to which family and friends repaired for blue-ribbon fishing.

The Ogden cousins and Stuie met me at the Lanceston Airport. First thing in the vehicle, Donny asked, "Do you want a piss?"

"Nope. Just used the MALE in the terminal," I replied.

"Right you are, mate. Yah. But would you like a beer, a VB, Victoria Bitter?"

I looked at my watch. Nine a.m. "Sure." I was thinking, drinking might allay concerns these guys could have about being with a minister—and for five days! So "on the piss" we drove through the area lowlands into Tasmania's highlands, my three compatriots all smoking—Donny, his own special roll. "We'll get some proper Tassie beer into ya tonight, Gem—and Friday," Donny assured me. "James Boag Draught. Once you've had the Boag, all others beers are boring."

On the mountainside in the distance we could see this giant, perhaps twelve-foot thick, pipe that brought irrigation water from the highland plateau to the lowland farms. We crossed a big river that the piped water created. Passing one especially green field in the otherwise straw-colored landscape of their midsummer, Donny said, "That's a poppy field. Only Tasmania, Turkey, and Pakistan are allowed by international law to grow opium."

"Tassie is the land of Oz," Oggie added.

Not in Kansas anymore.

An hour and a half's drive up winding roads—quite similar to going up the Pikes Peak Highway—and we were in Meina at Donny's shack. It was a house with two large bedrooms, one bath and kitchen, fully modern. It had a huge living room with a metal firebox in the middle. I was bunked in a room with the Victorians—but Victorians not like from the nineteenth century. Once unpacked, I assembled my eight-weight Orvis rod and was told to put on at least a six-pound test leader.

"We'll be sharking today," Stuie informed me.

Sharking

Sharking is when you drift in a boat, Glenn's fourteen-footer with a 25-horse Mercury motor, and look in the waves for fish whose dorsal fins and tails may be seen, like a shark's. "If it's a blue sky day with the sun behind you on the drift, you'll see 'em, dark brown shadows in the waves. Then cast and wait for the take," Oggie instructed.

Today, though, was mostly cloudy. So no fish were seen. Still Oggie, Stuie, and I, from Oggie's boat, cast to the possibility of cruisers. They were likely feeding on terrestrial insects blown in from the shore. I put on one of Oggie's greenback "Battles." He also presented me with a Red Tag dry fly. "Anything with a red tail," he said, "works." My Red Tag was on a #12 dry fly hook dressed with plenty of brown hackle. The Beetle and Red Tag together were tied to a nine-foot leader. Usually, I could see them bobbing on the waves.

Waves there were a-plenty, often whitecaps, caused by the strong northeast wind. "Yah don't mind the heavy chop," Stuie said, "if the sun is bright enough to see the fish. Yah." The sun, though, just wasn't there today.

Oggie motored us well upwind, then killed the motor so we could drift. We did not go fast because a drouge or drag was dropped off the windward side. This drouge was a 3'x6' plastic cloth spread between two sturdy two-foot-long dowels. The cloth was weighted down on the bottom by a chain and floated at the top by white, mango-sized foam balls. The support dowels had ropes attached to them, top and bottom, which ran to cleats on the boat's side. What the drouge did was slow the boat by using the weight of the water to detain us.

We floated and cast out our flies to a distance where we could still see them riding high. Then, as the boat moved toward the flies, we slowly stripped line in. After about twenty minutes, Oggie had a take. He struck back and his knot broke. "Buggers!" he swore. He went to rerigging while Stuie and I continued to cast.

Then, just as we were floating past the put-in boat ramp, Stuie exclaimed, "Crickey. I got one!" He just as quickly added, "Shocker! Lost him." We drifted on till Oggie said to pull in the drouge that we might return to the ramp area to drift again. Again with no results. So back to the first starting point, where again Oggie had a hit. Again, his leader broke. "Bluudy frickin' Maxim is too old," he lamented and began the rerigging, this time totally.

I reported that my Red Tag was sinking. So, from his big, flat, valise-size fly box—the one with 3,000 flies in it—Oggie pulled out a heavier-hackled Red Tag for me. This one I could see much better, it staying atop for several dozen casts. Suddenly there was a dorsal splitting the water—like a shark! My Red Tag disappeared. I lifted, felt the stop, and then a yellow-white missile burst out of the water, to quickly dive. I gave line, only to strip it in frantically as he charged back.

"This is a fish!" I exclaimed.

Again, he skyed. "Most unusual for a brown trout," I said aloud and thought, a rainbow maybe, but not a brown.

With landing net in hand Stuie assured me, "It happens here a lot."

Two more run-outs and the fish "came to Jesus" and was lifted into the boat. I took the hook out and asked, "Do we release him?"

"Not this one," Stuie said, administering last rites, three sharp raps to the fish's head with a wooden priest.

I held him up happily, a Tasmanian brown! A beautiful 19-incher.

"A bewdy!" said Oggie in Australian. "Let's get him in the hold with the ice and beer." So in went the bewdy and out came VBs for me—and Stuie and Oggie.

Popping the top and raising the can, I toasted: "Thanks, mates."

Together they said, "Good show, Yank!"

"How much do you suppose he weighs?"

"A kilo, maybe more," Oggie estimated.

"How much is a kilo?"

"Couple of pounds."

"All right!"

My fish was it for the day. Returning to the boat ramp take-out, we met three other boat fishermen who'd taken nine. They showed me their winner-fly, something they called a Black Mongrel, a rubber legged Madam X with black body, short tail, and swept back wing case of possum hair, the whole kept buoyant by two layers of extended foam, black on the bottom, pink on top. The fishermen said, "It's grouse!"

"Come again?" I asked.

"It's grouse, bonza."

"Huh?"

"It's apples. Very good. Keep it."

Thanking the fly-tyer, I put the Black Mongrel on my drying patch.

Boat on the trailer, we headed back to the shack. But first, a stop at the Meina Lodge, i.e., the piss shop. I bought the first round of Boags. There were three or four more rounds as evening came on. The conversation went everywhere, such as to a warning from the Victorians to watch out for these Tasweegians "'cause they have two heads—an isolation evolution mutation," I was told.

Oggie said, "In a boxing match the Tassie mutation gives us mainlanders unfair advantage —we get two targets to hit. I told me sister, fresh out of hair-dressing school, to think about coming to Tassie to get her business off to a fast start. Told her she could double her income."

Native Tasweegian Donny, who had joined us at the bar, let his cousin know, "Yah. And Victorians have three heads: one is out lost, the second is out looking for him, and the third won't work without supervision. So get nicked, wacka [that is, jerk], or we'll cut the cable from Australia and float off with paradise to ourselves."

"It'd only make for weirder mutations," Oggie retorted.

Ah, the banter.

The talk then went to various sports, little of which I understood. Some of the chatter was about cricket and cricket players but especially about football, which is not the same as American gridiron. "Gridiron players are sooks, wimps," Oggie said, "wearing pads and all. They oughta play Aussie rules with no holding back. That's the sport of real men." He praised someone named Ricco and noted that several Australian players had been hired in the AFL as punters. "They also know how to tackle—hard!"

I asked about soccer, and the guys said it was for poofers, that is, gays. I held my PC tongue, responding with, "How about rugby?"

"Leave it to the Queenslanders up north," Stuie inserted. "They're no-necked and cauliflower-eared. Something about the heat up there makes 'em drongo."

"Drongo?"

"Yah, stupid."

I commented on this rivalry among Australians. Bill Bryson in his book *In a Sunburned Country* reported one person from New South Wales saying that Queenslanders were "mad as cut snakes."

"Struth" [it's the truth], Donny replied, "Bent like a banana."

"Every one of 'em has a roo loose in the upper paddock," Oggie added.

"They're a sausage short of a barbeque, a sandwich short of a picnic," Stuie further illustrated.

So the conversation went, round after round until, with the rounds going down the gurgler, I could barely see my scribbled notes. So many new words and phrases coming.

Stuie said, "You're gonna need a bigger notebook, Gemmy. Otherwise you'll be up shit creek . . ."—an expression I knew.

". . . without a paddle," Donny added. Likewise, familiar.

". . . in a barbed wire canoe," Oggie finished freshly.

"I gotta stop," I said.

"It's okay, mate," Donny said. "We're just trying to get you in condition for Friday night. That's when we really get on the piss. Yah. But now, let's go to tea."

Tea, I thought, we're going to tea after all this beer?

But tea, it turns out, means dinner. Our tea, back at the shack, was overcooked hamburger patties, kangaroo sausages, and lamb chops. Except for some white bread and dead horse—that is, catsup—that was it: meat. And, of course, plenty of piss. We watched the video *Once in a Blue Moon* about mouse pattern fishing in New Zealand. Afterward, I showed the Aussies some Mouse ties I'd brought with me. They were fascinated. Then Donny said, "I'll show ya some new tying material, Gemmy."

He led me outside, and under flashlight beam we spotted two iridescent-eyed possums. They were right in the front of the shack, eating table scraps. Then, behind the house, Donny spotlighted a wallaby eating flowers. Unlike the possums, the wallaby bounced off.

"Often," Donny said, "there's a deer—a big buck—who hangs around. Maybe you'll see him in the morning."

Definitely not Kansas anymore, I thought.

Thus, day one in Tasmania.

I don't know what time the cobbers (other fellows) karked (corked) it, but it must have been late. I crashed about eleven.

Pulling

The ashtrays were empty when I awoke at sparrow's fart—"with the birds"—and all the empty VB cans were outside in a fifty-gallon drum. I looked for the sometimes buck, but he was not around. Only crows cawing, the wind blowing, and the clouds drifting swiftly by. Back inside the shack for several uninterrupted hours, I journaled and drank instant coffee—Nestlé's, not bad at all—and read *Tasmanian Trout Waters*. In it I learned that German browns from England were introduced to the island in 1864. Atlantic salmon were also put in about then too. The browns thrived. Some of the fish became sea-runs, going to salt and returning to the rivers in double-digit pounds and fighting ferocity. Such fish, I now understood, must be the fabled-from-childhood "hardest fighting trout in the world." From my catch of yesterday, I concluded that their lake-locked cousins weren't slackers in the fight department.

About nine o'clock, there were stirrings in the sleeping rooms. The first movements were toward the thunderbox (the head or dunny). Then it was to cigarettes.

After a while I asked about breakfast routines. Donny said, "We have a fisherman's breakfast around here. Do you know what that is, Gem?

"I'm listening."

"A fisherman's breakfast is 'a smoke, a piss, and a look around.'"

"Ah," I nodded.

Donny then sat at table to renew membership in the "Highland Greens Growers and Rollers Association." He put together a durry, a.k.a. a marijuana joint, big and firm. It was of tobacco and green "relish" from his garden, rolled up in a small piece of cardboard and licked together, thus to create a special fragrance for the room. Of all the weeds puffed by the mates, I enjoyed Donny's smoke the best.

Happily, Stuie poured himself a bowl of Wee-Mix, a kind of shredded wheat. I got myself a bowl of the same. Otherwise, the mates seemed to do without. "My main meal of the day," Stuie said, "is usually smoko."

My eyebrows went up. "Smoko?"

"Right. In the old days when the workers were allowed to come up out of the mines for a break, they called it smoko, and the name stuck. That's also when they ate. So we have four meals in Australia: breakfast, smoko, lunch, and tea."

"Right, tea," I responded. "Like last night: three red meats, white bread, and dead horse."

"Yah. Only tonight, veggies." Matter of fact, that evening we did have veggies: boiled potatoes, carrots, cauliflower, and pumpkin—a.k.a. sweet potato—along with lamb chops.

The fishing plan today was to return to Great Lake for sharking, as yesterday. So, about eleven we went back to the lake's put-in ramp. The boat was all but in the water when Oggie realized the bung, which drains water from the boat and prevents water from coming in, was gone. "Buggers! Buggers!" he cursed. (I wish I could convey the proper accent on this great word.) "No way to fish now."

Disappointed and defeated, we slowly headed back to Meina staring at the sides of the road with the unlikely prospect that we might spot the bounced-out black stopper. Shocker, in less than two kilometers, Oggie spotted it. We were unbuggered.

"Unfrickin' believable," I aussied.

Because the wind was even stronger today than yesterday, the decision was made to forsake Great Lake and, instead, go to Penstock Lagoon, a smaller, shallower body of water. I asked if Penstock was a name of some person and learned it meant, essentially, impoundment. Penstock Lagoon was a long NE to SW impoundment, so we again could float it, with the drogue behind, only this time using intermediate sinking lines. Our wet flies were an Orange Butcher, Brown Nymph, one something like a snail, and green and red-black Wooly Boogers. Thus, we were *pulling* or stripping as I had once done in Scotland. My mates dropped two flies off their nine-foot leaders and attached a third to the point. Cautious, I went with just two. With my Black Wooly Booger I had a touch early and then he hit the toe, that is, beat it away.

Stuie had one on for a three-count, but it broke off, and he then was caught in a horrible tangle. "Fouck!" he swore. There was a total rerigging to do. The wind, blowing our lines around and whipping our leaders, soon had Oggie snarled and starting over. "Fouck!" he too offered. It was frustrating fishing in the wind. It made me wonder if Tasmania, so close to Antarctica, might be subject to polar vortex conditions that create the famous winds in Tierra del Fuego, Cape Town, and Stewart Island. Or perhaps it is just the basic latitude winds. Sailing ships of yore took advantage of the "ferocious forties" to reach these climes. Whatever, it was windy.

As my friends painstakingly rerigged, I told them that, in my writing, I sometimes named chapters by the main goings-on in a day. "Yesterday, for example, could be called Sharking Day, but what would you call this day?"

Stuie looked up to say, "Fouck Day."

"Or Guys Fawked Day," Oggie added, "though it's not November 6."

"I'll consider it. Meanwhile, would either of you like a beer?"

"Yah," Stuie answered. "Get me one out of the slab."

"Which is . . . ?"

"A pack of 24 VB stubbies or cans on cardboard," he interpreted. "We sometimes have B & B in the boat: a slab of beer and a bag of ice. If you take out the middle four cans to drink right away, you put the ice in the hole created, then place the slab in an esky (Eskimo cooler). That's a B & B."

As "me mates" prepared to go back for another drift, I asked to be left on the shore, to cast from there. Shore, though, was a hard go. The lake's soft bottom put me in mud up to my knees. I had a feeling the musk ducks—coots, I think—and the black swans flying about were having a good laugh watching me. Having had enough of the futile exercise, I yelled that I wanted back on board. I was obliged. By this time, the pullers had had enough rerigging frustration to call it a day. We did.

En route to the shack, we got back on the piss and continued drinking into the evening. Stuie went to a Bundy—Bundeberg rum and coke in a can. It's a rum made up in Queensland and not bad.

Waiting for tea to be barbequed, I wandered across the road to meet the so-called "exaggeration" of fishermen renting the house there. They'd come down from Victoria and Adelaide. Two were named Ray. Younger Ray let me use his computer to check emails, and the elder Ray, my age, offered one of his just-baked scones.

"That's a biscuit," I suggested.

"Yah, but we call it a scone. Try it with marmalade." I did. Delicious.

From these guys I picked up more colorful words and phrases. Here are a few:[1]

she'll be right, mate = ok

cordial = watered fruit drink

going outside to roll a fag = for a smoke

hoo roo = see you later

long black = cup of coffee without cream.

I told the exaggeration that I was confused about negative names, like calling someone a drongo. "Who's a drongo?"

"That's a fool, someone with low IQ," young Ray told me.

"And a wally?"

"Similar, just someone who acts dumb, stupid—and is apt to get run over."

"And a tosser? What's that?"

"That's a bloke who plays with himself," older Ray interpreted.

"Like a whacka or a wanga or a flogga," younger Ray added.

"So what's the difference, say, between a wanga and a whacka?"

---

1. Here are other Down Under "Stine," words or expressions, I picked up later and greatly enjoyed:

Have a Captain Cook—take a look, Box of Birds—happiness, Speuth the Dummy [pacifier]—lose control, Strike Me Pink—I'll be darn, Do a Harold Holt—go drown yourself, Pardon Me Sticky Beak—being nosey, Drier than a Dead Dingo's Donga—really dry, He's a Happy Clappy—Pentecostal, Chuck a Leg Over—have sex, The Penny Dropped—it dawned on me.

"Just a stroke or two!" another of their mates added from the other room.

We all laughed.

For sure, this down-under language is colorful, unique, and great fun for me to hear and have explained.

Back at the shack, I told Donny that author Bill Bryson believes the Australians are the biggest gamblers in the world. Donny said, "Yah. Aussies will bet on two flies going up a wall."

Just about then, I noticed a spider on the ceiling—but no ordinary one. He was an ugly monster, six inches across, gray-brown and hairy.

Taking off my shoe for a dispatch-job, I asked, "What'll you bet on that spider up there surviving the night?"

"I'll bet you'll let him be. That's a Huntsman. He'll vacuum-clean his weight in mozzies, flies, and other bugs before the night is over. There should be two Huntsmen around. If ya feel something on your face tonight, don't swat too hard. I wanna keep 'em happy."

"Okay. They live, but let me sleep with the spaghetti strainer over my face."

Putting my shoe back on, I followed Oggie outside to the marijuana shed. There he hung my now-cleaned fish, said he liked fish to be dry before he filleted them—"and it'll be aromatically flavored, just right."

We had a great, Donny-prepared penne pasta dinner this evening. "Spot on!" I offered. About the Shiraz served with it, I said it was "bonza" and "a bewdy," believing I was using synonyms.

At 4:00 a.m., when I went outside for a nature call and looked about for the Southern Cross, I discovered snow! Yes, snow was falling, sleet more nearly, right in the middle of their summer—like our July.

Polaroiding

Next morning it was raining there in Meina. Donny said, "Tell ya what, Gem. I'll take ya on a big drive today, a sort of walkabout in me back yard. We'll miss the rain and can do some polaroiding, at least, on Dee Lagoon."

"Polaroiding?"

"Yah. Means you use your polarized dark glasses to spot cruising fish in the shallows. On a clear and calm day, we go to the western lakes, one of 3,000 up here, to sight fish. And, yah, there really are 3,000. This, though, is not a windless day. So our route will be a southern swing down to a Denwent River tributary and back."

"I'm game," I said, "and maybe my going out with you will take the hex off Oggie and Stuie's catching."

From the kitchen table, Oggie chimed in, "Probably not, but you're a bright bloke, Gem, for missing the rain. Stuie and I will be going to Woods Lake in it."

"Then, may the fish be with you."

So off we went in Donny's mud-spattered pickup. Donny drove us past Shannon Lake and River, to say, "Years ago, before the Great Lake Water Diversion Project cut it off, the Shannon River pulled in anglers from all over the world. They came to take part in a marvelous caddis hatch. Unfortunately, it's not much now."

Farther down the road, there was a gnarly forest of black stick-trees. Donny said the original cider gums had been killed by a destructive root bore. "That was bad enough, but what's most dangerous in this country is what is known as the kerosene bush, as in the next paddocks. When a fire gets going, this stuff explodes."

Suddenly Donny hit the brakes. "Here's someone you ought to meet, Gem."

He pulled off the left shoulder of the road, so I could look over an echidna, or Tasmanian porcupine. I got close enough to see his pointed little face before he pulled it back and into the earth, to become a veritable cactus.

"The foxes leave him alone," Donny said. "He's as slow as I am!"

"And how slow is that?"

"As slow as a wet week, both me speech and me lifestyle, especially since the divorce. Even so, I'm trying to be like the emblem-animals on our flag, the emu and the kangaroo. Neither can go backward, only forward."

"Well, good on ya," I said in Aussie.

"Yah. Yah. It's bewdy."

We drove on, he noting that the Black Angus and red Herefords in the fields were "good nick," that is, in fine shape. So were the white deer seen munching away in an enclosed paddock. We stopped. The buck had elk-size antlers. "One of those white stags got loose a few years ago," Donny said, "and would come around the shack. Some hunter, though, shot him and so no more. Bluudy shame."

"And that—that bird in the clump grass—what's he?" I asked. "Looks like a chicken."

"That he is, mate, a native chook. When they get to fighting, they make a hell of a noise. Worse than the possums you might have heard last night, but not so wild as when the Tasmanian devils go at it."

I wanted to know, "Will we see one?"

"Doubtful. Those little red-ear critters have about done themselves in. By biting one another, they've spread cancerous, life-sucking tumors. The government tries to protect 'em in various areas. If we don't, they'll go the way of the Tasmanian tiger, now extinct for a hundred years. Beautiful cat, now gone. You can see a painting of one in the Meina Lodge."

Now and again pulling our vehicle off the road so as not to be hit by logging trucks, we drove past Penstock Lagoon, where I'd fished yesterday. Then it was down a steep, steep grade for a couple of miles, down past the Waddamana power station and for the highlight moment of the trip.

We came to a barely running stream, the Ouse, a tributary of the Denwent. It ran in the bottom of a V-sided canyon. Coming to the edge, I stammered, "Stop, please! I want to see those rocks on the river floor!"

He did, and there, as the base of this river channel, were these hard, dark rocks worn smooth for vehicles to cross. They were fractured in parallel lines fourteen or so inches wide. "These rocks," I said to Donny, "I think, are the same ones my wife and I saw in a bridge in Warrnambool, western Victoria. English convicts built it in 1864. Blue stones they called them."

"We call 'em blue metals," Donny said.

"Perfect name. They're deep-earth rocks, metamorphized basalts."

"For sure they're old," he offered, "for Tasmania is one of the oldest land masses on the planet. Once it had mountains taller than the Himalayas. Over the millions of years the mountains wore down to what is here now."

So, it hit me, these flat riverbed blocks are "basement of time" rocks. I was stopped, recalling the concluding passage of Norman Maclean's novella *A River Runs through It*—my most read book. Here's the passage:

> *Eventually, all things merge into one, and a river runs through it. The river was cut by the world's great flood and runs over rocks from the basement of time. On some of the rocks are timeless raindrops. Under the rocks are the words and some of the words are theirs.*
>
> *I am haunted by waters.*

Hot as the day was, I shivered.

Raindrops on Rock, Albeit Sandstone

Here I was down under, down under even Australia, on the other side of
the world from Colorado. Here I was on the oldest chunk of planet earth,
feet on pre-Cambrian rocks. You are truly standing on the firmament, I said
to myself, billions of years old. A huge time connection for a man heading
towards four score years. Oh, my!

Thanks be to you, O God, for this moment in eternity.

"Well, let's be going, Gem. Got lots more to show ya. Yah."

And he did. Ghost gum trees, a three-foot-long tiger snake, and a Swift
Parrot, "fastest of the parrot family," Donny informed me. At one point we
had to stop and remove a dead tree the wind had blown across the roadway.
"Good thing it wasn't a big one," Donny said, "as I didn't bring me chain
saw."

I got a sense of what a big one might be when we came into an uncut
forest. One tree base was way wider than the truck and hundreds of feet
high. "Historically in Australia there may have been ash trees taller than the
American redwoods, but the tallest was cut down to measure it."

"Guess the loggers weren't up on their trigonometry."

"Just wallies," Donny summarized.

Finally we arrived at Dee Lagoon, most picturesque. We drove up to
the lake's inlet. Here was a river created by a huge pipeline of transported
water. "Okay, it's polaroiding time," Donny announced.

But it wasn't polaroiding for success as the wind whipped up the surface much too much. Moreover, pipeline flow was at maximum, creating
flood conditions on the stream and discolor for the lake. I tried dries, then

nymphs, and finally a streamer. Donny activated his spinning rod with a silver spoon. Nothing worked.

Driving away, Donny assured me, "We could have hooked into a 5- or 6-pounder there—just not today."

So we went on in the backyard, next to Brock's Bay of Echo Lake. Of all our stops, this looked the fishiest. I loved walking in the bay's two feet of water, pushing through emerald green aquatic plants, walking on firm sand, and casting a large Elk Hair Caddis to the clear holes in the flat. No action came of it, but the whole time I was thinking/feeling, "Well, all right, mate."

Finally Donny said, "We better get going. Clouds from the high country are coming this way."

In light rain we pressed on to Pine Tier Lagoon, where I fished a hopper-dropper and Donny in the truck talked on his mobile to his ex. Pine Tier was the last chance for a fish today. But nothing. Still, a great day.

On the way back to Meina we stopped at a roadside historical marker just off Bronte Bay. It had an inscription indicating we were at the center of Tasmania. Pressing on in the drizzle we sighted wallaby after wallaby on the sides of the road. I suggested, "We must have seen at least twenty!"

"And more than twenty wuzzas," he added.

"'Wuzzas'?"

"Road kill," he interpreted, "in this case, wallabies that once wuz."

"Gotcha," I nodded.

Shortly after we arrived the shack, Oggie and Stuie came in, sodden through and through but satisfied with fish to process: ten for Oggie and five for Stuie. The fish were up to 3 pounds and all browns. "Caught 'em pulling nymphs, eight counts for the sink and then a retrieve in three to four feet of water. I even caught two at one time," Oggie said.

"And we had a double once," Stuie added.

"Good on the both of yous!" I had to say, wanting to believe my jinx on their catching was now broken.

The VBs this evening were enjoyed with locals Rodney and Kim, who'd come by the shack for happy hour. Like Donny, they were full-bearded and long-haired. "That's the Tassie macho look," Donny let me understand.

"Beard and hair hide one of their heads," close-cropped Stuie inserted.

"Or the stitch marks on their neck, as with me cousin here," Oggie whispered aloud.

"To keep the flies outta me mouth and off me neck," Donny countered.

So, the talk. It went next to Aussie Rules Football, so confusing to me. Donny and Rodney, it turns out, were Richmond Tiger fans, Richmond being a suburb of Melbourne. Oggie and Stuie, on the other hand, were Hawthorn Hawk loyalists—the Hawks being premier, number one a year or so ago. For sure, these guys take their football seriously. One story is that a player from Ireland, Jimmy Stynes, was recruited to play here, so good he got in their Hall of Fame. Irishman Styles is reported to have said, "The great thing about Australia is they don't ask you what your religion is, just 'What is your team?'"

So the conversation went, with lots of sledging (verbal stirring). Great spirit among the Aussies and Tasweegians!

Toward the end I declared myself a Hawk fan, meaning, "I'd like a ride back to Lanceston with Oggie and Stuie on Saturday."

Full Tassieing

I told me mates that evening that angling gurus in America believe that trout come to the shores to feed in the evening and early in the morning. I was therefore resolved, before I left the island, to try fishing along the edge of Great Lake. Early the next morning, then, I drove Donny's truck down to the Meina Bay area. The water was amazingly calm, at least until the sun came on and beamed underneath the cloud blanket. Then came "breeze from the west" and expectation "fishing is best." Sad to report, though, the fish didn't know the rhyme. Not a touch for over two hour's casting. All was in vain, and I had to go with the consolation thought, "You never know if you don't go out." The only fish I saw turned out to be tiny gillixias, veritable one-inch transparent shiners, swishing around beneath a root wad. That was it. What I could visually appreciate along the shore, though, were rocks reddened from seeped-out iron oxide, white flowers on green bushes, and something like black cormorants flying about.

At 8:30 I was back at the shack fixing bacon, eggs, and oven-browned toast when the mates tumbled out for their first smoke and look-about. Oggie checked the overcast sky to conclude, "It's back to Woods, I think. Yah."

So we went to the previous-day hot lake. By the time we arrived, there were over twenty boat trailers in the parking area. Word certainly had gotten round that Woods was productive. Oggie's boat went in the water and then we motored to an area where four or five other parties were drouging along. Almost instantly Oggie had one on, and just as quickly lost it.

I said, "I want to rig up exactly as you are." So I substituted my single Black Leech for a three-fly assortment of a Brown Nymph, an Alexandra, and a bead head green Wooly Booger. To me, the rig was "The Full Tassie," so called after the movie *The Full Monty*, where all is exposed. Employing these flies also fully exposed us to line crossings and tangles—especially me, fishing from the middle of the boat. One twenty-minutes-to-undo bird's nest occurred.

The three of us cast using various retrieves: the five finger over and over, the quick-short strip, and the long-slow-steady pull. I learned a fourth, "the roly poly," in which you put your reel under your arm and then retrieve line from the first feral in a rapid round-and-round take. The most effective retrieve, however, was the quick-short strip. Stuie took one by the strip and, soon enough, I netted an 18-incher. The fish was on the slender side but decent and, as cleaning later revealed, was a female with eggs. Then Oggie pulled a male into the boat, a thick and strong male, about a foot and a half also.

"Nobody goes in skunked tonight," I was happy to observe.

"Yah, but it's not nearly so fast today as yesterday in the rain," Stuie responded.

"Now, I've another!" I shouted. "Feels like a better one." Strange, though, when this fish came near the boat, attached to the Alexandra, he appeared to be not more than 14 inches. "He fooled me," I admitted aloud, but then I saw that the leader to the point fly was under the boat. "Wait! I've two—for a single double!" So it was. We kept the larger of my two for the esky, Stuie's priest dispatching him.

Then another drift. Midway, however, Oggie looked at his watch. "Three fifteen, mates. Yah. Need to be heading back."

I must have given out a quizzical face, for he explained, "Friday's Happy Hour begins at 5:00. Piss time."

Yes, just enough time to get off the lake, clean the fish, get the boat on the trailer and us on the road back to Meina, drinking on the way.

Once at the shack I told me mates—they, spiffed up by clean jeans—to go on to The Lodge without me. I would walk down as soon as I got my stuff together for tomorrow morning's ride out. "Later this evening I may not have enough mind left to pack properly."

They went on. I dried my fishing boots and waders beneath the middle-of-the-room firebox and laid out clothes for the a.m. departure. Eventually, I made it to The Lodge. As I walked in, I was greeted in a loud chorus by my shack mates and others. "Welcome, Knackers!"—pronounced "knockers." It is Australian for testicles. Apparently the story had gotten around that I'd said that if any bloke came to Colorado, I'd be sure he was served Rocky Mountain oysters—calves' testicles, flattened, battered, and fried. "Just delicious," I'd said. "Tastes like chicken."

"'Knackers'?" Donny had uttered in amazement. "You eat knackers? Nah. *You're* knackers. That's what. Yah."

So I got a new name.

Our agenda for the evening was drinking The Boag at The Lodge, drinking VBs at The Great Lake Hotel, and drinking Boag and Bundies back at The Lodge. Whichever watering hole we were in, if someone yelled out, "Aussie! Aussie! Aussie!" other cobbers at the bar, tables, and porch rail would resound back, "Oy! Oy! Oy!" A great liturgical call-and-response, if ever I heard one. Can you imagine how that would sound when the Aussie Hawks played the Kiwi Blacks in a football stadium of 70,000 people? It could have been heard in Hawaii.

Now, as to what happened the rest of this evening, it's a bit of a blur. I'm not sure how smashed I got, but I had a number of VBs and Boags. The next morning my notebook indicated I'd said in amazement, "Look, the lake is finally still!" And it was. Totally placid. One Sheila—that is, woman, by no means a scrubber (prostitute)—at the bar affirmed my observation: "It's flat as a tack."

Donny seconded this with, "Flat as a shit carter's hat."

"What does that mean?"

"'Shit carter'? A shit carter is someone who emptied outhouses, putting the contents in a tub he slings over his back. As you can imagine, he walks very carefully, smoothly, like the lake now."

On my Aussie dictionary page I scribbled in other words, phrases, and expressions I heard during the evening. They were offered freely for my education into down-under language. A fellow named Clammer Hines was especially helpful with sayings, sharing,

- I'm talking to the butcher, not the maggot on the block—meaning, "Bug off, fella"

- There's too many lambs trying to be mutton and too much mutton trying to be lambs—meaning, girls acting like adults and grown women acting like young girls

About midnight we returned to the shack. I went directly to bed, "flat out like a lizard drinking water," that is, exhausted. The cobbers in the main room of the shack stayed on the piss, Bundaberg, and scoobies (weed), frequenting the dunny. At 3:30 I was shaken out of sleep by heavy metal music, the evening still full on. I stumbled out and turned my fingers in prayerful supplication to Donny to reduce the volume. Mercifully, he obliged.

When I got up at six to put my dried boots in the backpack, Spinner Hines was there, a fellow I met last evening. He was either "first one up" or "last man standing." In any case, as fire chief for the region, he'd come to do a training session in Meina. He handed me a cup of battery charger, coffee.

"It's quiet now," I whispered.

"Fair dinkum," was his answer, offered raising his coffee mug.

"Come again?" I asked.

"Frickin' oath. Same thing."

"And again, please."

"Like 'yes' or 'it's true,' fair dinkum. Another one for yer book, Gem. Do ya have 'wotdayadon' and 'hoyagoen'?"

"No, but I will now. Please spell 'em."

He did, and now they are here, open for translation.

At 8:15 Spanner charged into the cobbers' sleeping room and loud of voice exclaimed, "All right, tossers! Up with ya. Rattle yer dags! Knacker needs to go to the airport. Up, up!"

So, one by one, they did so, staggering to the thunderbox while lighting cigarettes and coming full awake with battery charger. By 8:30 we were making our way past the Central Highlands Shack Owners Association sign, and driving off the high plateau to the farmlands below. I noticed that the town of Longford had street signs in the shape of rainbow trout. Most charming.

Just before we arrived the Lanceston Airport, Oggie asked, "What was the most interesting thing you've learned these five days in Tassie, Gem?"

I said, "It is the word 'Yah.'"

"Yah?"

"Yah, yah, however it might be spelled"—yeah, yaah, yeh, maybe yueah. It punctuates almost every sentence you blokes speak," I said. "At the beginning of a comment, 'yah' is there—or at the end of a sentence, with rising intonation to make whatever is said more of a question than a declaration—certainly not an imperative. To my ear it is pronounced with a 'u' in it, that vowel included, like saying 'Good on ya!' as Aussies regularly say. 'Yah' seems to be a gracious affirmation of the one being spoken to, a taking into account of another's presence and person. It's gentle, respectful, and careful. 'Yah.' It's a great word. Thanks for embodying and offering it."

"Yah, knackers," they sang out together.

The fellows left me off at the airport. Oggie and Stuie were in for another week to take on "the hardest fighting trout in the world, the Tasmanian brown."

Segue to Manitoba

THE DAY I GOT back to Victoria from Tasmania, I joined my wife, her sister Robbie, and our brother-in-law Sid Shelton in Melbourne. There we four boarded a cruise ship, which took us across the Tasman Sea to—and around—New Zealand and, after ten days, back to Melbourne . . . to promptly return by plane to Wellington, New Zealand. There, in company with friends from the states and a Kiwi, we traveled into the North Island's interior, up to Lake Taupo, a lake made famous as a fishery by Zane Grey. I was able to fish the Tongariro River, Lake Taupo itself, and Lake Otamangakua, to take a "brace"—in my case, three—10-inch browns. The scenery about, however, was terrific, to include white flumes from volcanoes on dark green mountainsides.

Fishing Lake Taupo, Volcanic Fume Showing

Fishing luck improved when, after Wellington, Patti and I flew to Invercargill on the tip of the South Island, near Gore, "World Capital of the Brown Trout."

Welcome to Gore, New Zealand Granneman with Mataura Brown

Picked up by Ron Granneman—then on his "six months down-under" schedule—we three were able to fish the Mataura River, each trip successful for 14- to 20-inch browns. One afternoon on return from the river we had to wait an hour for 3,000 (of NZ's 30 million) sheep to pass.

Sheep on NZ Road

At his home, Ron showed us photos of giant rainbows he'd caught earlier in the season when fishing at night using a mouse pattern. Seems trout gorged on mice swimming the river, which eating enable them to become so monstrous and humpbacked as to look like B-747s. (Fish, I learned, store extra weight on their *back*, not just their belly.) One leviathan Ron cut open, showed remains of twenty-seven mice!

Our week with Ron included worship at the local Presbyterian church (lots of Scots in NZ) and a trip inland to the picturesque Mavora Lakes for couple of nice bows. One of the funny and mystifying things encountered in the town of Mataura was a sign on an old building that read, "Have You Remembered to Weigh & Mark Your Broke?" Whatever that means, I checked my wallet. For sure, New Zealand is a different country, yet understandably

English-speaking. Of all international places to live, I would choose New Zealand. For one thing, the Kiwis rightly and un-hypocritically—unlike *some* nations we can name—actually eschew nuclear weapons.

Fishing in Montana and states surrounding Colorado, most of my angling in 2010 and 2011 was not far astream but local, especially done at the Rainbow Falls Trout Club near Woodland Park, where I became a member. The well-stocked lakes and stream provided the catch of a 25-inch trout.

Daughter Cheril with 25.5 inch Rainbow Trout

Though I caught other good-size fish at Rainbow Falls and in the Trophy Pond at Bob and Bobbye Tucker's Ranch at Roaring Fork near Carbondale, it will be only in Manitoba where consistent catch of large trout is realized. I turn to that story next.

First, though, a little more set-up.

Ron Granneman, oft met in these pages, is also responsible for the trip and story to come. For a year or so his emails with photos spoke exuberantly about incredibly large trout he was taking in the Parkland Lakes of west central Manitoba. "You guys gotta get up here," he wrote. Thus the silver-tongued *pescador* persuaded Kuster and me to join him in the fall of 2010. We went back in 2011, '12, '13, '14, and '15. Snatches of these later trips I'll tack on at the end of the main account about to be given.

Though bordering the continental US, Manitoba is a world apart from most ordinary fishing realms. It is here Bruce and I take the largest trout of our lives, and it is here that we were acquainted with unique-to-us history, culture, religion, and geography. The people we met, Ukrainian descendants, made it especially great. For sure, on this trip things unexpected happened, such as "the almost international terrorism incident." Look for this story inside "Bonging for Bows—and More."

CHAPTER 11

Bonging for Bows—and More

including

The Almost International Terrorism Incident
Manitoba, Canada
September 21–October 6, 2010

If you're travelin' in the north country fair,
Where the winds hit heavy on the borderline.

—Bob Dylan

"OH, OH," HE GROANED.

"'Oh, oh,' as in 'Fiddlesticks' or as in 'Oh, oh, kimchi'?" I asked.

"Kimchi, deep frickin' kimchi! I left my fish-finder's electric adapter at home, charging away on the kitchen counter."

"You could run back and get it," I suggested.

"Right, wise one: 1250 miles of run back. Thank you, no."

"Then it's 'Oh, oh, kimchi, out of luck' for the ole trout stalker."

"Yip. Seems so."

So, part of the conversation our first morning in Manitoba, Canada. Little did we know what this "left behind" would portend. Bruce and I were here in the early fall to fish Parkland Lakes for what was reported to be here: monster bows and browns. Now poor Bruce had no equipment with which to locate the leviathans. Deep kimchi indeed. He may have to fish blind, but I assured him that I, with my battery-powered locator—the Fishing Buddy—would guide him into plenty of big fish.

These Manitoba lakes are all natural impoundments scooped out during the last glacial age, 10,000 years ago. What makes them different from most northern-clime waters is that these have had all the pike in them killed, and then the water restocked with trout. When such lakes don't ice over for too long, trout can survive. To keep Patterson, Tokaryk, Pybus, Twin, and other lakes open and oxygenated in the winter months, the local townships put in aerating pumps. Planted trout then can survive, stay healthy, and grow. And grow.

As noted, Kuster and I heard about these lakes from Ron Granneman. Over the phone to Bruce, Ron said, "I've been catching the biggest rainbows of my life in these lakes."

"How catching them?" Bruce asked.

"Mostly by stripping streamers, but some by bonging."

"Bonging? Which is?"

"That's what the guys from North Dakota call indicator fishing up here. They bong or bobber fish using chironomids."

Well, bobber and midge talk fired Bruce's fecund imagination. By late September we were able to go.

Going Up Days

Pulling my brother-in-law Sid Shelton's Star Craft pop-up trailer behind Bruce's Tahoe, we went Colorado to Wyoming, Nebraska, and into South Dakota. As we went I pecked at my laptop computer beneath what Bruce calls my "modesty screen," an auto window shade. We traveled US 83, the longest north-south roadway in America, running from Brownsville, Texas, on the Mexican border, into Canada, some 2000 miles, all told.

Highway Sign En Route to Canada

Traveling through North Dakota on the second day, shortly after noon, we crossed the border into Canada. The border guards seemed surprised to meet fishermen coming for *trout* in Manitoba, not walleyes.

Ten miles and ten minutes in, Bruce made conclusive observations about this *foreign* country: "Not many people live in Canada . . . they don't have American food here—haven't seen one McDonald's . . . how much is kilometers in American? . . . it rains too much . . . the border guard talked funny, saying "aboot" . . . they should move their border south cause it's too cold where it now is . . . Canada has nice hawks . . . they don't have the American flag anyplace, but, hey, your American computer works . . . did I say they have nice hawks in Canada?" And so on.

In the town of Virden we bought fishing licenses and groceries, then went farther north, noting that leaves on the willow and birch trees were turning yellow. It was, after all, fall of the year.

Reaching the municipality of Rossburn, we went twelve miles east on a dusty road to Patterson Lake to find our campsite slip. Once the camper was opened and readied, I set up my heavy canvas umbrella tent, in which to store "extra stuff."

Bruce inquired, "Where'd you get this mildewed monster?"

"It's an heirloom from my Great-Uncle Bonner, given to me in 1963. He said it was army surplus from the Spanish-American War. In 1898 Teddy Roosevelt, the old Rough Rider *hissef*, slept herein."

RV and Teddy Roosevelt Tent on Lake Patterson

"Be glad you got an enclosed trailer tonight."

"I'm glad."

That night in the trailer, my feet got cold, cold, cold. So I put on wool socks, and rolled out my sleeping bag as foot cover, saying, "We're not in Cuba anymore."

"What?" drifted out from the propane heater side of the trailer.

Big Brown Day

It was when we were inflating our pontoon boats and getting ready to launch this next morning, that Bruce uttered his sinking, "Oh, oh," regarding his fish finder's inoperability, an essential part missing.

"Electric charger not needed," I assured him. "Just stick with me and my battery-operated Fishing Buddy locator, and I'll put you on big fish."

He did not, however, stick. No, not he. Relying only on his "inerrant inner gyroscope," he anchored his Water Otter in the lake channel just across from the RV campsite. Sure enough, straightaway he was into fish.

Using a plastic minnow—a.k.a. "the Gummy"—and fishing it sixteen feet below a strike indicator, Bruce got into one, then two, the second a fat

23-inch bow. I began by flippering along the banks of the channel throwing a streamer. In nine feet of water, I had a strong take and the beginning of a deep down tussle. It was several minutes before I got a first glimpse of a brown trout quite yellow with red spots. In the fish's second pass I saw a massive head and majorly kipped jaws. When he finally was netted and could be measured, he was a full 23 inches, looking 25-plus. (I didn't get a picture of this fish but, later in the trip, Kuster took a similar-dimensioned brown.)

Kuster with Patterson Lake Brown

Bruce estimated my fish's weight to be 7 pounds. "You just caught the brown of a lifetime," he said.

"Weight size for sure, for sure," I agreed.

Little action happened after my brown-so-big-and-colorful. So I, then Bruce, returned to camp for lunch, a nap, and a drive south to the Shoal Lake RV Park for camper water. In the grocery store I got us a lemon to make the twists for scotch, a drink enjoyed upon return to camp.

Then came Kuster's "planned supper": plastic-like stroganoff in a plastic bowl with a plastic lid cooked in his brought-up microwave.

When set before me, I said, "I've never had plastic pasta before."

"But do you like it?"

"It'll eat."

"Well, get used to it, for I have twelve more bowls for you."

I thought he was kidding. I should have been so lucky.

Bladder Matter Day

Having had Grape-Nuts yesterday morning, I was surprised to see the same fare on the table today. Such breakfast prompted my question, "May I ask what we're having for lunch?"

"Tuna fish half-sandwiches."

"But that's what we had yesterday!"

"And what you'll have every day. We're keeping things simple on this trip."

"Oh." All I could say.

Lunches in our boat bags, we were on the water shortly after ten o'clock. I flippered my way down the campsite shore, casting into bulrush breaks. More than twenty yards from the dock, the Wulff went down and shortly I was admiring a 21-inch brown, four-open-fingers deep. I thought the catch signaled more to come, but that was the end of it. (Other "action" was precipitated by too much breakfast coffee, but more on that later.)

Bruce, meanwhile, positioned in his catching location of yesterday, put his Gummy Minnow in the water. After two hours of marinating it unsuccessfully, he was visited by Ron Granneman riding along on his Water Craft pontoon boat. "How're you doing?" Ron asked.

"Same place and offering as yesterday and not a touch."

Ron smiled, "Welcome to Patterson Lake," and moved on, powered by his electronic motor.

At 2:00 I came in beside Bruce to lunch. Afterward I went back to the camper to rest and to read Garrison Keillor's book *Pilgrims: A Lake Woebegon Romance*. It has this terrific passage:

> *I am not John the Evangelist*
>
> *Nor steeped in wisdom, not yet,*
>
> *But I know this to be true:*
>
> *Either we love or we die a living death.*

Truth, so well put.

When Bruce came in at 4:00, he reported catching four bows, one which was "really, really big," wider and deeper than any other so far.

For early supper we had—big surprise—plastic macaroni pasta and tomatoes in three forms: as a soup, in leftover motel pizza, and as juice in a beer. Just needed catsup to make it all complete.

Back out on the lake, Bruce went to place in the main channel, and I trolled a quarter mile south to a bulrush island. As I got near the reeds, I began to hear "ping-ping-ping" on my fish locator. So I dropped anchor and fished below with my bonging rod. About then another awareness: the bladder was speaking. What to do? Head toward shore? I decided on shore, but right then my indicator went down and I was fast to a good fish. Back and forth he went, finally to come close, then power away. Eventually the fish tired and entered the net. A great ending for the day, I thought.

Releasing the fish to the depths, little did I know I would soon be entering a watery world myself. For, in trying to row back, I couldn't hold it any longer, couldn't get my waders down fast enough, and, well, got wet in the waders. Yuck. Embarrassing.

That night Bruce was not the least interested in my unpleasant ordeal, however fully I described it to him. His only focus was on the fact that my Fishing Buddy had found fish. "I'm going to call home tomorrow," he announced, "and have my missing attachment sent up." As he turned out his night lamp, I was giving myself a sponge bath.

Buddas Day

Our fishery for today was Tokaryk Lake, a mile east of Patterson. Ron in his truck led the way and soon had his Minnkota-powered pontoon boat zipping across the lake to a reed island. Rowing there with the wind at our side, Bruce and I followed. For two hours we worked the edges of this island. Ron took one; Bruce two, the larger of which may have been a steelhead, so silver-bodied was it. As for me, I can only say that "sumpin'" took my bait, came back at me faster than I could strip line, and became untight.

After that, fishing was slow, slow. So, the decision to go back to the dock. Now the wind was blowing gale-like straight against us. It made for the longest and hardest row of my life. Pulling past me, chomping on his cigar, Bruce grunted, "Deal with it!" Next, Ron plowed by effortlessly, electrically taunting, "Next year, a Minnkota."

Eventually I made it.

We put our boats in and on the Tahoe and returned to Patterson to unload them. Then it was to Shoal Lake for that town's RV campground with bathhouse, the showers here working in three-second bursts of hot water. Still, quite wonderful. Then, as I filled the five-gallon jugs at the water faucet, Bruce got on his now-functioning cell phone—functioning because we were back in civilization—to call his sister in Fort Collins.

"Janice," he implored, "please go to my house, find the electric adapter for my fish locator—it's on the kitchen counter—and send it to me in Rossburn, Manitoba, general delivery. I need it bad, even if it costs $50."

Good person that she is, Janice agreed. (Later we learned that it cost $37 for a metal piece not much bigger than a restaurant saltshaker.) She sent it by Special Handling–Overnight Arrival–Air Orient Express–Guaranteed on Time Delivery.)

Phone call made and water jugs put on board, we went west to Rossburn, there to do laundry and have the smorgasbord dinner at the N&L Café, specialty "Chinese and Canadian Food." The buffet had a wide selection of deep-fried cuisine, high cholesterol but happily not plasticized, cost $8.85, drink included.

Before returning to camp, we stopped at the Olha Corner Store to purchase ice for the cooler. I asked the proprietor, Marion Koltusky, about the church building across the road. She said, "I have the key to it. Would you like to go in?"

We voiced "You bet!" together.

The beautiful white frame edifice is a Ukrainian Catholic or "Uniate" Church put up in 1904. That's when hundreds of immigrants from Ukraine still lived in the area. Marion said the church functions yet with about forty families, mass held four times a year. The icons in the church were spectacular, the archangel Michael being the parish's patron saint. The four evangelists were displayed in gold on the iconostasis with St. Luke mistakenly given a ram instead of an ox as his symbol. For the last thirty-nine years, Marion and husband Steve had lit the wood-burning stove in the middle of the sanctuary—the stove made from two 50-gallon oil drums.

Church's Oil Drum Heater

The faithful, you can bet, gather close around it on cold Sundays. We were exceedingly pleased to have had such a stunning introduction to the cultural and religious heritage of this area, the time also being an escape from the wind. Marion lent me a couple of books about the early settlers. She also directed us to an historic site a few miles farther east with restored *buddas*, Ukrainian pioneer huts. The buddas were 16'x16' shelters dug four feet into the earth, then covered with an A-frame roof thatched with native grasses. Livestock dwelt in there with the family through the harsh winters. Talk about primitive. Talk about incomprehensibly difficult. Only the hearty survived.

Restored Ukrainian Budda

I had fascinating and heart-rending reading that evening about the Ukrainians.

Our plan for tomorrow: go to Pybus Lake.

Two 2-Foot Trout Day

Pybus Lake, twenty-five miles south and east of Patterson, is also winter-aerated. By reputation the fish here are bigger than those in other lakes, but also harder to catch. On two previous trips, Ron netted none. This morning Bruce anchored north of the boat ramp. I rowed to the west bay. With his electric motor, Ron went all over.

Bruce struck first, capturing a thick 21-inch female whose girth was "ample," he said. Around noon he hooked into another—and what another! On its first run it went from near shore, where Bruce was anchored, to the middle of the lake, stopping with only a few feet of backing left on his reel. Then the fish turned for a series of in-and-out charges. When netted, measured, and weighed on Ron's scale, it was the largest rainbow Bruce has taken in North America,

BAK with 26.5-inch Pybus Bow

a 26.5-incher weighing 8 pounds! From my west-bay anchorage I heard the boys' excited voices and later marveled at the fish via the photos taken.

Though tempted to join them, I stayed west, hoping my Fat Albert dry and Waterboatman dropper would produce. I hoped for several hours. Then Fat Albert disappeared. And I had "Fish On!" Once, twice, three, four, and five times the fish ran out a long way, to be slowly retrieved to my large arbor reel. Though tired, he still resisted capture in my sixteen-inch net. Finally she—as it turned out—succumbed. What a sow, thick everywhere, even to the tail. At 24-inches she was the heaviest bow I have ever taken. Just sorry I couldn't get a picture.

After that there was no further action, though all of us kept trying.

Driving back to Patterson that evening, we were treated to a beautiful sunset of fluorescent oranges fully swept on the horizon north to south. Exquisite. Stunning.

Bad Start, Happy Ending Day

Let me say a word more about food fare on this trip: it has been only fair. Now it is simply monotonous, especially breakfasts. I've been singing Huddie Ledbetter's "Midnight Special":

You wake up in the morning

Hear the ding-dong ring

Go marching to the table

It's the same damn thing

And on each table

Knife and fork and pan

Say anything about it

You're in trouble with the man

Breakfast is getting close to being like Leadbelly's prison food. This morning, for example, Bruce put a huge spoonful of leftover luncheon tuna fish on my Grape-Nuts. Said, "It's topping."

I was slow getting it down. And slower getting down to fish. Arriving at the dock, I found my compatriots long gone. I would be still farther behind, for in starting out, I knocked my Fishing Buddy off the dock into the water and got my sleeve wet to the armpit retrieving it. Eventually I rowed out into the channel to put a trolling rod into service, but the reel fell off and sank into deep water. I retrieved it only by pulling up the line ever so slowly, ever so gingerly. Meanwhile the wind blew me into thick bulrushes. Here the oars would not function. All this before I'd cast even once.

Not a good start on this day.

Late then I made it to the southeast corner of the lake, where Bruce had recently ensconced himself in sixteen feet of water. Where Ron was, I had no idea. I anchored down a dozen yards from Kuster and straightway we both began taking fish, one brown colored by big gold and red spots. Through the morning we took eleven fish of 20–24 inches, mostly bows, doubling twice. Things were looking up.

Decidedly. So now, as I waited my bobber tranquilly slipped below the surface—always the sweetest moment in a lake fisherman's experience. Then came my lift and a solid stopping of it. "Got one," I spoke out.

"No doubt another 20-inch *dink*," Bruce commented.

"No doubt."

When the fish did not jump but submarined, I announced, "Think it's a brown."

Then wham! From down deep the fish took off. "This one's going to sea! It's a better fish!"

Better fish, for sure, able to run out fast and long. Though the drag was working, my reel was whirring. The fish then hesitated, so I quickly started to reel in. He again resumed speed, the reel knob banging my thumb and knuckles. Which hurt.

I ejaculated, "Jesus, Mary, and Joseph, what a fish!'

Bruce called out, "Stay with him, mister. You can do it."

I stayed and finally netted the fish, a fat hen, so thick the fingers of Michael Jordan couldn't encompass her. She was not the longest rainbow I had ever caught but was undoubtedly the thickest, the heaviest.

At 2:00 p.m. I went in, swept out the trailer, took a sponge bath, did a long nap, and began tending to the evening meal: chili from a can, unplasticized.

Meals readied, I went to the dock to greet incoming Bruce. There I fell into conversation with other fishermen. I told them about Bruce's fish locator problem and that the missing piece was being sent up.

Dave LaFrance from North Dakota informed me that the US postal guarantee is good only to the border, no farther. "With Canadian customs," he added, "that could take a few days—or a few weeks, depending."

"Depending on what?" Bruce, having arrived and beached his boat, wanted to know.

"Depending," Bob Morenski, another North Dakotan, said, "on how busy customs is, how the package comes to them, what its contents might be, and so on."

"If that package seemed to be of *uncertain usage*," I inquired, "could it be delayed?"

"Certainly," the fellows agreed.

"It'll come," Bruce asserted and then made his way up to the trailer for scotch, chili, and a good night's rest.

Unrelenting Winds Day

When Ron scratched on our trailer door the next morning, he announced, "Winds 20 to 40 kilometers today." I don't know how many miles per hour that is, but the lake was already in whitecaps, and the east shoreline was piled with frothy white foam, as if snowplowed into place. Some of the foam was blowing up the boat ramp road.

To row to the south end, where we had such luck yesterday, seemed an exercise in exhaustion. We could, though, make it across our camp channel to the island of high trees and thick bushes, to park our boats in quieter water. We fished without takes. I got a good photo of the island, clouds in the background.

At 1:30 I quit fishing and returned to the trailer to discover that its shade awning had blown off and my Teddy Roosevelt tent was flattened. There'd be no fixing of either till the wind abated.

The evening supper was again plastic pasta with two kinds of tomato sauce added plus some now unfrozen green and orange vegetables—a ghastly combination. Even so, it ate.

After dinner and dishes, I read aloud from the Rossburn-area history books Marion Koltusky lent me. It had accounts of the Ukrainians who immigrated here at the turn of the last century. One story was of a pioneer father who left in the spring to work on an Englishman's farm farther south. He returned in the fall with clothes and shoes for his wife and children, only to learn they had burned to death in their *budda* home. Another story was of a little girl who came to a neighbor's house asking help for her mother, then in pangs of childbirth. The neighbor came but knew not what to do. The birthing woman "cried out in unbearable pain for three days" until "she turned black as dirt" and died.

Hard, hard times, those years were.

Just south of Patterson Lake, I learned, is a mass grave site established in memory of forty Ukrainian children and women who died of scarlet fever and measles in a temporary encampment there. The year was 1899.

Ukrainian Mass Graves Marker

In comparison with those times, our discomfiting winds and tasteless suppers were Easy Street.

Wondering-about-Being-Arrested Day

The wind was gone when the alarm clock sounded at 5:15 a.m. "Let's get moving for the early bite," Bruce instructed. "We're going to the honey hole."

"And that is?" I asked from under the covers.

"Back to the southeast corner, outside the bulrush island."

"Okay." My mumble.

In lieu of Canadian bacon, which Canadians have never heard of, I made us eggs Benedict using what they call "bacon back." Same-same. Last bite consumed, Bruce was out the door in the dark.

When there was light enough, around 7:15, I followed. The lake was calm. Totally. You could see rises hundreds of yards away. Trolling, I snagged a 20-inch bow just outside where Bruce had anchored. For his dark-to-dawn vigil he reported "no action."

Ere long the sun came up, and wonderfully the water continued calm. Fishing, though, was slow. When Ron motored by around 10:30, he reported a better morning, three fish while throwing a bead head Black Wooly Booger.

"Congrats," Bruce said.

As the morning stretched out, our bongs not dipping, Bruce and I chatted. He said he wanted to go into Rossburn to check on whether his left-behind electric adapter had arrived.

Having meditated on things, I opined, "It has not yet passed customs, for it is a *suspicious* device."

He turned in his boat. "What are you talking about?"

"I'm just suggesting that the piece is, as we speak, likely precipitating great concern."

"Come again?"

I decided to share my evolving conjectured fears: "Bruce, there may be serious complications with this package, creating consternation at the border, the package perceived as a threat to Canadian security. We could have an international investigation in the making."

He didn't say a word.

I continued. "Consider it this way: that nondescript piece of hardware will never have been seen before by customs. Its intended use, for fishing, will not be self-evident to them. It's a metal apparatus with wires attached, after all, but perhaps awaiting connection to something else, which it is, of course, but *what*? Do you hear what I'm saying?"

He shook his head—not up and down.

"Look, your adapter is an electric device of 'some sort.'" I went on. "Perhaps for purpose nefarious, for all they can surmise. The border inspectors are likely to wonder, 'Is this something intended for—*perish the thought*—an IED?' Why, quite possibly. Just consider, it is being sent to Rossburn, Manitoba, for God's sake, which is a major agricultural area, an area with stockpiles of ammonium nitrate fertilizer. Are you getting my drift?"

I think he was. He started to pull up anchor.

"Wait," I insisted. "Let me finish. It is precisely by such devices that roadside bombs are detonated. Who knows, the Trans-Canada Highway could be the target. Maybe this is a part for a harness worn beneath the robes to enable a suicide bomber to get his seven virgins in heaven."

With that, I got his interest again, and he stopped raising his anchor rope.

"So the authorities will not know what this contrivance is. Once customs is alarmed, they will alert homeland security in both the United States and Canada. Soon—like, right now—an international search will be underway. A person of interest, of international interest, is on the loose somewhere in Canada!"

"Oh, stop it!" my friend exclaimed (faking bravado, I am convinced).

"No. Now listen. This is bigger than you think. Homeland security types in both countries will be more than just interested. They will be ecstatic, for at long last they will have found a genuine terrorist in their midst. Such a finding will be a windfall, guaranteeing the agencies significant budget increases, even during these hard economic times. The opportunity bells sound, and the Royal Canadian Mounted Police are being called in."

Now his anchor was up, and he was reaching for the oars.

"Be assured," I continued, "the Mounties—who always get their man—are coming for you, and it won't be a pretty scene here at Lake Patterson when, over the horizon, you hear, 'On, King, On you huskies!' and then all the descendants of Sergeant Preston and dog Rex, King of the Yukon, come mushing in, going around our pop-up camper in ever-tightening circles. Then you will know *The End Is Near*! After that, who knows? Certainly your arrest . . . then a trial . . . likely conviction . . . with a sentence of no less than nineteen years."

I'd lost him. He was well away.

"Don't worry," I called out. "I'll come visit you whenever I'm in Canada, and, further, I also believe that when you're let out of solitary confinement in a year or two, you'll be granted reading privileges. I promise I will send you my wife's old Tupperware catalogues as suitable literature. What's more, in your cell block there'll be Canadian hockey to watch, day and night, night and day, nonstop, with period breaks giving you updates on Italian curling competition."

My words of warning and consolation, however, did not reach the prison-bound. He was out of hearing range, where, unfortunately, he knew neither the water depth nor whether any fish were swimming beneath his boat.

Seeing him bobbing on the silver water beneath a cerulean blue sky, wearing his dark green jacket and brown waders, I wondered if Canadian prisoners wear fluorescent orange, as in the US. I hope not. Fluorescent orange is not on his color wheel. Too bad. If, on the other hand, Canada extradites him to the US, he'll be sent to Guantanamo and from there renditioned to Morocco or Bulgaria. In those locales, maybe they'll have a color-coordinated alternative attire for their waterboardee. Stripes in beige would work.

Oh, well.

We went to Rossburn that afternoon, Bruce directly to the little post office on Main Street. He inquired about his package. Pat, the postmistress, a charming redhead, treated him in a friendly way and said he might expect it in three days or so, "likely to arrive Monday." She'd keep her eye out for it.

Upon return to Patterson, I stayed in to journal the account above, while the boys went out. When I joined them, Bruce announced he'd caught two fish on a chironomid.

"On a chironomid? Chironomid? This time of year?"

He presented me a sample tie. I tried it for a while without success. He, though, caught two more on it late in the afternoon. The first was a 747, that is, humpbacked, brown. The second was better, making for quite a story. It seems a fish rose "out of the depths" with Bruce's orange bobber on his nose! It wasn't actually so, but seemed like it for a second, making it an unforgettable second. The fish was a large hen, and he landed Ms. Bobber-Eater.

Once we were all back at the dock this evening, Ron said, "Tomorrow let's fish Tokaryk again."

Jury-Rigging Day

It was much cooler this morning. The trailer's heater had run continuously. Thus we forwent cold Grape-Nuts in favor of warm instant oatmeal done in the microwave.

A report last evening of 9-pounders being taken at Tokaryk Lake stirred the camp to renewed enthusiasm for that fishery. Being "of the camp," Bruce and Ron made the trek over early. I, not so much "of the camp"—or the cold—spent the morning working on a story. After lunch, I drove over to Rossburn, and en route stopped to check out the windrows in the fields on one side of the road. The windrows were of canola, aka "rape" by the locals. Some weeks previously the fields were mowed, leaving the then green plants to dry in rows. The cut stalks, perhaps three feet tall, held long, thin pods, each pod encasing dozens of tinier-than-a-mustard-seed seeds.

Canola (Rape) Stock with Seeds

When the windrowed stalks and pods dried up completely—like about now—huge harvesting machines worked their way down each row, lifting up the piles and taking the dry crop into the internal works of the harvester to separate the seeds from the chaff. The seeds are later crushed to make canola oil. Pretty fascinating, I thought.

In Rossburn I got *petrol* for the Tahoe and use of the library's Internet, where 268 email messages were waiting. Finishing them, I next, "in fear and trembling"—so I reported to Bruce—approached Rossburn's little post office on Main Street. Upon entering I saw no uniformed or armed personnel. I spoke to the postmistress, "My name is Jim White, ma'am, and I have a friend, Bruce Kuster, who's expecting a package from the States. Might it have arrived?"

She looked at me kind of suspiciously, I later told Bruce, saying, "That which went to customs is still under review," like she knew more than she was admitting. She glanced at me and then at the wall with its wanted posters, seeming to conclude, "No match here." Next she said nervously, "Like I said yesterday, the earliest the person in question may expect his package is Monday, two days from now."

As I drove back to the lake, I wondered about that nervousness. Maybe that's the way she is all the time. I thought, "Don't be so paranoid, White. Let it go."

All this I later reported to Bruce, but he seemed oblivious to the warning signs.

I drove over to Tokaryk to find out how fishing had gone for my buds. Ron reported capturing a bow 26.5 inches, 8 pounds. Bruce had netted two 24 inch 6-pounders, the second taken by trolling a minnow pattern. This streamer, he said, was "attacked *with viga.*"

When Ron and Bruce got back to Patterson, they went into conference on something. I did the dinner, unplasticized rib eye steak (done on my portable 1959 charcoal grill), baked potatoes heated in the microwave, applesauce, rye bread spread with red raspberry jam—Bruce's fave—and Black Box Shiraz.

Kuster complimented me on the dinner, saying, "I knew you could do it Now let's get back on the lake."

"Now?" I asked. "Why now?"

"Because Ron has jury-rigged me a fish finder. Put it together from equipment he had on a previous boat. I'd like to see how it works."

So we went.

The jury-rigged fish finder operated well enough. He could read the bottom, and fish showed up on the screen.

"Good for you," I said. "Now you can let go all anxiety, forget the contraband adapter, escape the Mounties, and depart Canada unapprehended"

"No," he insisted. "I want my own fish finder. We'll keep checking at the PO. Meanwhile, this locator will lead me to fish."

But it did not, not this night. The bite was off.

With the sun setting, coolness headed for downright cold, the existential question became, "Shall we go in and miss the late evening bite, or stay out and miss the late evening bite?" Tough call, for sure. I went in to miss it. He stayed on for the missing.

Temperature overnight went well below freezing. To generate additional BTUs, we placed our cooking hot plate under the dinner table.

Miracle on Perfect-10 Birthday

I awoke to an almost-on-key version of "Happy Birthday to You" by the Bruster. So October 2 began, I thankful to be alive, wondering specifically what the day might bring. Providence had a doozy in store. Before the morning was over, I had taken eight (8!) beautiful brown trout on a chironomid, but the most interesting thing was that, in fighting fish number nine I knocked my second rod, unsecured in the holder, into the lake. Helpless I watched it sink down.

"Oh, shit!" I cursed—apparently loud enough for all the lake to hear, as that's what Brent Jakobson (fellow fisherman from Winnipeg) later told me—"I've lost my new Orvis six-weight rod!" And I now I have a big fish on.

"Forget the fish," Kuster yelled across. "What about your rod? Look for the bobber and pull it up, mister."

"Can't. It was my trolling rod, not bobbered."

"Then don't move. I'll go back to camp and rig up some kind of dredge." And off he went.

Meanwhile, Jakobson came in to assess the situation. Looking through his kayak bags, he said, "Let me see what I can do." What he did was put on a full-sink line and, in lieu of treble hooks, strung together three large pike flies, adding open-jaw pliers for weight. An awesome gang hook. With this rig he began to cast in the area where I believed the rod sunk. But was it really the exact spot? I wasn't sure. After a dozen pull-throughs, I knew it was hopeless.

Then Brent shouted, "Got it!" Up came the green rod tip followed by the rest.

As Brent handed the rod over, I was thinking, "It's a miracle, a special birthday gift." I sang out Handel's "Hal-le-lu-jah! Hal-le-lu-jah!"

Calmed down, I shared with the miracle-worker Brent that his save was amazingly reminiscent of one more than six decades ago. In 1947 for my tenth birthday I'd been given a white fiberglass Shakespeare casting rod and an Abu Ambassador level-wind reel. For first use, Dad took some neighborhood chums and me crappie fishing on Lake Carl Blackwell, near Stillwater, Oklahoma. As we were jigging among old, dead, still-standing trees, Ford Price, using my new rod, dropped it in the lake. Dad then said, "All right, boys, get naked and dive for it."

Ford and I complied and began diving into ten feet of murky, cold water. Several submergings found nothing, but in the last push-off from the muddy bottom my toes happened on, then clutched the rod. I brought it back. "That tenth birthday in 1947 and this one of 2010," I said to Brent, "shall be equally well remembered."

Bruce on shore, having heard my victory whoops, returned, smiling through his cigar. We bonged a bit more but had no new action.

Lunch was in Rossburn at La Choy's Café, where a phone call home got the answering machine. I left a message for Patti about my nine-fish morning and the miraculous "lost and found" fly rod.

Before leaving town, Bruce went into the grocery store for a chocolate cake and a large O or zero candle . . . "for the year of the decade," he interpreted, "not to be confused with any person living or dead."

"Thank you for that assurance," I responded.

The wind had changed a bit that late afternoon, so the bite seemed unlikely. My luck, though, held. I took fish number ten. Making it a perfect-10 day.

Birthday cake with coffee, also wine, was shared with fellow campers late in the evening. The caffeinated coffee, the dark chocolate cake, and vivid replays of daylight excitements did not a quick-to-sleep night make. But then post-midnight it was no longer my birthday.

Steelhead Day

On Tokaryk Lake the next day, a-*turning and turning in widening gyre* (Yeats) is what Bruce, Brent, and I did about this large impoundment. While a-turning, we did much a-rowing, a-casting, and a-bonging—all to no avail. At noon we rendezvoused on the bay closest to the dock. Bruce reported that a really good fish snapped him off mid lake.

"Too bad," I said to him.

"It was my own bad," he confessed. "I was using 5x tippet. Should have used heavier. But you might try my technique. I was trolling a Gummy Minnow hooked in the nose."

I decided to give his recommended technique a try, attaching a two-inch Gummy Minnow on a 2x tippet and adding a Backswimmer dropper held by 3x material. After thirty minutes of nothingness trolling, I called out, "Let's take it to the barn!"

Then wham! A huge—I mean huge—pull and immediately I saw a dolphin on the surface rocketing off. The fish spun out yards and yards of line, then jumped high in the air. He was truly a monster! As he turned and sped hard to the right, I got a little line in before he cleared the water a second time. A magnificent fish. A steelhead.

Next he went running hard, away, west, and into the wind. I was saying, "Turn back, O fish, turn back." But he did not. Instead, he went farther out—a lot farther out—and then sank into some weeds, leaving me beset with the problem of rowing against that wind to reach him while keeping a tight line. I just couldn't do both and, soon, there was no tight line. Reeling in, I found that the Minnow on the 2x was still there, but the Backswimmer on the 3x missing.

Undoubtedly this was the biggest fish I could have taken on our trip—likely 27-plus inches, maybe 9 pounds. Sorry it did not work out, but certainly the thirty-second attachment is the most action-packed half-minute I'd have in Canada.

Brent joined us at table this evening, our guest providing bean soup spiced by Ukrainian sausage chunks. Great fare—and without a trace of plastic. Afterward Brent told us about his maternal ancestors, who came to Winnipeg from Ukraine at the turn of the twentieth century. His great-grandfather arrived first with all his wife's inheritance money. The wife followed some months later in steerage passage, where she almost died, saved only by Brent's grandmother, then age three, stealing oranges and biscuits for them. Brent's father's side of the family was from Iceland, hence the "k" spelling in his name, Jakobson.

Nice evening. Tomorrow: Twin Lakes.

Tiger Burning Bright Day

Ron's truck with his Watermaster on top led the way to Twin Lakes, followed by Brent's Toyota carrying his kayak. Bruce's Tahoe was third in line with one inflated pontoon boat inside the vehicle and one on top. The caravan was off well before 7:00 a.m.

Driving through Rossburn in the dark, Bruce whispered, "Oh, adapter, be there."

"It might be," I empathized. "After all this is Monday. But right now everything's closed. So wait for it."

He sighed, "I know."

As dawn came on we drove past the Waywayseecappo First Nation village, then moved west on to Russell and Roblin, and north for Twin Lakes in the Duck Mountain Provincial Forest. The drive took two hours, but it was worth it to abandon flat farmland and see hills—actual hills—and then a pristine body of water surrounded by evergreens and birch tree. The lake is famous for having big tiger trout, a sterile cross between a male brown trout and a female brook.

As we launched, the lake was dead still, covered with a pollen film. Each guy sought to find a fly pattern to which the fish would respond. Ron started with poppers, Brent with streamers, I with a hopper-dropper, and Bruce with a chironomid. Just outside the passageway into the small twin lake, I took the first fish, a 10-incher looking to be 95 percent brookie. I netted two more.

When takes in the passageway slowed, I rowed into the smaller twin lake. Two anglers were moving about in float tubes. They were hooking up with some regularity.

I asked, "What's working?"

A full-bearded fellow answered, "Anything that floats—Chernobyl Ants, dry Muddlers, adult Damsels—you name it."

I tried to replicate their lake-to-shoreline casting, but in the wind couldn't. Just as I was ready to leave this lake, Bruce arrived to tell me of success with the three-inch Balanced Minnow, of which he was now out. He needed one. One of mine. I provided such and we both rebaited. Shortly he and I each caught a tiger. The one I netted was absolutely gorgeous, marbled dark paisley in green and gold, with bright red belly and the brookie's white-edged fin trademark.

We left the small twin for the larger. Kuster moved to the east side and joined Granneman. I rowed across the lake to the far west shore. Eventually Kuster came over. He told me he'd succeeded in taking a rising fish on a bass popper. While we were anchored there, Brent paddled by in his kayak, to report only modest success all day trolling. He told us he was heading home, back to Winnipeg. We bid him traveling mercies. As he paddled ramp-wise, he passed Granneman midlake, coming our way in his electric-powered boat. Granneman suggested we try a different technique: trolling bass poppers. "Troll them fast," he advised, "so as to create a wake." Both he and Bruce made this work. I started with the technique but could not go fast enough. So gave it up.

I backed off to the near shoreline, there to throw my popper into thinner bulrushes. Immediately prospects were encouraging. A couple of swirls happened right under my top-water retrievals. Then, when I inadvertently left the bug just floating on the surface, there was a loud swoosh. A 14-inch tiger took it and after a brief tussle was netted. This could be fun, I thought. I'm going to try the let-it-rest-retrieve some more. *Voila*, another attack, but a miss. Still, this was the way: cast in, do three or four quick pop-pop-pops, then wait, just let it sit . . . to be attacked.

In the course of the next forty-five minutes, I took eight healthy tigers, 18 to 21 inches long. Wow. What fun!

In running commentary, I described my newfound technique to my buds. But the more I described, the farther they seemed to move away. So I gave the blow-by-blow descriptions with full voice and enthusiasm.

(Bruce later told me that Ron asked, "Does he always talk to himself like that?" And Bruce let Ron know, "Oh, no. Just when he's on the lake. Also, when riding in the car working on his computer or when reading a book after dinner. Otherwise, hardly ever. His wife says she's sometimes awakened at night when he reads a sermon aloud. But, 'talk to himself'? No, not *always*.")

Such a friend.

It was now getting dark, darker to me because I forgot I was wearing sunglasses. Not to keep others waiting, I started rowing hard back toward the dock, trailing my popper. No more than thirty yards from the west shoreline came a wham-bam take followed by serious reel spinning outward. Then I went to spinning it in back-to-me direction. Then more out. Then in. Finally I netted a tiger of 23 inches, best of the day for me. The tiger was a grand finale and, as it turned out, the last of our fish-take in Manitoba.

Loading the boats back on the vehicle that evening, I said, "As pleased as I am with the day's fishing—and on my beautiful tiger especially—I'm actually ready to go home."

Kuster responded with something like, "Oh, I guess I could too, but I can't help but wonder how much better things would have been if I'd had my own fish locator."

"You could call up the Royal Mounties and ask them if they have statistics on success ratios with finders and without finders. If you did that, though," I had to add, "then they'd have a fix on your location. And who knows? Better jist fergit about it."

"White, you are such a comfort."

"Why, thank you. I certainly mean to be."

It was well past dark when we got back to Patterson.

TR's Day

At 5:00 a.m. I was awake, mentally figuring out how to break camp and pack for home. So was Bruce. By 11:30 we were on our way, having said goodbye to our compatriots still in camp. We stopped at Marion's Corner Store to return her books on the history of the area and then, throwing caution to the wind, went into Rossburn to check on whether Bruce's expensive Special Handling–Overnight Arrival–Air Orient Express–Guaranteed on Time Delivery—albeit highly suspicious—package had passed customs and was waiting.

Walking by a dog sleeping near the steps (King?), Bruce approached the little post office. I came a few steps behind, telling him I would be a witness if he was arrested by the Mounties and would thus be able to testify in court if he had been read his rights properly or been handled too roughly, even as a terrorist. "Then too," I explained, "I can tell your bereft grandchildren how you were at the last."

His only reply was, "Why don't you look for lost coins near the parking meters?"

"They don't have parking meters in Rossburn."

"Okay. You can come in. Just don't say anything. The postmistress is a very nice person."

Well, as it turned out, the Canadian terrorist capture squad was not there, and Pat the postmistress appeared calm. With a smile, she gave him his long-delayed package. I noticed, though, that she stayed behind the counter and kept one hand beneath it, probably near an alarm buzzer or on a .44 Magnum. My real suspicion, however, was that she was shining him on, leading him down the primrose path, lulling him into a false sense of well-being.

But I said nothing.

As he exited the post office, I held back inside the building momentarily, not wanting to get caught in the crossfire, if any. The streets of Rossburn, though, seemed to be clear. So I came out and got in the vehicle trying to figure out what might be happening. Then it hit me: they're waiting to grab him at the border! I told him my suspicions and added, "Not to worry. It's several hours before we get there. What I don't know is if it will be the CIA, the FBI, or both waiting."

Bruce seemed unperturbed by my prognosis. He said, "Haven't you got something better to do? This is getting boring. Just go compute some more."

Which is exactly what I did, so there might be an accurate record of the upcoming international confrontation.

When we arrived at the border check station, there were only two inspector guards on duty. They were friendly enough, asking about fishing and letting us come into the United States with contraband of two oranges and four apples. They did not even frisk him. One officer opened the rear of the vehicle and nearly gagged on the smell of wet fishnets and mud-slimed boots. Thus they failed to inspect and detect "the dangerous device." Moreover, let the record show, both these gendarmes said "aboot" and "shed-ual," so I think they were not Americans but Canucks, and Canucks are notoriously callow about iceback—as distinct from wetback—Islamofascists trying to crash our borders. The fine sand on the rear bumper could have tipped them off, raised suspicions that we could have been from the deserts of the Middle East, though it was actually from the dirt roads around Rossburn. But no. They missed telltale forensic evidence.

Thus Bruce escaped the clutches of the law. So far. I did not hear it, but he must have breathed a sigh of relief.

My compadre was now in a more relaxed state. So I asked him to do an appraisal of Canada, as he had done upon first entering.

He waxed eloquently. "As we reenter the US of A in North Dakota and turn toward Teddy Roosevelt country, I think, 'Bully!' I want to return to that foreign land of Manitoba next spring, because I like those big northern trout on a chironomid. And that's all I've got to say about that.'"

"Well, thank you, Forrest Gump. I'll make a note. Now, dear friend, I must share my remaining qualm about our situation. Most likely those sneaky G-men are still gunning for you. They probably want you to be farther into the country so that a full battery of TV cameras and reporters can be present for your apprehension. Their trap is set and right now they have surveillance planes tracking us. Drones equipped with air-to-ground missiles are above us."

Driving, he stayed below the speed limit, I noticed, and he kept looking in the rearview mirror. Without incident, though, we went through Minot and Bismarck and headed west on I-94, seeing only a few highway patrol officers, and they feigned disinterest. At Dickinson we turned south, and as the orange twilight faded into black, Bruce seemingly was at peace.

I, driving this section of the trip, now shared recalculations. "They're waiting for you at Devil's Tower in Wyoming, readying a close encounter for the adapter kind, you."

He responded petulantly, masking his deep-seated fears. "Just keep the car between the fence posts." Then he turned to bury his face in the window pillow.

Coup de Grâce Day

Having spent the night at the Motel 6 of Belle Fourche, for breakfast we rightly went to the Belle Restaurant. We each ordered the 18-wheeler: two eggs, three bacon strips, hash browns, french toast, and coffee, cost $4.77 per.

Following breakfast, we made our way from South Dakota into northeast Wyoming, headed for America's first national-natural monument, Devils Tower, so designated in 1906. The giant rock column, core of an ancient volcano, now stands 867 feet above the valley floor. "This is a place of symbolic significance," I said. "Be ready for anything here."

"I'm ready," he assured me.

Devil's Tower National Monument, Wyoming

Our 1.3-mile walk around the base showed us the monolith's columnar sides, which look as though a bear had in fact clawed the rock, as Indian legend suggests. A highlight of the walkabout was seeing wild turkeys, our *almost* national bird. They crossed our path.

When we returned to the visitor center, Bruce went to get a drink of water. I then approached one of the badge-wearing park rangers and asked a favor. So when Bruce came back, the ranger came up beside him. I then said, "Bruce, this is the hour of reckoning." With that signal, the ranger put his hand on the back of Bruce's neck.

"You are under arrest," I said for the ranger, then got a picture of the nabbing.

The Almost International Terrorist Nabbed

That'll teach him to leave his adapter behind!

So ends the *almost* international terrorism incident.

And so may conclude the first tale of travel into the north country far.

The "More": Later Years in Manitoba Things

Because Manitoba is so alluring, so eye opening, creative of events and stories, I want to add *pieces* from trips made after 2010, when the just-told
story happened. I'll take an incident, paragraph, or topic and bring material
to it from records made earlier or later.

Don't Need a Weatherman (Spring 2011)

"In the spring of the year, the time when kings go forth to battle" (2 Samuel
11:1), Bruce Kuster and I again went to fish in Manitoba. It was a different
world from that experienced the fall before. The area was in flood condition.
The Missouri River in Bismarck, for example, was flowing at 75,000 cubic
feet per second, the highest it had been since 1912. The creeks and lakes
everywhere were full, the land sodden.

In the fall, things had been dry and the nights cold. Freezing weather
would be ours in other years too. This year, however, rain was the main

thing. It socked us in some days, and seeped through openings in Sid's trailer to give us wet blankets and clothes.

Then there was the wind. Yes, the wind, ole *Mariah*. Last year she flattened my Teddy Roosevelt tent. This year she did so again and ripped the awning off Sid's trailer. One afternoon she was fierce enough on the lake that she drove me into shore where I had to "abandon ship" and walk back to camp.

Time and again in the years to come, we repeated the line, "I fought the wind, and the wind won."

I remember only a time or two when it ever was hot up here. But occasionally. On such days there were flies to swat, mosquitoes to battle, and ticks to check for—not always found right away, as the back-home dermatologist's exam and bill revealed.

Manitoba Fauna, Fall 2011 (and 2015)

An account from my journal:

Restless from all-day confinement in the camper (to stay out of the wind), just at dusk I went for a walk down the road south toward the mass grave site, and had the highlight moment of this Manitoba trip. The wind was at my back this fall evening and cool as I walked. No cars or trucks kicked up dust. Then on the hillside of recently cut canola, something white caught my eye. Looking, I saw it began to move. There were several somethings. What? Sheep? Goats? Not cows or horses. Not that big, but somethings, somethings clearly white, moving out there and seemingly moving away from where I was. I decided to investigate, so I crossed the road and fence to go into the field. Perhaps I could get close enough to know what they were before "what-they-are" ran off. Just past the barbed-wire fence, however, the white somethings changed direction. They no longer went east. They went up. They were geese! Snow geese. As the flock of twenty lifted, they were joined a quarter-second later by an equal number of Canadas. So, white and black in the gray eastern sky. The forty were no more than up and squawking when some two hundred more Canadas, just down the slope, also arose in a great noise. Then the whole hillside, for a quarter square mile, exploded! Geese—likely ten thousand—took to the air from the stubble. What a racket. What a long, dark "coattail" they made across that sky! Never in my life have I seen so many wild geese at one time. It was an awesome/ wow moment. Thousands of honks filled the now-night air.

Such was my journaling about wildlife seen on Manitoba trip number three.

As to what "other game" might be around, this year—and other years—there were deer, elk, bear (seen by Bob Morenski), and, hard as it is to always believe him, Kuster swore he saw a mountain lion!

The most wonderful, almost unbelievable, game story, however, happened four years later, in the fall of 2015. It involves two big game hunters we met up here: Bob Chabbo and Ken Daufault, genuine Royal Canadian Mounties on vacation. The two had a cabin in the woods some miles north of Patterson Lake. Bob told of several easy successful hunts he'd had for moose in recent years. So Kuster predicted, "The next hunt, of course, will be hard."

"No doubt," Chabbo replied.

Three days later, Bob and Ken came through to report on their "most strenuous hunt ever" (which Bruce predicted). Ken shot a big three-year-old bull moose in their back yard. Shot it at nine o'clock a.m. out their kitchen window. He and Bob were still in pajamas at the time, recovering from too much Black Box wine the night before, Bob said.

That's one for the books. They promised us moose steaks, and so delivered two days later.

Delicious.

Trashed Trailer to Taj Mahal (Spring 2013)

"It's smoking!" he yelled, slamming on the brakes, pulling to the shoulder of the road.

"What?"

"The trailer!"

I looked back and saw smoke pouring from the top vent on our pop-up trailer. Fire was also flaming out the hole where the propane line connection was.

So begins "The Thedford Tragedy," a write-up I did that details our going up to Manitoba in 2013, effectively destroying my brother-in-law Sid's camper, having to abandon it to a field in Nebraska, near the town of Thedford.

Inspecting the Trailer Damage

Sans trailer we eventually made it to Oakburn, Manitoba, where—grace prevailing—a resident provided us, for a modest fee, a much bigger, more commodious RV trailer and hauled it to Patterson Lake for us to use.

Bruce Manuliak of Oakburn is a "prince of a fella" who made this accommodation for us. Quite an upgrade it was, with electricity, water tanks for washing dishes and taking showers, plus a CD player and TV screen. As soon as our old fishing friends in camp got acquainted with the trailer, they called it the Taj Mahal.

Good name.

The Taj made for dry sleeping, hot meals, spread-out space for fly-tying, and room enough for entertaining. Its comfort enabled me to wake up singing "Oh, What a Beautiful Morning." The day awakened to was beautiful indeed, in deluding "winds zephyr-ish." We launched the boats and quickly anchored just beyond the Patterson dock, thus to work back into the spawners channel. In the hours that followed, BK took twelve fish to 26-inches. His biggest one I ferreted out of the reeds for him, getting wet up to my armpits from pulling cattails, all the while creating new words for an old church hymn, "Be not dismayed whatever you do, Jimmy will take care of you." He was happy with my ferreting result, if not my singing.

I was happy too with ten nice bows averaging about 23.5 inches. Wowsers!

So, yes, there were blue-ribbon fishing days. And days you couldn't buy a touch.

About the fish up here: 80 percent of our catch has been rainbow, the other 20 percent browns. Some years the average length was 23 inches. Other years, closer to 19. Whatever the average, consistently big fish, compared with any Kuster and I have ever caught domestically or in other international water.

The flies that were tried through the years have been many: Balanced Minnows, Backswimmers, Bob-in-a-Tors, Ayr-in-a-Tors, Beaver and Purple Leeches, the "Secret (Gummy Minnow) Fly," Chironomids, the Golden Horde, Sheep Creek or Biggs, and Squiggly.

Early on—before macular degeneration—I was able to tie flies, but later Bruce became the master tyer and constant experimenter.

The Manuliaks (Season 2013 through 2015)

Paragraphs from my journal:

> *Driving back from Rossburn this evening with the Manuliaks (Bruce, Kim, and eleven-year-old Alyssa), I asked, "In Ukrainian what does Manuliak mean?"*
>
> *Quick as can be, Alyssa asserted, "Awesomeness."*

Right translation, for sure.

The Manuliaks, Kim, Alyssa and Bruce

Let me say a word about this special family—and extensions of it. Bruce, large fellow and large-event food caterer and part-time farmer, originally offered us use of his camper trailer, our Taj Mahal. He set it up in the Patterson RV Park, regularly brought water for it—and, for us, rib-eye steaks! Kim, who works for the Canadian Mounties, has opened her house and table (wine on it) time and time again. What a delight has been Alyssa, growing-up through the years, playing hide-and-seek with her friends in the camper park and her threesome singing to us like The Wailin' Jennys.

We've loved and appreciated the Manuliak aunt, Marion Koltusky at the Olha Corner Store, from whom we've gotten ice, rye bread, eggs, Magnum ice cream bars, and many a delicious homemade pie (banana cream, Saskatoon berry, and pecan). She also made us Ukrainian borscht for one of our suppers—and frozen borscht to take home. What graciousness!

Author with Marion Koltusky at Olha Store

Our RV campsite has been kept by Bruce's cousin, ever-pleasant Ruth Kawchuk, whose husband died a year before we came up. He left her with the largest collection of martin houses one could ever imagine. Simply exquisite.

Then there are Bruce Manuliak's brother and mother. At his mother's home Bruce maintains an enormous kitchen in which he prepares catered meals for up to 500 people at huge weddings and community celebrations, e.g., Ukrainian Day.

One evening at Kim and Bruce's we met her folks, Laurence and Sheila Stebelski. Laurence is my age exactly, and still actively farming.

It's an amazing and gracious family, fully living out *awesomeness*.

Eastern Orthodoxy in Manitoba
(Spring 2015 and earlier)

Hospody pomyluj, Hospody pomyluj—"Lord have mercy, Lord have mercy." Must have said this 150 times Sunday at the Ukrainian Orthodox Church.

Seems that Ruth Kawchuk (caretaker of the Patterson RV site) picked me up and took me to her church located east of Olha.

The Manuliak's Ukrainian Orthodox Church

We arrived early to set up the community house for a post-service meal. Then to the onion-steeple church itself.

Father Michael, out from Winnipeg, (for $400) conducted the Divine Liturgy in his native tongue, Ukrainian. Nick Durand from St. Vladimir's Seminary in New York City was his deacon, assisted by the priest's seven-year-old son. There was much icon kissing, incense burning and swinging, kneeling/standing/sitting, and the holding of eight-foot-tall candles—especially by the Manuliak men.

The Orthodox Service in Progress

All the long, in and out, back and forth liturgy was prefatory for Communion—but Communion only for the "confessed," this day the priest's mother, the priest's son, and Deacon Nick. Seems no one else had been properly
confessed, as the priest arrived too late to hear confessions. (When, in other
years, I attended the *Catholic* Orthodox service at Olha and Rossburn, the
priest, by a thin spoon, dropped bread mixed with wine directly in my
mouth.)

A choir of four, led by a deep-throated, defrocked (because of alcohol
abuse) priest, did the chanting. We in the congregation did *Hospody*-ing—
that is, "Lord, have mercy-ing,"—all the while standing. Burning incense
was swung in a thurible. I was helped through the service by Bruce's Aunt
Pat, who turned prayer book pages for me and explained that there are *different tones* for different chants of the Divine Liturgy. I could sort of hear
the differences.

The most holy moment of the morning was when shafts of light cut
through the smoke from the thurible incense burning. It was a "thin" moment in time and place.

"Jesus Rays" Inside the Church

After the Liturgy was a blessing of the graves in the churchyard's cemetery. The priest recited prayers and threw holy water on each grave by an aspergillum—a silver ball on a silver rod. Ruth's husband's grave was so sprinkled. Before his stone grave marker she presented a woven ring of bread with a candle in the middle. Bruce M., his brother, and another man stood solemn and at attention all the while with pole banners.

Ukrainian Cemetery Blessing

After all the graves had been blessed, we repaired to the community building for Ruth and company's soup and sandwich lunch. I sat with the un-understandable priest Michael and the deacon-in-training Nick. We talked about Orthodoxy that I might distinguish Ukrainian *Greek* Orthodoxy (Ruth's and the Manuliak's) from Ukrainian *Catholic* or *Uniate* Orthodoxy (Marion and Steve Koltusky's at Olha). The small differences date back several centuries when Orthodoxy in Ukraine was heavily influenced by Polish Roman Catholicism—or something like that.

After the meal cleanup, Ruth brought me home. I felt mercifully blessed—*Hospodyed?*

Manitoba Farewell (2015)

At the end of Kuster's and my seventh trek to Manitoba in 2015, we agreed this was the best trip up here ever! But the last, because of my failing eyes, the grueling thousand miles each way Bruce has to drive alone, and the cost, generally $1,000 each. Still, we've had great fishing, unique experiences, new friendships, and all creating beautiful memories.

Segue to Venezuela

AN IMPORTANT THING FOR me happened in April 2010, right after we got back from Australia-New Zealand (on which the Tasmania adventure took place) and before the Manitoba trip just described. That important thing was issue of my long-worked-on fishing book, *Round Boys Great Adventures: Fish-a-logues through Rocky Mountain Trout Waters.*

RBGA Book Arrives for Author

Much of the next several months—and into the future—was spent promoting the book. I did recitations and book signings at the library, bookstores,
and fly shops. Folks in my church were interested in the book, even had
an "Evening with the Emeritus," having me read selections "Chauncey vs.
the Antelope" and "Batter Up on the Missouri." At that occasion the host
provided attendees with cuisine touted in the book: saltine crackers and sardines floated in mustard sauce! Newspaper stories appeared with headlines,
"Retired Pastor Hooks Fishing Tales" and "Reverend Releases Book."

I sent notices to family and friends of the book's existence. Then I
mailed out copies to those requesting one.

In the summer, when I went to Tennessee to be guest preacher at a
family gathering—and fish for bass—people took a copy or two. As did old
high school classmates at a reunion in Oklahoma City. In January 2011 at
the Denver Fly-Fishing Show, I sat at the "authors table" with distinguished
angling writers Ed Engel and John Gierach. Several copies, happy to say, of
Round Boys went out.

Later that winter, at a church's men's fellowship evening, I did a presentation on "Fishing and Faith" with Anthony Surage.

Ah, Anthony! I must introduce him more fully. He is an incredibly
accomplished fisherman, thoughtful Christian, nature mystic, and friend—
also author, in 2018 of *Bringing Back Eden: Meditations of a Fly-Fisher.* For
years Anthony had been saying, "There is too much shallowness in this
world. We ought to engage fly-fishers in serious consideration of this sport
and life."

So I set up a "Spirituality and Fly-Fishing Retreat" with *strong* women
in my church, basically women who'd read *Round Boys* and told me they
wanted to try fly-fishing. The called-together "interesteds" were then taken
on a 24-hour retreat.

Author with Strong Women on Spirituality Retreat

On the retreat we'd meet at the John Wesley Ranch near Divide and begin with casting lessons, followed by ranch-pond fishing. After supper we conversed on an "Anthony Topic" (e.g., "Going Deeper," "Where Is God?"), and I usually introduced the retreatants to centering prayer—"it's not unlike concentrating on a floating dry fly," I told them. The next day we stream fished the South Platte River in Eleven Mile canyon, concluding the twenty-four hours together with shared reflections and Holy Communion.

These overnight retreats, begun in 2010, continued for several years, eventually to be done also with men.

Thumbs up on Men's Fishing and Spirituality Retreat

A time or two, Anthony and I did co-led getaways. On some occasions folk shared poetry or reports on books that shaped their life.

Much of what I learned from the doing of them has gone into this book.

Now to March 2011, when there was an interruption in the book promotion and retreat leading effort. Albeit, it was a grand interruption, with a new continent to be touched and a new fly-fishing tried, in Venezuela.

On the trip I took lots of photographs and, afterward got copies of pictures from other fishers. It would be fun I think, to do a no-text, photos-only account of the trip, but I'll use words this time, and be content with a limited number of pictures.

Let it begin.

CHAPTER 12

The Salts Of Venezuela

March 5–12, 2011

VENEZUELA.

I was going there to "fish the salts," my trip occasioned because I took the almost-canceled reservation of my friend Jon Thomas who had suffered a "no fly" cornea detachment. In Atlanta on the way to Venezuela, I met up with Jon's brother-in-law, Donn Erickson, my roommate and boat partner for the next seven days.

Our first night was spent at the Tamanaco Intercontinental Hotel in midtown Caracas. There we met six others from the States going on this trip. The excursion was arranged by Larry Schoenborn's company, "Fishing with Larry," our coordinator being Californian Phil Lighty, who'd fished here previously.

In Sunday morning's darkness, our gang made a black-market currency exchange. It was done via Antonio, travel guide for the day. Host for the whole trip was native Venezuelan Eduardo Pantoja. He supervised getting our luggage, fishing gear, and us onto a bus with blacked-out windows.

Getting on board I asked, "Why the blackout?"

"For protection," Antonio replied.

A voice behind me whispered, "So *banditos* will not know it's *Americanos* on board. We are capital candidates for ransom." The voice was that of Kent Saltonstall from Seattle.

"Oh," I exhaled.

By dawn's early light the bus passed through the streets of this million-person city. The hillsides revealed that the poor resided in quite fragile housing. For some reason, police cars were everywhere. Out in preparation for Carnival/Mardi Gras, someone suggested. Maybe so.

After a two-hour drive, the bus arrived at *Parque Nacional Laguna de Tacarigua*, just past the town of Rio Chico. The park, essentially a mangrove estuary on the Caribbean, is the size of Rhode Island. Its brackish water creates a nursery for baby tarpon, our primary fishing target this leg of the journey. Having delivered us safely to the lagoon's main docks, Antonio left, saying, "*Hasta tres dias, amigos.*"

Largish motorboats then transported us across the lagoon to its seaside, passing through mangrove canals and beside islands, eventually to plunge us into a narrow channel. The channel led to a dock in the middle of a marsh. Via a quarter-mile-long wooden pier the dock connected to terra firma, a spit beach with the Caribbean Gulf on the other side.

Walkway to the Tortuga Compound, Phil and Kent at Abandoned Lodge

Gear was transported over the pier planks in wheelbarrows pushed by eager-to-help-and-be-tipped teenagers. Younger boys then carried the baggage to our assigned bungalows of this the Tortuga Lodge. The two-person stuccos had okay amenities: air conditioning, indoor plumbing, and big hammocks on each porch, quite wonderful. The Tortuga Lodge's main building was not the abandoned two-story structure encountered when entering the grounds but a large bamboo and wood open-air "watering hole" called the Bar Corocora, so named for the scarlet ibis of the lagoon. The menu at the thatched-roof Corocora included *cervezas* at all hours with specialty of fresh-caught *pescados*—mackerel (a.k.a. kingfish) and snapper.

At lunch we got better acquainted. First off was the beautiful, ever-smiling Jeanie Koeneman from Georgia and her quick-with-a-story husband, Lynn, a medical pathologist. Two other MD-types were with us: my roommate, Donn from California, and Kent Saltonstall from Washington State. Hailing from Oregon were Russ Davis and Tom Minihan, engineers by profession and longtime friends. Our expedition's tour leaders were, as noted, Phil Lighty and Eduardo Pantoja. All of us were experienced anglers—"old salts," you might say, though saltwater fishing like what we were about was all new to me.

The order of each trip out was to meet at the Corocora and walk the planks to the motorboats. There, twosomes were paired with a guide. These guides were Jose, Elias, Alejandro, and Braulio. Most knew little English. Happily, they knew the lagoon and its fishin' holes like the back of their *manos*. Each guide poled his boat out from the crowded dock area, then raced full throttle down the narrow channel to open water. From there they sped us to various locations in the lagoon, slowing down only when entering a fishing site. Selected bays and coves were approached quietly. In each we cast streamers big and bright into likely spots, such as at the base of mangrove trees.

Mangrove Water of the Estuary

We'd let the fly go down for a *cinco* count, then retrieved it in short jerks, ready for a take at any moment. If all went well in cast-and-retrieve, we'd have a take and, one time in five, we'd set the hook successfully for a fight. The bigger fish caught we'd photograph. Still, all were released. Then it was back to casting, moving, and casting some more. Like most others in the party, Donn and I fished with eight-weight rods and twenty-pound test shock leaders.

We boated tarpon and snook in equal numbers, their size ranging anywhere from 15 to 20 inches, 1 to 3 pounds in weight. Occasionally, someone caught a fish larger than that. I, for example, took a 24-incher and had on another "really big boy." Braulio thought that fish might have gone 6 kilos/14 pounds. When hooked, the tarpon exploded into the air, then rocketed himself into a root wad to break off at the knot connecting thirty-pound tippet to twenty-pound.

I also netted a mackerel and in the El Guapo River channel caught a catfish, a small jack with yellow fins, and a petite ladyfish. Fascinating variety. Other anglers reported landing barracuda and groupers. One trip my count was "touches 24," "on briefly 5," and "in the net 4" (2 tarpon and 2 snook). Last afternoon with Braulio, Donn and I boated twenty-four of sixty-four takes. Though several different fly patterns were used, my most successful was a Black and Silver Minnow imitation about four inches long. Also effective was the purple Egg-sucking Leech.

After a morning of fishing, it was to the beach, or hammocks, or showers or, certainly, to the Corocora for refreshment. Tuesday happened to be Carnival/Mardi Gras day itself, when many people from the mainland came to enjoy the sea. Sunbathers and shade-seekers were lawn-chaired on the sand, while children made sandcastles at waves' edge. Throw-net fishermen walked along, looking for mullet school disturbances. A skinny fellow with a big beach towel over his head and shoulders walked by, prompting Lynn Koeneman to remark, "Are those his legs, or is he riding a chicken?"

Drummers placed themselves beneath palm trees, and before them were salsa dancers—the girls most appealingly underclad.

Beach Dancers and Drummer

I, having watched, became overheated—because of the sun, of course—and went for a swim in the surf. That was a near disaster, because I forgot that my sunglasses were still on. I almost lost them in the breakers.

There were gulls on the beach in addition to terns and other shorebirds. Backs from the waves' reach, on the upper beach, were crimson and yellow hibiscus and bougainvillea. Such color! Through the days here I'd seen bright scarlet ibises, flocks of snow-white egrets flagging at us from emerald trees, pelicans sailing high in the blue, and brown-back turtles splashing off logs. Not by me, but by Davis and Minnhan, a crocodile was spotted near the dock. Eye-candy also arrived each evening in the sunsets over Rio Chico Lagoon.

After two and a half days fishing the lagoon, we set out on the second leg of our Venezuelan salts adventure. Boated back to the harbor docks early that morning, we reboarded our black-windowed bus, Antonio again supervising. He sped us to a small airport. At one checkpoint en route, we spotted a semi-symbol of Venezuela, a *militario* with an AK-47 on one knee and a pretty girl balanced on the other.

While waiting for the flight to Los Roques, individual and group pictures were taken.

Pescadors Ready to Fly

Then it was off to the archipelago in the Gulf about 125 air miles north of the mainland. As the plane slowed and dropped in approach to the islands, exhilarated exclamations arose: "Look at that!" "Wow!" "How beautiful!" Indeed, this tropical place of verdant islands, ivory beaches, white sand spits, opalescent waters, and silver flats was a sight beautiful. Phil Lighty, however, reminded us why we were here, saying simply, "Bonefish, folks."

Islands of Los Rogues

Passing through a sort of customs with flags whipping in the wind, we walked to our hotel, La Posada Arrecife los Roques, most comfortable. A couple of large tortoises roamed the floors, while a brilliantly plumed parrot squawked in the lounge. Evening meals were served on the hotel's open-air rooftop and do-it-yourself breakfasts taken in the lobby. Sack lunches were picked up by the front door on the way to the boats.

Our boats here were moored to the harbor's beach by guylines. Most boats had 225-horsepower motors, more powerful than those used in the lagoon. One craft was a cigarette speedboat—the kind used in drug smuggling we were told! Each craft had a crew of two: the pilot who drove it and the fishing guide. Our crews were Julio and Vladimir, William and Danny, Claudio and Exis, and Achilles and Luis. Achilles and Luis took Donn and me out the afternoon of arrival day.

The leeward side of a sand island was Captain Achilles's first stop. Guide Luis then walked us to the windward side. It had an expansive flat. One at a time Luis led Don or me out to hunt for bonefish, the bones themselves searching for crabs in the mid-calf to knee-deep water.

Luis and Don Looking for Bones

Unfortunately there weren't many around just then, and those present spooked easily. Most of all, they were hard to spot. Indeed, I couldn't see a single one. Only Luis could. He would point "There!" to direct a cast. *There* was a particular spot in front of moving, blue-gray mini-torpedoes. Get the fly *there,* and maybe one will go for it.

So you may ask, "How'd you do?"

I confess that I was not only slow with the long cast needed, but also inaccurate. Blame it on the wind. Only one time that afternoon did I successfully cast to *there* . . . for no-pick-up by a cruiser. (The next day, wading another flat, I got it together well enough to actually take two.) Others in our gang, I believe, had somewhat greater success. Wade fishing for bones is not, by any means, akin to "shooting carp in a barrel."

After a couple hours pushing our legs through the shallows, Luis returned us to the boat. Achilles then pounded us away over blue water in search of some that was milky, it called *aqua la leche* or *la mancha* (of mud/*lodo*). *La mancha* is created when a population of bones—maybe thousands—move along in four to five feet of water looking for crabs. The moving school effectively stirs up the silt, turning the teal water into a light brown cloud. With these bones of *la mancha* we had greater success.

The pilot would position the boat to be either just ahead or just to the side of the moving swarm. Then we'd cast toward the cloud, letting the fly sink and drift with the current, retrieved by deliberate pulls, a stop to let the fly resettle, followed by another pull. When the crab-imitation bait was taken and you felt the touch, instead of lifting the rod to strike, we did a strip-strike, which consisted of pulling the line straight back hard. With hook in its mouth, the fish would start to run, and we could give line and not let him break us off. *Then* the rod was lifted, and the fight began in earnest. These fish were not monsters—as those perhaps found on Christmas Island—but they were rod-bending speedsters nonetheless. Our bonefish were in the 14- to 19-inch range and seldom more than 2 pounds—but always worth the action. First afternoon I took one bone, which weighed 4.2 pounds. Several times in the next two days Donn and I doubled, with Donn sometimes using his spinning rod armed with a Clouser Minnow. Invariably my fly of choice was the Crazy Charlie.

Author and Erikson Going for Bonefish and Beautiful Bonefish

The other boats, occupied by Russ and Tom, Kent and Phil, and Jeanie and Lynn, did much the same. I believe Jeanie caught the biggest bonefish of all the anglers, one weighing close to 5 pounds. One day Kent recorded his strikes, and the number came out about thirty. That suggests double digits for actual landings per fisherman per day.

Each day we changed guides and therefore went out in different boats. During one trip, Donn and I pursued permit . . . and saw one! The sighted fish fled off the reef so fast I had no time to unspool line. Twice we saw large barracuda, and each sighting excited the guides immensely. With a large lure of a silver fish attached to strong cord, they tried desperately to catch the sighted barracuda, with no luck.

Twice we went to a particular semicircular bay where "glass minnows" schooled. Here large tarpon were feeding on them, we hoped. Only Salton-stall, however, using spinning gear loaded with a Castmaster and a Gummy Minnow dropper, managed to hook one and hold it.

Tarpon by Saltonstall

(Any *hooking* of a tarpon is special; for tarpon have ceramic-coffee-mug mouths.) Kent's tarpon went for the dropper and when netted and weighed, went 20 pounds, the largest fish caught by anyone on the trip.

Each day all day I reminded myself to reapply sunblock. Several of us—including our well-tanned guides—wore full-face scarves and/or broad brim or high-UVH hats. Lots of water was drunk under the dehydrating sun, but no beers were on board, lest the *cervezas* too quickly go to *la cabeza*.

Flora and fauna of the islands were wonderfully different from anything mile-high Colorado offers. Fascinated by this tropical island ecosphere, I took photographs of sea urchins, crabs, conchs, and coral-red starfish. We learned that at one time in the waters of Los Roques, conch snails were massively abundant, then massively—and tragically—too well harvested. Evidence of those days could be seen in the giant mounds of conch shells on one island's shore.

Conch Shells on an Island Shore

If I were a botanist, I also would give names to the plant life in the water: various grasses, varieties of kelp, etc. But, alas, botanist I am not. "Palm trees *of various kinds*," though, I can say, "are on the islands."

The water itself was beautiful, transparent yet vibrantly colorful, depending on the conditions of depth, bottom material (e.g., sand, grass), overhead sky, and wind. In the main harbor and on open water were big and little sailboats and ostentatious yachts. Did any cruise ships pass by? Maybe. I don't remember.

Each afternoon, sore of shoulder from casting, we came back to port ready for libation. Our party's drink of choice was the *caipiriña*, three-fourths Brazilian rum and one quarter Chilean *vino tinto*. When we gathered, jokes and stories were let out, the best of which was Lynn Koeneman's:

> A Floridian went to north Georgia fly-fishing with a guide. The
> client, bothered by biting flies, asked, "What are these, anyway?"
>   The guide replied, "Zoom-zoom flies, sir."
>   "'Zoom-zoom' flies. Never heard of 'em."
>   "They're a species that usually hangs around horses' asses."

*"What?" the Floridian glowered. "You callin' me a horse's
ass?"*

"O no, sir. . . . But you can't fool a zoom-zoom fly."

Dinners at La Posada had more red meat on the table than at Tortuga
Lodge, but still—and mostly—there was fish, delicious fish, well prepared.

After dinner one evening, Jeanie, Donn, Eduardo, and I wandered *el
pueblo*. (Quite a treat let me say, to be walking a desert isle with a former
cheerleader for the New Orleans Saints!)

Two on Los Roques Town

Eduardo told us this had been his home for a number of years, so he
knew some of the folks and introduced us around. One person's *tienda* featured black coral jewelry, exquisite and expensive. "No, but *gracias*," just the
same. Eduardo led us to the beachfront to look inside the small Catholic
church facing the bay. Its bright white exterior was matched by creamy interior beauty, punctuated by ebony tiles holding the fourteen stations of the
cross. The Virgin of Guadalupe was above the altar, keeping watch over this
wonderful little village.

Los Roques Church by the Sea

On Friday we flew off The Rocks in two small planes, this time able to recognize some of the islands, coves, sand beaches, flats, and waters we'd fished. Leaving the islands behind, the bright blue waters gave way to dark deep blues.

Once in Caracas, we spent the night at the Hotel Euro, a three-star establishment with one-star cuisine. Last pictures were taken and email addresses shared.

Next morning early and late, our gang of eight departed for the States. Phil, Donn, and I traveled together to Houston, then took different routes home. I gave each a copy of my fishing book, *Round Boys Great Adventures,* and while flying over Texas, I wrote in my journal, "The salts—people and water—made for yet another."

Segue to Bali

IT'S A LONG WAY from Venezuela (story just told) to Bali, Indonesia (setting for the next tale). The locales are 12,227 miles or one Pacific Ocean apart. Much less *time,* however, exists between visiting these places, just a year and a half. In this brief period, piscatorial and ministerial things per earlier reports transpired. I fished the Bighorn, Spinney Mountain Reservoir, Rainbow Falls, the Arkansas, and, streams in Rocky Mountain National Park. Bruce and I rejourneyed to Manitoba; and with the Moorhusens, Patti and I did another Ontario fly-in.

Anthony Surage and I continued our spirituality and fly-fishing retreats, and I did occasional pulpit supply (guest preaching). In September 2011, however, I began a five-month ministry in Bali, Indonesia, Patti sojourning with me. How that pastoring in the Southern Hemisphere came about needs background.

Return with me to 2008–9, even before the first Manitoba trip or the Venezuela adventure. In '08–'09 I was engaged in a second post-retirement interim ministry in Seattle, Washington—some of this ministry already told about. During this twelve-month charge, in lieu of a parsonage, Patti and I did much housesitting, made terrific new friends, and I got into trout, salmon, and steelhead angling. A couple in the congregation, the Reverends Greg and Kathy Turner (who in the 1970s served a Denver church, as did I), told me about short-term *international* ministry opportunities. They had done one such in Belgium. "You, Jim, could do one in Bali, Indonesia, for instance, in an English-speaking church," Greg suggested.

Now as it happened, Patti had just finished reading Elizabeth Gilbert's *Eat, Pray, Love,* a sweet travelogue story that ended in romance on that island. When I floated the idea of going to Bali, she had visions of riding her bike beside lush green rice paddies on quiet, peaceful paths.

"I'm in," she said. "Work it out."

I did.

Two years later, right after I officiated at a niece's "9-10-11" wedding in our backyard, for which Patti twice catered more than a hundred meals, we flew to Bali. For us two from the cool and dry Rocky Mountains, Bali was not a paradise—not with its heat, humidity, and human congestion. The archipelago island, two degrees below the equator, was made famous in the musical *South Pacific*. It is the same size as our El Paso County in Colorado with 600,000 residents, but Bali's population is 4,000,000, most of them traveling too fast on their motor scooters with two, three, or four aboard.

Even so, being there was a rich cultural, religious, and living experience. Our Protestant church in Nusa Dua was on a hill, side by side with a Hindu shrine, a Buddhist temple, a Muslim mosque, and a Catholic cathedral. That's ecumenicity writ large.

Protestant Church in Bali

... with Assembled "Family" on Chancel

While in Bali, I also got into fishing quite different from most I'd ever done. We made it up to beautiful Lake Bratan. To fish here, our guide's outrigger was secured to the lake's bottom via a bamboo pole stuck in the mud twenty-four feet down. Patti, our driver Wayan Suwinton, and I together took two dozen 3-inch perch-like fish.

P and J Ready to Fish Lake Bratan ... for Small Perch

The opportunity to fish the Indian Ocean also came. That's the story that follows.

CHAPTER 13

Gambling For Tuna

Bali, Indonesia Indian Ocean
December 9, 2011

"IT'S A GAMBLE," THE booking agent at the marina, explained. Still, we booked.

"It's a gamble," the fleet coordinator repeated the morning we arrived. Still, we went.

The odds of catching skipjack tuna by trolling—what the agent and co-ordinator were lowering expectations about—were, we knew, not high. Our expectations were not unrealistic; most in our party had gone deep-sea fishing before and on occasion experienced zilch results. So, what else would be new? Regarding reef fishing, however, the cautionary promoters were more sanguine, said we could be winners, "It's just that the fish will be smaller." With regard to the third item on our agenda this excursion day, snorkeling, they said the tropical fish would be in the coral beds, "guaranteed."

So, out of Bali's Benoa Harbor, five of us went a-fishing: Sunny and Jim Moorhusen from Illinois, our Balinese automobile driver Wayan Suwinton, my wife Patti, and I. Wayan came with fresh-water telescoping rod and spinning reel. We went out into Bali's Badung Strait of the Indian Ocean, toward the nearby islands of Lembongan, Penida, and Ceningen.

Our boat was *The Tropical Express*, our captain a sun-weathered man of fifty years, quiet and quite dour, name of Bogan. He knew some English. Kadet, his well-tattooed, twenty-something first mate, knew almost none. So we communicated through Wayan, fluent in both English and Balinese. Bogan and Kadet bore sticky-rice grains on their foreheads, a Hindu piety. On the dashboard of the boat's cockpit was a small basket of fresh flowers. The little bouquet also held a stick of burning incense.

When I asked about the rice and basket, Wayan explained that all was for the god Vishnu to give "good fortune."

"They're like a gambler's totem," Moorhusen suggested.

"Sort of," Wayan agreed.

These sailors wanted good fortune, since all fishing boats out of the harbor the last two days had had zero catches of tuna. The odds were not in our favor.

First Dealing, Tuna

About twenty minutes out, Captain Bogan quieted his two 115 Suzuki engines, lit himself a cigarette, and began a steady troll. Kadet came to the back of the boat with a large Styrofoam board wrapped by three heavy monofilament lines, each about twenty feet long. He got out a ten-inch, bright yellow, fish-shaped float with flanges on each side. By a swivel he connected the float to the line on a heavy-duty level-wind reel. The reel was seated on a stout six-foot rod. To the tail of the fish-float he attached the mono, and at the end of the mono was the bait: three two-inch bright streamer flies arranged in line. Flies, mono, float, and line were then let out into the wake of the boat, to go back—way back, like 150 yards back. When the payout of line was complete and the reel braked, a just-visible spray of water appeared, created by the flanges on the float.

Satisfied that rig number one was set up correctly on the port side of the boat, Kadet turned to rig number two on the starboard side. Just as he began to put on the second yellow float, he suddenly let it drop and lunged back to rig number one. It was hit.

"Keno!" I heard myself say.

Kadet lifted the rod from its seat and set the drag for play, cranked a couple of times, then turned to look. "Who wants it?"

I pushed Moorhusen to the task, and he knew what to do: let the fish run and then, when the fish calmed down enough to be moved, lift and reel.

It was a good fighting fish, for sure. Once Kadet saw that Moorhusen was in control, he grabbed a belt with a rod-butt holder to strap around Jim's waist. I noticed he let it out considerably before he snapped it on.

Patti said to Sunny, "The belt was last used by Twiggy."

"That's generous," she nodded.

Anyway, Moorhusen was doing lift-and-pull, lift-and-pull until Kadet patted his palm down in motion to say, "Just reel, just reel."

"You mean 'horse him'?" Moorhusen asked.

Kadet continued patting. "Just reel."

Jim did and, after a bit, we could see a silver flash in the water. Actually, flashes. Jim had hooked two fish, two tunas! When close enough to the boat, Kadet grabbed the line and lifted both in. They were iridescent, each about 20 inches long. They flopped their tails madly when thrown into the Styrofoam box well. Beautiful.

I congratulated Moorhusen with, "Way to go, old salt. Lady Luck is riding with you. If we get another, let's let Wayan have the rod."

"Good idea."

"It'd be a first for him."

It wasn't long before Wayan got his chance, as rod number two, set to work, started bouncing. We put him into position. Sunny grabbed the fish-fighting belt, and Kadet pulled the belt strap in—way in. Wayan went to work and soon a third beauty was in the cooler. For the picture, Patti instructed Wayan how to hold the fish. "Way forward, Wayan, way forward, to the camera." (So a 19-inch fish looks like a 3-footer.) Patti, of course, has taken a lot of pictures of Jim White and made-monster trout.

Soon we were back to trolling, going in a wide elliptical circle, hoping that Lady Luck was still with us. She was. Middle rod, a rig without a spray-up indicator, was hit, and ere long Sunny was grinning broadly, having caught the biggest tuna so far, one about 21 inches, 4 pounds.

"I think I hit the jackpot," she said.

Then it was Patti's draw, but when rod number one went to pulsing, rod number two did the same. Patti took number one and I number two. "Doubles!" Her catch, however, did not come in quickly. Mine did. Too quickly. The fish was off. I reeled in the float and put the rod against the side gunwale. Then I turned to Patti. She was in harness, put on by Sunny, and working hard.

"This must be the biggest yet," I encouraged.

"Stay with him, Pattigirl," Sunny added.

She stayed but was unable to crank easily. A strong fish indeed. Nay, not fish singular nor fish plural, as in double, but fish plural as in *triple*. Patti had a tuna on each of her three streamers!

Patti with Jack Tuna (Two others in Hold)

"That's my technique," she said, reminiscent of this same line when she caught a 39-inch northern using a hooked walleye as inadvertent bait.

We were all shouting "Ohhh" and "Aaahh" and "Amazing," and I think I saw the captain smiling. I wondered if he'd ever had a client do a single triple. Patti's three then made tuna number seven for his boat. If they hoisted flags out here, the skipper would have had a seven-card flush to show.

Then eyes turned on me. Moorhusen asked, "What became of your fish?"

"Think Patti's three-of-a-kind aces trumped my singleton. He got away."

"Seems like lessons in rod-handling skills are in order."

"Just dealt a bad hand," I offered.

When Kadet went to reset the lines, he discovered that my placement of the rod against the gunwale had let the monofilament leader tangle in the prop. So the engine was cut, and Jim helped Kadet disentangle it. Afterward, Moorhusen said simply, "Guess every poker game has a fish in it."

"Like a donk?"

"Exactly."

It took a while for Kadet to get all three rods back in action, but he did.

Now it was my turn to roll the dice. Happily the middle rod was hit, and Kadet handed it my way. Wayan strapped me in with the fighting belt, graciously saying nothing about lengthening it. So I was onto a fish. He was big, I was sure, for it was not easy reeling. Why? Because my fish immediately crossed two other lines. I was dragging in three rigs at once. This was *a horrible, terrible, no good, rotten* mess, for which the captain had to kill the motors and come back to help untangle.

Moorhusen just said, "*Donk* still works."

Still, we had eight tuna.

Second Dealing, Reef Fish

Once the lines were unsnarled, we trolled a bit more. Shortly, though, the captain had us haul in, and he picked up speed to take us toward Ceningen Island, the smallest of the three islands to the east. Kadet now went below deck and came up with five cardboard boxes with five crustless ham sandwiches of cardboard bread and similar-composition cold french fries. Gluten-free Patti was spared the sandwich bread. I asked for a beer, but was provided only water. So we ate and drank. Once he'd fed us, Kadet went to work putting together reef rigs.

He made a loop in some monofilament and hooked the loop over his second longest toe and proceeded to affix two silver hooks on six-inch snells about a foot apart. The hooks were long shanked. When all was ready, he tied a three-ounce barrel weight to the bottom of the rig with a swivel on the top. The bait for each hook was a three-inch shrimp, head pinched off, its shell removed.

With the boat now drifting in the wind, we dropped the sinkered-baits off the sides. Each weight went to the bottom, maybe thirty feet down. When the spinning line, twenty-pound test, went slack, we cranked the reel handle a time or two and jigged. Moorhusen and I each had a rod. The third stayed in the hands of Kadet, and he caught the first fish, a 10-inch red snapper. Having demoed how to do this, I thought he'd hand the rod over to Wayan. But he did not. He simply returned to jigging.

It wasn't long until Moorhusen announced, "Got one," and brought in a purple hand-sized fish, a triggerfish, about 8 inches long. Jim showed Wayan how the unbendable horn on the top of the fish could be lowered simply by touching a trigger in front of the horn. Pretty neat.

I missed a couple of hits. So I gave my rod to Wayan, and he proceeded to take a 9-inch white snapper, then returned the pole to Kadet.

Right away Kadet landed a koca, brilliantly orange, armed with lots of sharp fins.

About then the captain came to the back of the boat, and he rigged up rod number four. This I thought he'd hand over to Sunny or Patti. But no, he was there to fish. I looked at Patti. She was reading a book. I looked at Sunny, and she raised her eyebrows as in, "I don't get it." I looked at Wayan. He was assembling his freshwater, lightweight telescope rod. His brittle line in preparation, however, kept breaking, and soon he realized he did not have weights enough to get to the bottom. He might have used a sinker from the captain's tackle box, but none was offered.

We paying passengers were all nonplussed. Never have I seen a fishing guide push clients away that he himself might fish. Strange by Rocky-Mountain-guide etiquette anyway.

Finally I said, "Captain," and he turned his head, "the girls would like to fish too."

He did not say anything, but handed the rod to Sunny. The hand-off did not stop Kadet. He kept on angling and no longer put shrimp on emptied hooks. We ourselves did—but not very well.

Captain Bogan went back to the helm and took us to another location. It was shallower. No fish were to be caught there, and I think he knew it. He was pissed at me for having interrupted his fun. After a while, though, I caught a smaller red snapper. So the captain moved us again. In the new drift location, there were more bites and more takes. The bites-'n'-takes were now for Sunny, inveterate walleye-snagger. She caught a triggerfish here. On a fourth drift she took another, as did Wayan, who was finally given the first mate's rod. I caught a kota, equally as bright as the earlier one, but smaller than Kadet's. Moorhusen caught a bigger trigger.

Our reef catch now went to about a dozen fish, in weight equal to one tuna, and it was eleven o'clock. The captain asked, "Enough?"

I looked at Patti, still reading, and she nodded, "Enough."

Third Hand, Snorkeling

Bogan took us into a cove on the middle of Lembongan, the midsize island. Four other boats were in the cove ahead of us, each hooked up to a planted buoy, as no anchor dropping is allowed here. Such caution prevents damage to the corals below. With a long-handle gaff, Kadet pulled in a buoy and tied us in. The motor was cut, and a box with snorkeling equipment brought forth.

Outfitted, Moorhusen was the first in, then Wayan—he'd done this before—followed by Sunny and Patti. As the swim fins given me were size 12—and I'm a 10—I put on extra thick socks, then skillfully back-dropped into the water, as I've seen scuba divers do. Such sheer grace a camera would not show, just a rookie snorkeler with salt water up his nose sputtering deleted expletives. Still, I was in.

Well, it was a wonderland: fishes of every color and shape . . . fishes striped front to back . . . fishes striped up and down . . . fishes blue, golden, some with long antennae . . . fishes big, like four pounds big, and black with a white ring in front of their tail . . . fishes so thin they disappeared under you . . . fishes of all kinds, and each one extraordinary. Common names included angels, parrots, neons, and grunts.

More amazing than the fish was the coral. It too was of every color and combination of hue, and every shape, from a thin ruffled fan to a thick coral as big around as a kitchen table with scoops and mounds to it, as if it were a sculpted river boulder. Sunny and Jim identified types of coral as staghorn, elkhorn, and fan, plus some that looked like cabbage and mushrooms. The one that most fascinated me had a rough heart shape to it and was about ten inches across, greenish-purple with edges iridescent blue. I wanted to show it to Patti. So I popped my head up to find her swimming nearby. She couldn't hear me call so I swam up beside her and pinched her leg. Her head came out, dark hair sweeping her mask. Her eyes were wide in fright. It wasn't Patti.

"Sorry," I gurgled.

The girl did not reply, but her head went searching for someone, someone I knew must have tattoos and massive upper-body strength.

"Sorry. I thought you were my wife," I gurgled again.

Eventually, I found Patti and showed her the iridescent fringed coral. It became her favorite also. Together we explored till returning to the boat. Once on board, the look "Enough?" was in the eyes of the captain again.

Enough.

After all, it was lunchtime.

Fourth Dealing, Shore Cuisine

Captain Bogan next took our craft to a beach on the big island, Penida. Quite a few boats of various sizes were moored here, including a huge, bright-orange *Water World* barge with slides and diving boards. We passed it to get in close for a shallow wade to the shore. The captain held Sunny's hand across the slick grassy bottom. Kadet brought in our catch of fishes. With Wayan's linguistic help at the restaurant, we ordered one tuna to be grilled, one tuna to be cleaned but kept whole for Wayan to show and tell his family, and all the rest to be filleted, skinned, and deboned for us to take home. About half of the small fish were fried and the other half went to somebody, perhaps the kitchen crew.

The wait for our fish dinner was well worth it. The fish came with white rice, fried rice, and tasty pepper-like compote.

Fish Platter at Penida Isle Restaurant

Houseflies enjoyed the cuisine too, as we were told the reason for so many: "It's mango season." Four recently born, skinny kittens also came around looking for scraps. At table next to us were six young Russian adults. They said they were "escaping Siberia." The six ate their whole catch of the day—two tuna. At both tables Bintang beer, the culture's uniting elixir, was enjoyed.

Through heavy seas we pounded our way back to Benoa Harbor. Moorhusen instructed us to sit on "the hinge" of the boat, that is, the back seat, where there was less bucking. We did and bounced along in silence, all five of us immensely satisfied with the winnings of the day. The gamble paid off.

Segue to Europe

AFTER BALI, AND FOR the next five years, my international fishing was a return to Ontario's Keeper Lake, a return to Cabo San Lucas, and five returns to Manitoba.

As noted in the Manitoba write-up, there I got acquainted with Ukrainian Eastern Orthodoxy. Such exposure prepared me for touching Russian Orthodoxy. In the fall of 2014 I co-led a group of twenty-five American church folk to Russia. We were in many historic churches and monasteries, as well as Moscow's Red Square and in the Hermitage in Petersburg.

Author before St. Basil's on Red Square

On the Volga River we saw wee perch fished for and caught. The seeing made me wish for my fly rod and a #22 Red Annelid.

Canada, Mexico, and Russia, then, were my away-from-the-USA adventures prior to fishing in England, Germany, and the Czech Republic, as recounted in the story to come, "Europe on the Fly."

Home-water angling during this period was "the usual" Bighorn, Spinney, etc. The usual "Fly-Fishing and Spirituality" retreats continued. That topic was also considered when I rendezvoused on the San Juan River in New Mexico with old fishing friends from First Plymouth Church in Englewood. The subject was also well discussed on a wilderness horsepack trip taken with Bob Tucker, his daughter Polly, and my daughter Melissa, our "little fisher girls" become "mature, thoughtful women" and adroit fly-fishers.

Fathers & Daughters on Horsepack Trip

Then too the "meaning of fishing" was broached at Ring Lake Ranch, summer of 2015, in a panel discussion with "Holy Joes" Andy Blackmun, Ron Dunn, Brian McLaren and me, all of us in Dubois, Wyoming for a "Theology and Culture" seminar.

Author, Ron Dunn, & Brian McLaren

So lots of significant in-depth thought and conversation with many *compadres.*

During this period, the big thing for me was publication of *Brief Christian Histories: Getting a Sense of Our Long Story.* The book came out in 2014. Brian McLaren (see photo above), a JWW lecturer, wrote the foreword. In my estimation, that foreword, a four-times-walking-down-a-river-bank analogy, alone is worth the price of the book. Publication of *BCH* sent me on promotional preaching-teaching trips to denominational conferences, former parishes (Denver, Moline, Wichita, Seattle), other locales (Norman OK, Creede CO), and "I don't remember where all." I believe the writing of the book, its earlier iteration (*Christianity 101: Tracing Basic Beliefs*), with the books' subsequent promotions and interpretations, worked to ground me well in understanding the Christian faith—at least *historic* Christianity. So maybe I know what it is and is not. You can decide, reading the last two chapters of this book.

As macular degeneration, first diagnosed in Seattle, continued to be my lot during these years, angling facilitation has come via friends and family. Never could I say fishing is an *individual* sport. It takes a lot of ghillies to put this fella on the water.

Let us then go to the next—and last—story *qua* story.

CHAPTER 14

Europe on the Fly,
Learning to Fish Blind

September 2015

Do not go gentle into that good night,
Old age should burn and rave at close of day;
Rage, rage against the dying of the light.

—Dylan Thomas, Counsel to his dying father

FOR THE LAST SEVERAL years I have been meditating on the poet's words introducing this chapter, for "the dying of the light" is happening to me via macular degeneration, an eye disease that is progressing well, thank you. So, burn and rave and rage is what I do—or feel like doing. Yet I believe there can be a "good night" with the One Who Keeps Eternity, who has been just-all-right-by-me for fourscore years now.

Said another way, if loss of eyesight is the primary problem in these last years of my life, then, "Get over it, White!" There are other infirmities more devastating with which you might be dealing—pancreatic cancer, collapsing arteries, unrelenting dementia. None of these, so far, have hit me. Just blurring of the central focus of my seeing.

My low-vision doctor rightly says, "Your only problem, Jim, is between your ears." If that is so, the question becomes, Can I make the mental adjustments toward the night, generally, and specifically with regard to fly-fishing? I have been an angler since childhood, and fly-fishing has been my passion––along with ministry, some women insanely, justice and peace issues, and writing. Still, it's been fly-fishing. As sight blurs, questions appear with which I now must wrestle: Can I continue to fish? If so, how?

I've got to learn coping mechanisms; for example, when I tangle my line, leader, weights, flies, and tippet into a chocolate mess, I cannot see to untangle it. When a dry fly floats on the water, unless it's big and contrastingly bright, I can't see it, much less any take of it.

Oh, oh, poor, pitiful me.

No, self. Now stop it! You're "pouting and acting like a baby," as daughter Melissa described you one no-fish morning on the Bighorn.

So, coping mechanisms.

In the last several years, increasingly I've had to get by with more than a little help from my friends. Bruce Kuster found me a large red and white plastic bobber to use in lake fishing. Anthony Surage crosses the river to change out a fly. Guy Fredello on the San Juan tells me when to "Hit it!" Peter Thomas will drive me to the fishin' hole, then help. More than once streamside, only the "kindness of strangers" enabled me to untangle a bird's nest. All of which is to say that the most important thing I've learned in the last year or so is that I can no longer fish alone.

This lesson came in spades when fishing a glacier-cut stream in Wyoming. The stream was like hundreds I've fished for years and years. It was clear, open, readable, deep-holed, and well populated with cuts and brooks. Perfect for the right hopper-dropper combination. While all others in our backcountry party of six went upstream, I went down alone. I was convinced that if I could get a mile below where most anglers worked the water, I'd be into fish. I got down there and after a couple of refusals realized my Joe's Hopper was too big. All right. Change it. You've always been able to do that. But I couldn't. Having clipped off the hopper, I could not see to put the 5x tippet through the eye of the #14 Elk Hair Caddis, much less a #20-Adams. That combination, I think, would have worked. A hundred stabs with the tippet, even using my flip-down magnifiers, and I still couldn't do it. I wanted to cry.

Truth be told, on the long walk back to the car, that is what I did. I cried. Defeated. I waited two hours for the other fishermen to return. It may have been the lowest day of my fishing life. I kept saying to myself, Norman Maclean in his old age might have fished the big waters alone, but not you—not even a tiny brookie stream. No more.

If I can learn the lesson of necessary dependence, there are still other coping skills I'm going to have to acquire to stay with this sport. Perhaps I can attain some from other, different fishermen, specifically European anglers. Patti and I had plans during the fall of 2015 to visit friends in England, Germany, and the Czech Republic. I thought, maybe I can engage with other fishermen in the places where we'll be and get some helpful fishing pointers. In planning each visit, I asked our overseas friends if they could possibly set me up in a guided fly-fishing opportunity in their country. Specifically I asked Audrey and Terry White, our "cousins" across the pond, if I could fish one of the waters of England where Izaak Walton angled. Graciously, Audrey set it up with a guide. Our German "daughter," Annegret Höerrmann, whom we met and adopted in Bali, said she'd see what could be done. Maybe there'd be opportunity on a friend's farm pond. Then in Prague Jan and Jana Vales, theological "siblings" whom we've thrice visited, used the internet to find a Czech Nymphing School workshop for me.

Perfect, I said to myself. I can go to school on the guides, both to learn some European fishing techniques and to discover something helpful to this less-than-keen-eyed old guy.[1]

For the trip I put in my suitcase a seven-piece pack rod, a five-weight reel, a tools necklace, sundry accessories, and flies. Oh, that I might use them to learn piscatorially useful things as I "go into that good night" . . . *sans* raging?

England's River Dove (and Scottish Waters)

My middle name is Wilden, from my maternal great-grandfather. All I know about him is that he was married to my great-grandmother, whom I "met" when I was less than a year old. My mother told me Grandmother Wilden always called her husband "Mr. Wilden." I've liked the name, though it is often mispronounced as "Weldon" and "Wild'one." I've never been sure where great-grandfather Wilden's family came from, but I assumed England.

En route to Dubois, Wyoming, for a two-week theological seminar—with fishing on the side—my wife and I listened to Sir Izaak Walton's *The Compleat Angler* on audiotape. Part I of this 1751 classic mentions the River Dove, a stream in northwest England, Derbyshire district. Part II of the volume, the part written by Charles Cotton, speaks in detail about this stream. Cotton relates that he and a companion went on horseback to fish the river. As they went, they rode through the town of Wilden!

"Whoa!" I said to Patti. "Could this be the place from which my ancestors drew our name?"

"It's possible," she allowed.

"Well," I told her, "I want a picture of me beside the signpost for Wilden Town when I go a-fishin' the River Dove next month on our trip to England."

"Maybe the angling guide you've scheduled can take one of you."

(As it turned out, he couldn't, as Wilden—actually "Wildon," for I misheard the name— is about a hundred miles from where my River Dove

---

1. Since 2015, fishing life has ben further compromised by a 2016 stroke, which has left my casting hand somewhat "wanting." Still, I persevere. Successes known. (See next segue.)

guide would take us. Even so, I felt a kind of strong two-and-a-half-centuries reach to my ancestors and to "the father of trout fishing," Sir Izaak himself.)

When we reached Liverpool in September, "Cousin" Audrey White had signed me up to fish the Dove with John Machin, Anglo-American guide. He met me at the train station in Rugely, south of Stafford. As we drove in his car toward the river, we went by the Walton Inn, and John told me the train I'd come here on passed Walton's historic home. "Down the river is Charles Cotton's famous Fishing Temple. Have you ever fished in England before, Jim?" he asked.

"No," I confessed. "But twenty years ago I twice fished in Scotland. I was in Edinburgh for a conference and got to fish then."

Then I explained that the year had been 1996, and I stumbled into John Mackay's fly shop in Edinburgh. Mackay, the proprietor, was a really gracious guy. When I told him I was from the United States and interested in fishing here, he said, "This is your day, Yank."

"How's that?"

"Well it's the Fourth of July, and if you want to go fishing, I'll take you."

"When? How?" I stammered. "All I've got is a pack rod."

"Bring it and come back at eight tonight."

"All right," I answered happily. "But why so late?"

Because it would be light until almost midnight, Mackay explained, it being just two weeks since the summer solstice. "Scotland, if you haven't noticed, Yank, is in a northern clime."

"So it is," I remembered.

That evening my host took us to a small loch, Loch Portmore, south of Edinburgh in the Scottish borders region. He set me up with a pair of too-big waders and rigged my reel with a leader at least twelve feet long. To that leader Mackay fixed three wet flies, names of which I've lost, but they were no bigger than size sixteen and most had swept-back, blue-gray wings over dark bodies. (Some of the flies I later placed in a shadow box, which has a print of a picture, titled "Preparation," showing an old Scotsman, tam-o'-shanter on his head, carefully winding new thread on a bamboo rod. Now, as I look at these flies, I see subtle differences in color, silver, red, and blue. A few have gold wire segmenting and two possess golden pheasant tails.) The flies we cast well out, let sink, and then retrieved by slow, two-foot strip backs, giving them a sink again rest and another slow stroke. Mackay called this technique "pulling." It worked. I caught a couple of nice rainbows in the 16 to 17-inch range. Mackay and a friend landed several more than this, with a couple up to 23 inches. Someone not in our party netted and kept a 5-pounder, probably 25 inches.

I also told John Machin (of England) that what I remembered most about that high-latitude experience was standing in the water with two

Scotsmen right behind me talking. They were speaking English, I'm sure, but try as I might, their brogue was so thick that I got not a single word. Even so, it was an evening that Norman Maclean's Scots Presbyterian minister father would have called "beautiful."

Machin said he'd fished Scotland a few times, mostly for Atlantic salmon, but had had minimal success. "I like English streams best. You'll see why. But your other Great Britain fishing experience was . . . ?"

I then recounted the second, which also took place in '96, also in Scotland. Seems we worshiped at the John Knox Church in Edinburgh, the church where a woman threw a chair at the priest for introducing Anglican liturgy in this strongly Calvinist land. There we met an affable Scot named Bill Scott from the Isle of Bute, west of Glasgow. He invited us to visit him. We accepted and, after a week on the Isle of Iona, made it to his isle. One morning Bill took us on an excursion to see an historical kirk with connection to the Lamont/McGregor clans. This was amazing to me for, as I'd heard my family genealogy story, these clans were my ancestors on my father's side. You know the song, "The Campbells are coming, tra-la, tra-la"? Well, back in the day, the Campbells would execute any persons of a rival clan who gathered in groups of three or more. So my ancestors sought clan anonymity. They changed their surnames to Brown, Black, and White. The bad part about this is that I now must admit that I come from a long line of cowards—albeit survivors, thank you.

After visiting the kirk, Bill dropped me off at a tiny stream nearby while he took Patti to gather thyme or something. Using a #16 Royal Wulff, I succeeded in catching a 4-inch brown trout.

"That's it?" Bill later asked.

"Guess so."

"Be assured," he said, "in the winter sometimes large salmon come here to spawn. But this is summer."

I was quite satisfied to know that my American fly worked in Scottish waters.

At this point I turned to John Machin to say, "And that, my guide, is the full extent of my fishing British Isle waters."

"Today, though, you get the best of England itself, with the chance to catch both brown trout and grayling." He then set me up with waders and a nine-foot Orvis Helios five-weight rod. Later, he let me try an 8.5-foot bamboo rod, and I asked, "Is this what Sir Izaak used?"

"No. In those days they had twelve-foot or so cane rods without reels. The thing most similar to Walton and Cotton's time is the fish: they're hundred generation plus direct descendants from those of the mid eighteenth century."

The water of the Dove was maybe thirty cubic feet per second and clear, seldom more than a few feet deep. What made the river so distinctive to me was the number of overhanging tree branches: birch, alder, oak, and willow. These created casting challenges. The banks of the stream were thick with vegetation. As we entered the water, John said to watch out for a particular weed, which would cause a horrible itching rash. I said, "In and out, after you, Alphonse."

"Okay, Gaston. But tell me about your eyes."

"Not much to say, except the macular degeneration is there. Part of what I'm hoping for today is to discover what I can and cannot do with my eyes. For sure, I'll need you to tie on flies and untangle my snarls."

"I can do that. Now let's fish."

John armed my first cast with a tungsten-bead Pheasant Tale nymph. Quickly enough, though, when he spotted rising fish, he changed us to a dry fly. First he had me cast straight upstream, as if to do a quality control check on this client. Then, because he could see rises better than I, he directed my casts, saying, "Nice," and "Nice cast." I appreciated the encouragement. Not all casts were nice, especially to begin with, as I kept back casting into the bushes and weeds. Then he had to go and free me. Finally, though, I made a nice one against the bank between overhanging branches and had a take, which resulted in a colorful eleven-inch brown trout.

Cast and Take on the River Dove

"Now you're in kin with Walton and Cotton," John said, "but better than they, because we release all our fish these days."

"Of course. Thank you."

"Now, let's see if we can't get you a grayling. You can recognize them by the little bubble they leave when taking something off the top. Their mouths are more under their nose than that of a trout, causing the bubble."

"I'll take your word for it. It's enough for me to see the ring made when anything surfaces. In fact, I'm seeing something else, something weird."

"What's that?"

"Well, in the space above my casts I'm seeing what appears as a cluster of lightning bugs, fuchsia in color. They seem to flicker around over the water in a clump." (As best I could figure out, they were refraction in my cornea of same-color flowers on the bank—except they didn't go away when there weren't such flowers. It was just weird, and it's never happened since.)

John said, "Never heard or seen such a thing, but if you can see a rising-ring, aim your cast above it, and I'll say, 'Lift,' when there's a take."

In this way, casting straight upstream, but after two misses, I stuck another brown trout. Joyfully, this little beauty was followed by a grayling. A grayling! My first since 1982 in Alaska. I was thrilled. Then there was another . . . and another . . . and one that was 12 inches long. For the graylings, the dry fly of most worth was a black-bodied Klinkhammer, size 16.

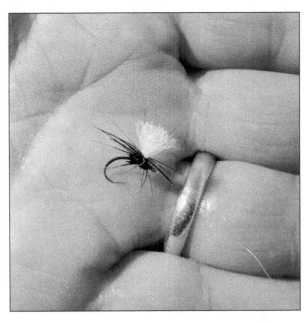

The Klinkhammer Fly

What was so good about it was the white parachute topknot, which I could see just well enough without John having to say, "Lift." The Klinkhammer, I thought, could become my new favorite dry fly/emerger.

Then something even more special happened: I caught a chub. This is a fish named in *The Compleat Angler,* but I had no idea what it looked like. It was a silvery sort of fat whitefish. Mine was about 9 inches long. John was pleased too, saying, "In all my years of fishing the Dove, that's only the third chub I've caught here."

I thought to myself, if I were to also catch a roach and a dace—neither of which is in these waters, John said—I would have an English slam. Even so, I was happy with my three species.

The main new thing I learned from Machin was how to side cast successfully. He said to imagine a postal slot in your door and then putting your fly into that postal slot. To do this, you have to stop and start the side-arm casts earlier. That gets the fly to land straight upstream, not swing off to the side. Casting downstream in this side-arm way also decreases snagging on the side bushes and into the overhanging tree branches. When I did it successfully, John would say, "Nice."

After a while, my casting hand began to lock up and spasm. So I insisted that John take the rod. His casts were Maclean "beautiful" . . . and he caught many more per cast than I.

At lunch, enjoying Audrey-prepared sandwiches, I learned that John guided in Florida estuaries during the winter months, getting his clients tarpon, snook, red fish, and others. In modesty he said he has a world-class record for catching a grayling on an 8x tippet. I was impressed.

Following lunch, we fished new waters upstream of the morning's beat and then, later, down from the beat. As the afternoon came on, both he and I had more refusals than takes. Still, we got a few. I was impressed by a picturesque stone bridge, which we fished above. It felt like something that could have been over the stream when Walton and Cotton angled here.

"Like it, do you, Jim? I'll send a photo of the bridge in snow, taken last winter." (Happy to report, he did. It was quite stunning.)

John Machin and River Dove Bridge, Summer and Winter

I loved my day on the River Dove, and though I didn't get to Wilden-town, I felt I'd made some kind of holistic circle back to where it all—or a lot of me—began. On leaving, John said, "Watch the rises, not the fluorescent lightning bugs."

"I'll try," I promised. "And every time I place a cast through the postal slot, I'll think of you. Thanks, guide extraordinaire."

On Germany's Golden Pond

One of my goals going on this European trip was to catch a German brown trout in Germany. With my own eyes, I'd seen brown trout in nearby Austria. That also was in 1996 on sabbatical. Patti and I had two-nighted on Lake Hallstatt, just east of *Sound of Music* Salzburg. From our pensión, we went for a picnic on the lake where a stream came down from the high mountains. Curious as to what was there, I worked my way through thick bushes to peer into the water. There they were: two olive-backed brown trout, about 14 inches long, with their haloed black and red spots showing. Beautiful. Right then I resolved to come back one day and catch a German brown here—or better yet, in Germany.

Home of origin for *salmo trutta*, I believe, is Germany. I've taken this species in New Zealand, Tasmania, Canada, the US of course, Scotland, and now England. The fish were planted around the world in the nineteenth century, including in Argentina, Chile, South Africa, some island in the Indian Ocean, and I don't know where all. Now, on this European trip, I was in Germany, with a chance to fish for one.

"Can we?" I asked Michael Feuchter, who picked us up at the airport in Stuttgart. "Can we?"

"I'm sure it can be done," Michael said.

"But . . .?"

"But it's complicated."

Michael, affectionately called Michi, was the since-June husband of Annegret Höerrmann Feuchter, our adopted-in-Bali daughter. That was two years previous, when I was serving an English-speaking church there. Physical therapist Anne was a volunteer at an inland medical center and part of our expat church. She weekended at our parsonage residence on the beach, thus escaping inland island heat. Patti and I were simply smitten by her charm. On parting Bali, I said to Anne, "When you get married, we'll come over for the wedding."

Well, early last winter she announced her engagement and plans to be married in June. Our European travel plans so began. I said, "We'll come, but not at nuptials time—we'd never see you. How about September, well after your honeymoon?" So it was set.

We were now in Germany and, forgive me dear Patti, for thinking not, "Be an attentive guest," but "Go get a brown trout." On the day of our arrival, Anne had to work. So husband-Michi picked us up and drove us east to where they lived, Schwäbisch Hall, an ancient city famous for its salt. As we rode along, Michi explained the German fishing situation: "There are hurdles one has to jump over to fish in this country. First of all, you have to take a how-to-fish course and pass a graded exam. After that you can get a license. Then you need to hook up with someone in a fishing club who could get you on what is essentially private water."

"Does sound like a bit much," I had to agree, for we'd be here less than a week.

"Even so," Michi continued, "if you're still interested in fishing, Anne's brother-in-law is a really good angler. On his family farm pond, he can take us all fishing. It's good—excellent, really. We could do that."

"Yes. Let's. I'm grateful for the opportunity. It'd be a special experience." This special experience, I knew, would not be for *salmo trutta* but of *cyprinus caron carpio,* that is, carp.

Carp are a trash fish for most American anglers. Growing up in Oklahoma, if we caught one, we'd throw it to the bank. "A *racial minority* fish," my raised-in-the-South, prejudiced father would say. "Much too bony," mother would add.

I thus inherited a prejudice against carp.

(My father's racial bias obviously extended beyond fish, but, happy to say, in the late 1950s, his mind began to change. It happened because Prentice Gautt, the first black player on the University of Oklahoma football team, made the Sooners winners. Such success pleased my father exceedingly. By then other teams in the then–Big Eight Conference, notably Nebraska, had black players on their squads. One Saturday afternoon when OU played Nebraska, I was sitting with my father in the stadium watching the game. Prentice Gautt did an end run and in the attempt was crushed by two Cornhuskers. With that bruising tackle my father turned to me and said, "Did you see what those niggers did to our colored boy?" It was the first chink off the armor of his prejudice ... but not against carp. That remained.)

In most parts of the world carp are prized and, when cooked and plated, are considered most delicious. I learned this when visiting the Sea of Galilee in Israel. There Patti and I were served a St. Peter's fish—not a carp—but we were told that a cousin of the carp, the barbell, was an even greater delicacy. Furthermore, the barbell carp was likely the fish involved in "the marvelous draught of fishes" caught by Jesus' disciples.

Carp, I've learned, originated somewhere in middle Asia. They were transplanted widely. Japanese koi, for example, are a carp, and so are common goldfish. Sometime in the Middle Ages, the fish made it into waters of central Europe. Here they became a food staple. For people in the Czech Republic and Slovakia, carp are prized above all other species. In December 2005, when Patti and I were in Karlovy Vary of the Czech Republic visiting friends—whom you'll meet directly—we went to the supermarket for groceries. To our wonderment there were horse-size watering troughs outside the market brimming with live, large carp. One fellow came by and said, "I'd like one of five kilo." The fishmonger dipped into the tank with a long-handled net, pulled out a fish, weighed it, and said, "Only four." So he returned it to the tank and then dipped out one the right weight. He then put the fish in a plastic bag for the purchaser to carry home. My friend and Czech host, Jan Vales, said, "Likely the gentleman will keep that fish in his bathtub till Christmas Eve, then kill, clean, dress, and bake it for his family." Two days later Jan went back for a 4.5 kilo-er, which we enjoyed that Yuletide with his family. It was delicious.

(Upon return to the States, I read *How I Came to Know Fish*, by the Czech novelist Ota Pavel. It had a World War II story about a carp pond owned, loved, and kept by Pavel's Jewish father. This pond, however, the Nazis took from him after their invasion of Czechoslovakia. Pavel's father, of necessity, accepted the confiscation until December. Then, late one freezing night, he and his father chopped a hole in the ice of that pond. The opening allowed the oxygen-deprived carp to come to the surface for air. When they did, he and his father netted them, put them in gunny sacks, and carried them home, where they reimpounded them to live in pails, buckets, the sink, and of course the bathtub. They kept the carp to sell to and barter with their Christian neighbors. When the Nazis later came to drain the pond, they found it mysteriously empty!)

So my acceptance of going to a farm pond in Germany to fish for carp.

When Michi and I arrived to fish, Annegret's brother-in-law, Daniel Pfeiffer, was setting up. The pond, I estimated, was 50 feet across and 300 feet long. Though fed by a clear running spring, the water in it was murky gray. Michi commented, "I believe the carp keep the bottom stirred up."

I'm sure he was right. I could see down into it only six or eight inches. To protect the fish from winged predators, they had crisscrossed 40-pound test monofilament line over the pond, so birds flying in would hit their wings and miss their prey. The taut crisscrossing meant that one had to cast into small pie-shaped sections, otherwise get hung up on the mono.

Daniel and Michi came with spinning rods, I with my seven-piece fly rod. As I started to assemble it, I noticed the guys were using pencil bobbers.

Three or four feet below each bobber were a weight and a #10 barbed hook. Daniel next opened a can of corn and put three kernels on the hook. Before casting, he tossed a small handful of corn on the water. Then he carefully threw out his line. It wasn't but a minute until the bobber went down, and he pulled in a golden carp about 12 inches long, maybe half a pound. Soon he had another, as did Michi working another pie section.

Observing this, I thought to myself: I can take these fish on a crawdad pattern. So I gave my copper Meat Whistle a try. But nothing. I let it sink deeper, where it began to hang up on the bottom. Several successful dislodgments later, it hung up for good, and I had to break it off. I then struggled to tie on a Pheasant Tail, operation completed when Patti with her good sight came by to put the tippet through the hook's eye and tie the knot. The nymph was no better. So I recruited Daniel to tie on an Elk Hair Caddis. I saw it sometimes, but Daniel saw it more. "Hit it," he instructed, but I was too late. Someone told me that carp have a brain six times bigger than a trout's and are harder to fool. I may have missed another one before my fly was too waterlogged to float.

By then Daniel was approaching double digits on the carp, and Michi was not far behind. I asked for a corn rod and was outfitted for one with a larger and brighter pencil bobber. This I could see, and ere long it moved to the side. I lifted and caught a fish.

In the course of the afternoon, I saw the bobber go down a half dozen times but landed only two more carp, all about the same foot-ish size.

Then Daniel shouted, "I got a big one," and his rod was bending. The fish moved about the pond, so Daniel had to manipulate his rod over and under the stretched mono lines to stay with his quarry. Eventually it tired and Michi got the net under him. A magnificent fish, dark gold, almost 2 feet long, weighing perhaps 8 kilos. Once photographed, the fish was returned to the water.

Golden Carp on German Pond

Daniel said, "I caught a bigger one last week near my village, and we'll have steaks from him at supper tonight."

"All right!" Michi and I said together.

The picnic supper by an open fire with the family was just wonderful. We ate fresh vegetables from Anne's parents' garden, brats and blood sausage on rolls, and baked beans. Treat number two was American s'mores, which Patti introduced. Made with roasted marshmallows and chocolate pieces smooshed between graham crackers, they were a surprise hit. The kids loved 'em. So did the adults. Treat number one, however, at least for me, was Daniel's carp. Cooked on a grill over red-hot coals, it was tender, bony—yes, Mother—and quite delicious. Its color was golden brown. So I had my "German brown in Germany."

Mission accomplished.

Now, on to Bohemia.

The Czech Republic's Vltava
(Dinners with André)

Patti and I went by train to Nuremberg and then by bus out of Germany into the Czech Republic. Our dear friend Jana Vales met us at the Prague station. She escorted us on the subway to their flat on the campus of Evangelical Theological Seminary, where her husband Jan is dean. Within an hour of our arrival I was talking by phone to Milan Hladik, director of the Czech Nymph Fly-Fishing Workshop, offered twice a year on the Vltava River in southern Bohemia, near Austria. Milan said, "Come down as soon as you can. The sessions have begun, but there is room for you. We have fishermen from many countries."

"And English, a problem?"

"It's the lingua franca."

"Good, 'cause I'm monotongued."

A day later via Student Agency bus, I was on my way south to Český Krumlov, a UNESCO World Heritage city. Riding along, I remembered my previous experience fishing in this country. Ten years ago the Valeses had taken us to southern Bohemia to their family cottage. From there we visited Jan's uncle, Jiri Vlk, who had a place on the Berounka River. Jiri invited Jan and me to fish with him. How he fished was to squeeze dough bait onto a small treble hook, which, he threw out by spinning rod and reel. He then let the bait float down the river and swing around. Some small pan fish would take the bait. We caught half a dozen. To my surprise these little fish were kept, destined for the frying pan.

That was what I knew about fishing in the Czech Republic. I was certain, though, that fishing on the River Vltava would be different, involving the fly rod, flies, and trout.

When the bus arrived I was met by Karel Krivane, who drove me up the Vltava to Rožmberk nad Vltavou—or Rožmberk. Here the workshop was headquartered in a quite nice pensión. Going to Rožmberk, I learned Karel had been coach of several Czech fly-fishing teams that won international championships. Wow! No ordinary angler he.

No sooner was my suitcase in the room than I found myself in a photo of the school's fishermen and guides: one fisherman from Belgium, four guides from the Czech Republic, four anglers from Germany, two from Switzerland, three from South Africa, and one from America, me. It was a distinguished bunch of casters, all accomplished, with several on national fly-fishing teams.

International Fishers

Still, from the Czech teachers, all wanted to learn how to fish better, especially Czech nymphing. Besides just learning the technique, my other objective was to see if this style of fishing would help me to fish in spite of visual impairment. If Czech nymphing was about *feel* as much as *sight*, then it might.

I considered this feel dimension a possibility from a brief exposure I'd had to Czech nymphing in the mid nineties. A presenter did a seminar at the Anglers Covey Fly Shop in Colorado Springs. I attended the man's seminar, watched his video, and bought some flies. A few days later I tried Czech nymphing, as I understood it—that is, with no strike indicator. It didn't seem to work for me then. Still, I believed it an effective technique. Why? Because in the international fly-fishing competitions, Czech teams were regularly the winners.

So here I was in eastern Europe for schooling. After introductions and the serving of Pilsner Urquells, I fell into conversation with an affable guy from South Africa, André Steenkamp. He asked, "What's going on in America? Donald Trump for president?"

"Yes," I said. "But we're willing to trade him for 100,000 refugees."

He laughed. "You know the man wants to put up a border fence bigger than the wall of China."

"You heard that?"

"Yeah—a wall that could be seen from space. What's he got against the Canadians?"

"Beats me. Socialized medicine?"

"You don't fool me," André said. "I believe you're a Trumper."

"Right—and hotels will fly."

At table that evening I asked André to tell me a little about himself. I learned he was a lawyer and his wife a theologian, with a PhD in spirituality. Together they'd traveled much of the world, she to ashrams, he to fisheries.

"Come to Colorado," I suggested, "and I'll find her a pulpit and you a stream."

"You know, we might."

I then noticed that André ate and led with his left hand, using his right hardly at all. So I inquired, "Do you fish as a southpaw too?"

"Ah," he responded, showing me his right hand, badly scarred, "I'm really right-handed, but a decade ago I fell through a plate glass window and severed almost everything in this mitt. Fortunately, the doctors were able to connect a nerve to my thumb, so I have feeling there for line control. I had to learn to fly fish all over."

I shivered a bit in self-reflection, then told him that I was having to learn to fish all over again too.

"How's that?"

"Macular degeneration. It's progressing well. But I'm going to use your story as inspiration. So, Lefty, how'd you do today?"

"Very well. I got a lot of little brownies in the river and one big brownie in the woods."

"Oh, most interesting."

Gavin Cooper, also from South Africa, seated beside me, whispered, "We just can't stop him."

After Thursday's breakfast in the pensión, Milan fitted me with boots for use with the waders I'd brought from the States. Then he told me I'd be guided today by Martin Musil Jr. "Martin," he added, "won the world youth fly-fishing championship a few years back, and his father is manager of the current Czech fly-fishing team."

"Impressive!" I heard myself saying.

Seeing that everyone was wadered, Martin nodded and said to David Hood of Switzerland, Marc Sonck of Belgium, and me, "Please ride in my car." We did, downriver several miles to a pullout parking area. Martin there rigged my brought-from-Colorado rod, the one I used for carp in Germany. He took off my tapered leader and tied on an untapered one, of .152-millimeter fluorocarbon.

"What 'x' is this?" I asked.

He looked at the spool and read, ".006-inch diameter, 4.74 pound test, 5x. 5x is your answer, but we go by millimeters here."

I said, "That's different," and thought, we should have gone to the international measuring system when President Eisenhower proposed it back in the '50s. Not having done so now makes figuring out speed limits and other measurements difficult in Canada, Europe, and everywhere for me and other Americans. Oh, well.

Next, Martin tied flies on the .152 mm leader. The upper fly, called a Red Tag or Hotshot Nymph, went on a dropper of 6-inches/15-cm length tied at a 90-degree angle from the leader. Two feet or 60 cm below went the point fly, essentially a Pheasant Tail. Both flies had tungsten bead heads, sizes 14 and 16, tied on nymph hooks.

Alerted by Milan to my vision problems, Martin put white Pulsa pinch-on indicators to my leader, not one but two, seven feet above the point fly. As a result I could sometimes see the indicators floating down. After several casts and drifts, I detected a take, lifted my rod, and hooked up. Turns out it was a nice rainbow, about a foot long, 30 cm. (I'm getting this metric stuff.) Later in the morning I got a second bow.

Now here's something quirky that happened. Preparing to cast up-stream, I let my flies drop into the water, next to the bank behind me. In casting forward, I was suddenly hurling a small fish through the air. He had taken the fly just as I cast. It was a 6-inch/15.24-cm chub, making me think, "An Izaak Walton fish in Bohemia." In truth, such fish are probably all over European waters. Not only did I catch a chub, but also, later, a dace, which is a whitefish. The dace was 8-inches, 20.23-cm long.

Nymphing School Shirt and Nymphing the River Vltava

After getting me stationed in a good run, Martin went downstream to check on others—and to fish. He was gone almost two hours. When he came back I asked him, "How'd you do?"

"Oh, I probably took eighty or ninety fish."

Oh my. Is this guy for real? He probably is.

What Martin most wanted to tell us about, however, was something strange. "I'd caught a small rainbow and had him just at my feet when, all of a sudden, this giant bow came up after him. The bow was way over 60 centimeters, way over." Better than two feet. "Oh my," Martin finished. "What a fish! I couldn't believe it!"

After this report, we drove to meet up with all the fishermen for lunch at a small town hilltop restaurant. The fare was of German and Polish sausage on top of sauerkraut, with sliced dumplings and red cabbage. Different. Simply Bohemian.

After lunch I was given a new guide, Jiri Pejchar, the school's deputy director. Jiri took three of us upstream of Rožmberk to where the water was quieter. He too was most competent, a ranked competitor on the Czech fly-fishing team. Happily for me he also was attentive to my sight issues, thus instructing me to do these things: cast to the side —not upstream—and do regular little strips to let the flies rise up, then drop back down, all the while swinging around. "Forget dead drifting," he instructed. "Just bring the flies back in by short pulls. What you're doing in this way is using your flies as both nymph and as streamer."

Sure enough, especially on the swing, fish would hit. One did, and I landed a dace. So I said to Jiri, "I can do this—fish by feel, more than by sight. Thanks."

He then went off to see how others were doing, but came back half an hour later. "How's it working for you?"

"I don't know. Something's wrong. I've now had six hits in a row, and they've all come off."

"Let me watch you," he said. On the next hit I lifted, connected, and immediately disconnected. "Ah, I see the problem. When you strike, you lift your rod straight up. That's a mistake. Hit the takes to the side and then reel with your rod to the side. With these flies the heavy tungsten beads tend to let the fly drop and come loose."

So next take, I responded to the side and brought the fish all the way in, holding my rod level with the water. I now enjoyed five straight catches. So my numbers for the afternoon went up to 6 for brownies, 2 for chubs, and a 4-incher called a gudgeon, which, Jiri said, is seldom caught in these waters. The little fish had hang-down tentacles on each side of his mouth. So I speculated he might be in the carp family. Adding the gudgeon to the variety of fish I'd already taken—rainbow trout, brown trout, dace, and chub—I wondered, does this constitute a Czech grand slam? Add a grayling, and it should.

Lost in such speculation, I failed to hear voices and laughter behind me. Jiri, though, spotted pilsner-filled celebrants coming down the middle of the river in pontoon boats lashed side to side. He shouted, "Watch out!"

Turning to see the flotilla coming toward me, I started to move away but found I couldn't go fast enough. Anticipating a collision, I heard myself thinking, you can just push the craft away. I tried to do that and was, instead, pushed back into the water and knocked to my knees. Water was coming in over the top of my waders when, suddenly, Jiri came in behind, grabbed me around the waist, righted me, and yelled at the frolickers, "The man is seventy-seven years old and you knocked him down, you idiots"—or "shit-heads" or "bastards" or something else strong in Czech.

He was furious, as a responsible guide might be. I, though, thought the whole thing ludicrous, and so was laughing. Perhaps it was nervous laughter, as more than a "getting a little wet" might have happened.

In any case, thank you, Jiri.

Taking off our boots and waders that evening, I told others how Jiri had pulled me from the drink. With that, Andreas Meder of Germany reported, "I pulled a big one out of the river this afternoon myself. A rainbow. He went 62 centimeters."

"How big's that?" I asked.

"About 2 feet," Martin answered. "Where'd you get him?" he asked Andreas.

"Downstream from the lower parking area."

"Well, well! I'll bet it's the same fish I saw this morning."

I then confessed, "I didn't think there were fish of such size here."

"Indeed there are," Milan, regional aquatic biologist and part-time fisheries manager for the region, inserted. "Last fall we planted some brood stock in the Vltava. Andreas's fish must have been one of them. Nice to know some survived."

That evening the group went downriver to the medieval walled city of Český Krumlov. Leaving vehicles outside the walls, we passed through the town's thick gateway on foot and walked cobblestone streets to a well-known restaurant called Gipsy Pub. There at the table, Andreas of Germany showed a cellphone picture of his catch. He passed it around as pilsners came and dinner orders were made.

Dinners came.

Fishermen at Gipsy Pub Dinner

"But," André of South Africa asked, "What is this?" He looked down at his plate and extended open palms on each side of it. We looked at our plates too. "This" was smoked pork and sauerkraut along with (1) white flour dumplings, (2) brown potato dumplings, and (3) beet red dumplings, and, I swear, a half-pound of each was on every plate—plus the usual red cabbage. André then began to raise and lower his open palms, roll his eyes searchingly, and say, "I have no words for this."

With that I snorted my beer. André repeated himself: "I have no words for this." I don't know exactly why, but his plaintive question-with-comment struck me as the funniest thing. I went to sleep that night thinking about, "What is this? I have no words for this," and laughing. I woke up at 2:45 to laugh some more.

The next morning I gave André my last copy of *Round Boys Great Adventures.* Apparently he got into the book, for on Saturday, the day the workshop ended, he urged me to stay on and fish with him and the other South Africans.

"Wish I could," I replied, "but the wife . . ."

"No, no. For, how can your wife *miss you, if you never go away*?"—to quote the dedication page in the *Round Boys.*

He had me, of course. Good man. Funny man.

On Friday, our last day on the river, Milan took me under his wing. "We planned to go after graylings today," he said, "but the grayling stream flooded overnight." So it was back to the Vltava but to different sections. "I want you to really learn the classic Czech nymphing technique with floating line and short leader." Milan led me through woods and down an embankment to a river section with good pocket water and a couple of deep runs. Looking over my rig of yesterday, Milan removed the Pulsa pinch-ons and went with eight feet of unencumbered light fluorocarbon to the double flies, saying, "Fish with the rod held high and watch only the line just where it barely enters the water. If you see any movement of the line or if you feel resistance, strike." That was the drill. He then demonstrated the way. Almost immediately he had a nice rainbow. "Now you get in there this way."

I did and, watching the line only, I saw a hesitation, so I lifted and was onto a nice rainbow myself.

"That's all there is to it," he said. "Simple."

Milan then went off downstream, fishing as he went. Before going out of sight he called back, "Look!" I looked. He had a fish thrashing on each of his two flies.

"Nice going!" I shouted, and then returned to line watching. Before long I hooked another bow, the nicest of my trip. Now I felt pretty confident, though without any more landing success. I missed a couple because it was still hard to see the line. "Doctor, my eyes," I kept singing.

Milan returned with a "Hallo!" from downstream. Just as he halloed, I had a hit. By the time he reached me, I'd landed a 10-inch fish. "A roach," Milan said, "recognizable by its orange framed eyes. He's in the whitefish family."

I replied, "I am now, even more, a compleat angler."

"If only I could have gotten you into grayling."

"No regrets, my friend. I got several *braces* on the River Dove. Think all I need now is an eel, and I'll truly have Izaak's menu."

The two of us then went upstream and, while Milan caught five or six, I managed two: a chub and a dace. Coming back, Milan forded deeper water just above the original run and proceeded to hook two rainbows. One ran him from bank to bank until netted. It was a full 18 inches and the biggest trout I personally saw taken.

Lunch again was at the hilltop restaurant. Smoked pork was served along with the usual dumplings. When the dessert came, it was two long pancakes crisscrossed, clumped with whipped cream, topped by raspberry preserves. I thought, "Pancakes on steroids!"

Heavy Crepes for Lunch

Looking at André, I saw him raise his hands and lift his eyes ceiling-ward, as if to say, "I give up!"

Tactics for fishing changed somewhat after lunch. Volker Hufsky of Germany gave me an indicator of tied-together bright strings: three inches of orange backing, followed by three inches of yellow, by three more of orange till there was a foot all told. At each end of the string were tiny O-rings. He said, "This could be something you can see better." How thoughtful.

When we made it to the river section behind a roadside service station, Milan tied on Volker's string indicator, fixing the line to the upper O-ring, the fluorocarbon to the bottom one. My flies were six and eight feet below that. He instructed me to keep the multicolored string just off the water, as I had my line earlier.

Thus armed, we crossed the river's slippery bottom to the opposite side. All the way across copious light green grass was undulating in the currents. Getting almost to the opposite bank, I saw fish rising in a slot behind a rock and, in four good casts, caught two brownies and missed a third. "Think I got it," I said to Milan.

With that, he left. Now alone, I proceeded to take four more amid the rocks and grass. Milan meanwhile went upstream and got into what must be "competitive mode," as if in a fishing tournament. Every time I looked upriver he was fighting or releasing a fish. He was a machine. Twice he doubled. When I crossed back over the slippery bottom, got out, and walked up to find him, he'd switched to a dry fly with a nymph dropper. It was a deadly combo. I myself would have switched over to hopper-dropper too, but I would have had to call him out of production to assist me, and I was content to watch. He was a wonder. In just a little over an hour he landed fifty fish! I managed to miss a fourth that number. Finally I snagged a lonely chub—my last fish of the trip.

After roast duck dinner this night, with no dumplings, Milan presented all the fishermen with a diploma saying we'd graduated the fly-fishing school. I wrote on André's diploma that he graduated *magna cum laude*

André replied, "Aw, shucks"—or its equivalent in Afrikaans.

Most happily for me, André indicated that he would seriously entertain a trip to fish Colorado waters. I hoped that yet can happen. He'd be great company, as would be any other graduates of Milan's academy.

Saturday, on the bus riding back to Prague, I made notes on why and how Czech nymphing differed from my usual way.[2] My final note reads, "I hope I can put these lessons into action when I return to Rocky Mountain waters."

By no means have I solved the main visual problem I brought to European waters for cure, namely, that of fishing through "the dimming of the light." Now, though, perhaps between the ears I have a few ideas enabling me to "go gentle into that good night" fly-fishing, not raging. Let it be so.

---

2. Several things went on the paper, the first being that one does not use a bobber. An indicator, the Czechs contend, creates unnatural movement of the flies. Second, use only 5x fluorocarbon. No tapered leader for these fishermen! Third, have tungsten beads on the flies or, conversely, use no weights. Fourth, tie the upper fly to come off the fluorocarbon at 90 degrees, thus the upper and the point fly swim freely. A couple of other things were suggested. One is to be sure your flies land on the water first, before the leader and line come down. This is facilitated by checking the forward stroke higher in the air, thus dropping the weighted nymphs in first. In addition, when doing a dry fly with a nymph, always attach the dropper to the eye of the dry, not to its bend. That way the dry floats upright, and there is one less impediment—that is, trailing tippet to be in the way, when a fish goes for the dry.

Segue to Ixthus and Closing Cast

2015 to the Present

The young man Tobias and the Archangel Michael started out toward Media, taking Tobias' dog along with them. They walked on until sunset, then camped by the Tigris River. Tobias had gone down to wash his feet in the river, when suddenly a huge fish jumped up out of the water and tried to swallow one of his feet. Tobias let out a yell, and the angel called to him, "Grab that fish! Don't let it get away." Then Tobias grabbed the fish and dragged it up on the bank.

—Tobit 6:1–4[1]

THE YEAR AFTER OUR "Europe on the Fly" trip was a year most satisfying. It included angling at Pyramid Lake in Nevada. Bruce Kuster drove me there, and we met up with Andy Blackmun, Ron Dunn, and Brian McLaren. Casting from ladders placed in the lake, we caught a few of the fabled Lahontan cutthroat trout and continued conversation about faith and fishing begun the previous summer at Ring Lake Ranch. Much of this conversation goes into the chapters to come. To be included there too are insights of Anthony Surage and Colorado College Professor of Religion David Weddle.

In 2015 into 2016, of course, I fished my "usual" Colorado, New Mexico, and Montana waters, trying out River Dove postal-slot casting and Czech nymphing.

Then came disaster.

On June 17, 2016, when Patti and I were visiting friends in Albuquerque and planning a morning walk, I went to reach for my ball cap and couldn't grasp it. Forty-five minutes later I was in the hospital, clot-buster medicine at work to slow the effect of a stroke. A week later I had carotid

1. Roughly the New Revised Standard Version of the Bible is used here and elsewhere.

artery surgery. My casting arm and page-turning right hand were rendered practically useless.

Much occupational therapy later—two years' worth—and my mind is now rightly telling my hand what to do, maybe 97 percent of the time. I bear on my neck the scar from a carotid artery operation. One scoff-at-my-plight thought has come to me, though: in *A River Runs through It,* Norman Maclean says his brother Paul believed that if he had just two more years of fishing, he would be able to "think like a trout." After neck surgery, which left a scar, I now at least can "think like a cutthroat"! Seriously though, because of the neck surgery and attendant tiredness and with my macular problems to get on the water or to proof a normal-font paragraph, I rely on a lot of help from friends and family. For that I say, "Thank you, Jesus"—Jesus, who comes to us yet, I affirm, as of old, "in human form."

Some human forms that I especially appreciate are the "Old Salts of 1937," fishing friends Dick Anderson, Joe Field, Stan Harwood, and Jim Vandermiller,[2] now all over eighty. These fishermen are also solid church-men who, I do believe, keep their passion for fishing and for Christ rightly aligned. In the summer of 2017 the octogenarians gathered at Patti and my Casablanca mountain cabin to fish, eat, imbibe, and share two hundred years' worth of collective wisdom regarding fishing and faith.

2. With Vandy, in particular, I have fished, backpacked, played guitar, composed songs, smoked and quit smoking, and seen same-age daughters grow up. For a while, when divorcing, we shared an apartment and, always agreed on politics, culture, and the religion. Quite a friend!

The Salts of '37 at Casablanca

Also in 2017, Patti and I took immediate-family members to France and Italy on vacation. It was a marvelous trip for which I told the daughters, "I'm happy to blow your inheritance on the granddaughters." A highlight of the weeks was to fish the upper Tiber River.

Daughter Melissa and Author on Tiber River

The Tiber starts in the Apennine Mountains of Tuscany, where we were ensconced, and runs past Rome to the sea. Using my recently acquired Czech nymphing technique, I managed to land a half-dozen nice brown trout and one feisty chub. Melissa took a dozen fish on a dry fly. It was an immensely satisfying international fishing day on St. Peter's river.

Speaking of St. Peter, here let me insert a story Father Richard Rohr tells about a little guy who with a group of tourists visited St. Peter's Basilica in Rome, the largest church building in the world. As the diminutive fellow looked about this cavernous, beautiful, statue-rich space, he said to the tour guide, "Pretty nice tomb for a fisherman."

Just love that story.

Now let me look ahead.

Please consider *prayer forms* remembered in the ACTIP formula: Adoration, Confession, Thanksgiving, Intercession, and Petition. It's the T-prayer I say most fervently, especially after I receive the bread and wine of a Sunday morning at worship. Eucharist/thanksgiving fills and restores my very soul—and not just on the Lord's Day. Almost every morning all through my life I've awakened saying "Thanks, God. Where's the party today?" Usually I've found it somewhere, especially with Patti-the-Party-Planner's creativity. In addition now, life's *little things* mean more: predawn hot coffee, walking Gilda in the dark, chirp of an early-awake songbird, and the fact that I can highlight text on my computer screen, press ctrl+esc, and *hear* what's said there, then use Dragon-Speak to put words on the screen to work with. All this before 6:00 a.m.

Life is full. Life is good. Later, daughter Cheril may call and ask, "Can I take you fishing today?"

Wow. Thank you, Jesus.

Beyond that day on the Tiber, I have no other international fishing accounts to share. But I have a national *wunderbar* moment in Montana to lift up. This was when I was fishing "by feel" more than "by sight." On Kuster's and my 52nd or LII—same number Super Bowl this year—trip to the Bighorn River, a gift of grace came. Here's the story:

> Starting beside a seam in the Upper Snag Hole, I began tossing my streamer rig. Much to my surprise, right away I hooked and landed a dark and beautiful 18-inch brown. I said, "My day is made, my existence justified. I can quit." But more blessings were to come: browns two, three, and four came, all by swinging my shad streamer into, then out of the current and along the seam of still water. I felt great.
>
> Kuster meanwhile nymphed the middle of the Snag. When I joined him, I threw my streamer between the main channel's flow

and the skinnier side-channel flow, to have seven or eight "touch-es" and the capture of one small brown. Going back upstream I was desultorily casting my streamer to the shallow-run side when it stopped. As I attempted to pull it out for another cast, it stayed put. Then I felt movement and saw a silver side. "Foul hooked," I thought. But no. The fly was actually in a fish's chops and the fish headed downriver hard, to soon turn and come in, seeming to say, "I've been in this rodeo before, done all the bucking I need do."

Seeing the fish, I yelled, "Bruce, I got a big one on. Come help."

He yelled back from way upstream, "Where's your fucking net?"

"In the car," I shouted.

"Of course it is," he groused, sloshing his way downstream, thus to scoop up my rainbow in his tiny net. Doing so, he exclaimed, "This one is 25 inches!"

"No way. Maybe 21."

Not having a measuring tape with us, we laid the fish alongside Bruce's rod, tail at the bottom of the butt section, nose one inch below the first feral. This "taping" we later measured out to be 25 inches, So, the longest trout I ever caught on the Bighorn.

The story above is told to say that I've had remarkable luck on the river and on lakes in spite of AMD (age-related macular degeneration) and a less than fully functional right hand. Every time I go out—albeit, transported by others—I'm giving thanks to God for "one more day."

Stay with me in the forthcoming attempt to connect the fly-fishing life with Christian faith, avocational spirituality with historic Christian religion.

CHAPTER 15

IXTHUS and Ichthyology

The earth is the Lord's and all that is in it,
the world, and those who live in it;
for God has founded it on the seas,
and established it on the rivers.

—Psalm 24:1–2

THE LAST ADVENTURE CHAPTER, "Europe on the Fly," recounted travel, fishing, and learning experiences in England, Germany, and the Czech Republic. What I want to restate is that these international opportunities happened *because* I am a Christian clergyman. This point was made previously: ministerial sabbatical studies landed me in Scotland where fishing happened; ministerial colleagues pointed Patti and me to Bali with its Indian Ocean fishing opportunity; etcetera. In broader consideration now, let us investigate how this Christian faith of mine—which may be yours too—connects to my passion for fly-fishing, which could also be yours. What's their relationship or *non*-relationship, and how might they be better aligned?

"Fish Worship" T-Shirt

In the 1960s, when I was doing campus ministry, I led weekend spiritual life and fishing retreats with male students. Some of those retreats went by the name "Ixthus and Ichthyology." Similar title was given to retreats I did with men in my Denver churches in the '70s and '80s *and* with women and men in the 2000s in Colorado Springs.

Let me begin by unpacking the "ichtus" word, say how it was and is used, and reflect a bit on the two uses in the title of this chapter. Ixthus or Ichthus or IXΘΥΣ in Greek simply means "fish." In the early church, the IXTHUS became an acronym for Christ, thus:

I=iota=J=*Iesous*=Jesus

X=chi=Ch=*Christos*=Christ

Th=theta=*Theou*=God's

U=upsilon=*huios*=Son

S=sigma=*soter*=Savior

Taken together, IXTHUS means "Jesus Christ, God's Son, Savior." Thus the fish became a—if not *the*—primary symbol in and for Christianity. Tradition has it that Christians under persecution might draw a convex line in the sand and, if another person scratched a concave line alongside the first, crossing the ends of the lines, there was a fish shape. So drawn, each sand-scratcher knew a sister or brother "in Christ" was beside him or her.

The fish stood for Christianity. I mean IXTHUS to be so understood here.

Next, regarding *ichthyology*. Ichthyology literally means "theory or knowledge or study of fish." It's a science, an academic discipline, a branch of biology. In these pages, however—as on spiritual life retreats—I use ichthyology to mean, "fishing" generally and "fly-fishing" specifically.

As noted, wherever I've been in ministry I've led versions of the Ixthus and Ichthyology retreat. Often enough, to be truthful, more of the emphasis was on the latter, ichthyology, that is, fly-fishing. In some years the retreats got other names: "Faith and Fly-Fishing," "Poetry and . . . ," "Casting and Conversations around . . ." I've probably instructed five hundred people regarding the practice of centering prayer and a thousand in the art of 10-to-2 casting.

Those who have gone on a retreat with me, sharing stories and "waving the wand" (W. B. Yeats)—as well as those with whom I've stood in awe and fished distant waters—are for me part of God's family. In my system of values, with loyalty to God through Jesus and knowing the compassionate ethics of Jesus, people are not chopped liver. They are divine-spark beings, often creative, always complex, and never uninteresting, well worth remembering—and so are lifted up in the appendix of this book. I thank them for being great co-angling and, often, co-believing companions.

In light of people valuing, consider my friend Bruce Kuster, often met in these pages and trip companion for almost six decades. A religious skeptic himself, Kuster nevertheless joins me in theological ruminations, has twice read my *Brief Christian Histories* book, and tolerates my saying grace at meals. So he is not coreligionist in the church but *mystically more* than mere acquaintance. When he says, "Put on a second weight," or "Fish the head of that pool," I *also* hear Jesus' words to his disciples, "Cast your net on the right side of the boat." If and when I follow Kuster's sagacious instructions and thereby take a fish . . . well, I can sometimes recognize that it is not "any ole Joe" standing with me there in the water.

Grace prevailing, I would so regard all whom I meet in life.

The retreats I've led in the last decade have been with Anthony Surage, mentioned earlier. Anthony was—is yet—a hard questioner, a man biblically and poetically literate, mystically inclined, and one ever given to existential angst. I love his "struggles with life" and the fact he can see fish and put me on them when there aren't any.

Both Anthony and I recognize that fly-fishing, almost inherently, has *spiritual* dimension. Certainly. So do many outdoor activities—hiking, gardening, sailing, etc. These outdoor pursuits regularly open up men and women to what may be beyond, underneath, or above whatever they are engaged in. An "awareness of Otherness" or mystical presence may be attendant to other out-in-nature doings. This is simply all to the good, and I certainly don't denigrate it. I affirm it.

But let's not deceive ourselves: such spiritualities are not Christianity. Some might want to suggest that it is so, saying, "I am closer to God on the river than in church." That is true for many. It's just that that that experience is not Christianity. Neither is "doing good" or "being a moral person" Christianity, as many seem to believe. Nor is assent to a creed or having been baptized or a number of other possible "religious" evidences. Christianity, while involving all the possibilities just now cited, is more complicated. Why? Because it is a full-blown *religion*, whereas outdoor spirituality is not.

"Awe" born of nature does not constitute the fullness of any world religion. "Sense of the nearness of God" on a mountaintop or on the seashore is not fullness for religious faith. Such numinous moments, however precious for the individual, lack philosophical underpinning, can't handle questions of ultimate meaning, and have little or nothing to say about ethics.

How often have you heard someone say, "I'm spiritual but not religious"? The statement always seems vacuous, usually meaning, "I eschew organized religion with its services, rules, practices, hypocrisies, and, especially, calls on my money. Give me freedom to relate to God and the world—or not relate—in my own private way." (This is, I believe close to what Robert Bellah calls "Sheliaism," making oneself the center of the world.)

Thus folk pursue their spiritual path, and, if it works for them . . . fine. What I suspect, though, usually is no spiritual practice at all but a "going with the flow" of whatever is the drift in culture—consumerism, twittering, entertainment absorption, following sports, or patriotic militarism. But say there is something deeper, even transcendent, that guides them, and not just "getting blown around by the culture." Say they experience holy highs in horseback riding, rock climbing, or jogging. I'm thinking here of Eric Liddell in *Chariots of Fire* proclaiming, "When I run fast, I feel His [God's] pleasure."

Please note, I am not excluding fly-fishing, for it too has spirituality in it, or, as I say, *can* have such.

In any and all of these, though, I wonder, if we haven't shortchanged neighbor, the world, God, and ourselves.

There are, I am contending, important things absent in most spiritualities, whether *intentional spirituality* (Native American, transcendental meditation, integral yoga, etc.) or *coincidental spirituality* (as in fly-fishing, skiing, walking in the woods, etc.). Consider what might be missing.

The first is community. In my way of thinking, spirituality is too individualistic. The "I alone" deciding what is the good, true, and beautiful is too easily in error. There is limited *socii* to support or challenge the "I." Community usually does exist in religions, wrapped up in synagogue, mosque, temple, or ashram. In Christianity it is called "belonging to the body of Christ." The body exists to nurture, support, instruct, correct, and motivate the individual to wholeness in a faith *not* of his or her own making. Religion connects one to others and broadens boundaries. That is certainly Yale Divinity School Miroslav Volf's point in *Flourishing: Why We Need Religion in a Globalized World*.

Consider too that most spiritualities are just too caught up in the moment, too much "here and now," too transitory. They lack backbone supplied by the past, and they have limited vision of the future. The roots are shallow and the hopes dim, being so caught up in the now. Guidance from *Torah, Qur'an*, or *Bhagavad Gita* is not sought, nor are hope and work for the kingdom of heaven or nirvana entered into. Where is Moses or Lao Tzu to guide one or the Buddha or Muhammad to beckon? Answer: they in their ancient wisdom and prescriptions for the future are lost in "the present moment," however titillating that moment may be. People of substantive faith need historical grounding and enlivening vision.

God found on the golf course or encountered by the lake, however wonderful, is short on many essentials that make and keep life human. Let me list some from Christianity. Consider caring community, education for children and adults, attending to and debating sacred texts, being sustained by helpful ritual and ceremonies (e.g., confession and absolution or those for "hatching, matching, and dispatching"), praying with the saints, chanting and hymn singing, going on a work project, and, shudder, other *institutionalizations*: "Pass the offering plate, please." Spare me from people who are more spiritual than God, who know nothing about incarnation—the Spirit becoming flesh.

About the arts, a person not in a "thick religion" may miss much, for example, in Christianity, Bach's *Mass in B Minor*, Rembrandt's *Return of the Prodigal*, Michelangelo's *Pieta*, Divine Liturgy/Drama (which could include "bells and smells"), or preaching of the Word which "comforts the afflicted and afflicts the comfortable."

While fly-fishing and travel, the foci of this book, are pastimes of significant personal satisfaction, even a comfort to the soul, we'll not call such Christian.

Now I'm pressed to define what escapes facile definition, namely, *Christianity*. It involves (1) believing, (2) belonging, and (3) behaving: *believing* in God through Jesus as God's Anointed (Christ), *belonging* to the body of Christ (the church), and *behaving* in Christ-like ways (lovingly, justly).

I am struggling, I believe you can appreciate, to find a way to adequately describe how my *religion*, Christianity, is or can be compatible with—even complementary to—my *passion* for fly-fishing, and vice versa. They are different yet overlap. Consider the two coming together in a VENN or primary diagram.

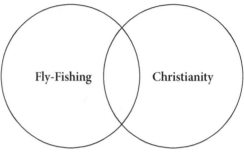

The circles overlap—or *can* overlap—each other in two ways, by (1) intentional connection and (2) awareness of grace. There can be a *bringing of* known Christian things to the activity of angling, and the blessed *discovery of* faith-enhancing dimension in fishing. Thought and awareness are each involved.

By "taking thought" one may connect something experienced on the water with what he or she knows to be part of his or her basic faith. For example, when we have a trout in a landing net, we might consciously recall "the miraculous draught of fishes" (John 21:11) that the disciples, rightly following Jesus' instructions, successfully lifted up. Such might even lead a person to rejoice in his or her being lifted up, "by the Savior," from spiritual or moral degradation, if that is the case. Both these illustrate bringing one's Christianity *to* the water.

A second way of understanding faith and fly-fishing's interaction is "by becoming aware." Recognize that unbidden precious Christian gifts can come *from* angling, if we are attentive and appreciative. Restoration of the soul, for example, much needed by folk caught in burnout, can come with time on the water. To this point I am much impressed with the thought of Jesus saying, "*My peace I give you*—which you, O man/O woman, can't grasp. It's a gift." By grace we also may become aware of individual and corporate sin. Last year I caught a fish using a barbed hook. Such for me is a "don't do that," a sin. To make the wrong convict me further, I also discovered that fish's mandible (part of its outer jaw) had been torn off by an earlier fisherman who'd likely used a barbed hook too. Then the words of Isaiah 6:5 came crashing in: "Woe is me! For I am a man of unclean lips and I dwell in the midst of a people of unclean lips."

We are called to take our faith to the activity of fishing better and to better attend to what is happening while fishing that goes along with our religion, not compartmentalizing either.

Let me give additional illustration of *taking faith* to fly-fishing by thought and *drawing out from the sport* by attentiveness. Start with "taking to." Consider the fellow who comes onto your beat and messes up the hole. You may want to yell at him, "Get the *blank* out, jerk," but you *could* remember he too is a child of God—even one for whom Christ died—and respond with gentler words, "Hey, brother, I wonder . . ."

Illustrative of "drawing out" from fishing that, which aligns with faith, we can be more fully appreciative of a mayfly hatch that comes on pretty mysteriously—by grace—to turn catch-less hours into a double-digit morning. For which we ejaculate, "Thank you, Lord!" whether God had anything to do with it or not. Rising, hungry, fly-sipping fish come as a gift, an amazing grace.

Consider something as simple as shore lunch shared with com-*pan*ions—that is, those with whom we "break bread." Luke tells us that at the table on the road to Emmaus the disciples' eyes "were opened in the breaking of the bread." If we are attentive, it could happen again, beneath a pine, overlooking the Arkansas River, chicken salad sandwich in hand, seated beside a bud.

The idea in "taking thought to" and "becoming aware of" is ultimately to positively "relate all things to God." If we want. If we choose. If we're open.

One foggy morning on Patterson Lake in Manitoba, I was rowing my pontoon boat out to find my friend Bruce. He and his boat, though, were lost in the mist. I thought I saw him. Then I didn't. I decided I was close to being in what the mystics call "the cloud of unknowing," such as caught up Jesus and the disciples on the Mount of Transfiguration. My moment was not, however, overwhelming *mysterium tremendum*, which biblical scholar Rudolf Otto talks about in *The Idea of the Holy*. Yet it was, made so by intentional connection and awareness.

Which is my point.

A Misty Morning Begins to Lift

That is, I think, how one's Christianity best relates to angling, by act of conscious will, albeit sometimes aided by the gift or grace of the Spirit who "In the beginning moved over the face of the water" (Genesis 1:1) . . . and still does.

Feel for it. Think on it. Pray for it.

In this book I have let my Christianity and clergy perspective slip in on the fishing travels at times but, I pray, never offensively or—horrors—boringly so. The Christian way and fly-fishing are both too life-vitalizing for that to happen.

Let Christians and fly-fishers, perhaps one and the same, say, "Amen!"

CHAPTER 16

Closing Cast: On the Meaning of Fishing

I live my life in widening circles
that reach out across the world.
I may not complete this last one
but I give myself to it.

I circle around God, around the primordial tower.
I've been circling for thousands of years
and I still don't know: am I a falcon,
a storm, or a great song?

—Rainer Maria Rilke, *Book of Hours: Love Poems to God, I, 2*

I RECEIVED A POSTCARD, quite provocative. It shows a man in a boat with a large fish and a caption reading, "Many men go fishing all of their lives without knowing that it is not fish they are after—Henry David Thoreau." Doubtless most anglers have heard the quote.

Thoreau Quote and Picture to Ponder

The quote certainly sounds like something Thoreau, author of *Walden Pond* and a fisherman himself, would say. He didn't pen it though. Its most accurate wording resides in E. T. Brown's *Not without Prejudice: Essays on Assorted Subjects.* In that essay Brown says, "It is really not fish men are after. It is philosophic meditation."[1] Brown speaks true—and, I will come back to his truth shortly—but Thoreau, however misquoted, is heuristically useful. So . . .

"Not after fish?" I stammer. How can that be? If it is not fish, then for what have I given so much of my life, spent so many dollars, and for this book alone traveled over 100,000 miles? Consider with me *suspects* for what it might be we have been "after."

Begin, though, allowing that Thoreau could be in error, wrong in suggesting men and women are after something other than fish when going down to the crawdad hole. Maybe it is *fish—and only fish*—for life and livelihood most are after. The purpose is to put food on the table or in the market. For most of the hungry world, for sure, this is the truth. Likely such is not so for readers of this book. You, I suspect, are into catch-and-release. Something other than trout almondine is what you are after. But let's not forget it could be physical life itself that motivates probably 95% of the world's anglers.

Beyond physical sustenance, suspect number two is *escape*—escape from people and escape from work. Some years ago the Colorado Division of Wildlife did a survey of fishers. They wanted to ascertain the reasons men—and I think it was just men—go fishing. The number one reason given, as I remember, was "to get away from my wife." Escape may be what many are after when they go a'fishin'—or when other people (often women)

---

1. E. T. Brown, *Not without Prejudice: Essays on Assorted Subjects* (Melbourne: Cheshire, 1955), p. 142.

go a'shoppin'. Truth be told, lots of us live in houses so hot, we need cool water or air-conditioned malls to continue to function.

Related to escape from domestic tension is escape from work. What we do to make a living may be so unfulfilling that time chasing trout is the best remedy for job stress. Regularly you can hear folk repeat the bromide, "The worst day fishing beats the best day working."

Getting away, then, is suspect number two in this investigation to discover what anglers are after, if not fish.

A third major suspect in the line-up motivating piscatorial effort is *challenge and accomplishment*. That may be what most makes the angling life alluring. Anglers keep a pretty close tally of the number of fish caught on their trips and always take pictures of the big ones.

Trophy Trout ... and ... Typical Take

Definitely there can be personal satisfaction in having pitted one's skills against an oft-elusive quarry to come out the winner. Never mind that a fish's brain is no bigger than a breadcrumb! Challenge and success are not unimportant to humans. What Spanish philosopher Ortega y Gasset says about hunting applies equally well to fishing:

> One does not hunt in order to kill; on the contrary, one kills in order to have hunted. If one were to present the sportsmen with the death of the animal as a gift he would refuse it. What he is after is having to win it to conquer the surly brood through his own effort and skill.[2]

Another thing about challenge, competition, and winning: it is not just with fish we engage, but other anglers. Sad to admit, it seems that our little egos need to be bolstered by besting a fella or fem fisherperson. What we may be after is self-affirmation vis-à-vis others.

These things about food, escape, and challenge/accomplishment, I believe, are not that to which Thoreau alludes. So what other possibilities are there for the meaning of our sport?

Here's one: fishing is for *excitement*. Who is to say that joy and elation are not what we need to make and keep life human? I tell you, it is simply the best to hook into a big fish, have him catapult into the air, throwing water as he turns, then dive to the depths, there to shake his head, having gotten you well into your backing. What a thrill! The adrenaline rush could be what it's all about. To push fishing into deeper socio-psychological consideration, much less philosophical-theological speculation could be beside the point. One song says, "Girls just wanna have fun." Guys do too. That may be reason a-plenty for many—perhaps most—to engage in angling.

Readers uninterested in further reflection on "meaning" could close the book here. You would depart with my thanks for going this far.

Still, I believe with Thoreau that, in the fishing life, ultimately we are after something less transitory than streamside excitement. Something of existential importance is involved in this passion of ours.

Consider yet another suspect. It is *peace*. Let me illustrate. My wife says that when I come home from a day on the water, I appear settled, "becalmed," she says. If that is so, I know why. To have concentrated the mind for several hours on a little puff of fur-and-hair floating over riffles fixes one's attention and excludes all other thoughts. The mind is cleared for a spell. Fishing, then, becomes a branch of soul-satisfying meditation, even as suggested in Izaak Walton's classic, *The Compleat Angler*. Here are his words spoken to his colleague Charles Cotton on the subject:

2. From his *Essay on Hunting,* exact citation lost.

Indeed, my good scholar, we may say of angling, as Dr. Boteler said
of strawberries, "Doubtless God could have made a better berry,
but doubtless God never did"; and so (if I might be judge), "God
never made a more calm, innocent recreation than angling,"[3]

In angling something like an alternate state of consciousness, of which the
Buddhists speak, may transpire. What we receive by fishing could be tran-
quility of soul. That is most excellent. If found or given, peace could be quite
enough, the answer for what is sought.

Peaceful Rest on a Riverbank

3. Izaak Walton, *The Compleat Angler* (New York: Weathervane Books, 1975), p.
114.

So again, my friend, no need to go deeper in this inquiry. Stop, if you're satisfied. Depart in peace.

For me, though, the meaning of fishing has not yet been fully plumbed. I posit that *something ultimate* may be what we are "really after." Begin in consideration of longing, deep longing, longing for that which is more illusive than the wariest brown trout but ever more important.

William Butler Yeats's poem, "The Song of Wandering Aengus" sets the search scene. In this poem the fisherman catches a "little trout" that becomes a "glimmering girl with apple blossoms in her hair" who calls his name then "vanishes in brightening air." Aengus longs for her, saying:

> *Though I am old with wandering*
>
> *Through hollow lands and hilly lands,*
>
> *I will find out where she has gone,*
>
> *And kiss her lips and take her hands;*
>
> *And walk among long dappled grass,*
>
> *And pluck till time and times are done.*
>
> *The silver apples of the moon,*
>
> *The golden apples of the sun.*

This great poem resonates with anglers—this one, anyway. We long not for a literal glimmering girl but for what she symbolizes, namely, the Good, the True, and the Beautiful, a.k.a. the Platonic Trinity.

Fishing, like gardening, great music, and a few other activities, can intimate—and "intimate" is the operative word here—the numinous, open us to the eternal verities, even the Divine.

Do we ever really get there? Probably not. The girl with apple blossoms in her hair is ever elusive. Plato has it right: we are prisoners in a cave, our backs chained to one wall. On the opposite wall of our cave we can see flickering shadows of what is real as the real passes on a ledge behind us in front of fire light. We prisoners, however, can never see the Perfect Forms themselves. By the shadows, however, we get intimations of that which is real, is eternal, is essential.

What "all their life" anglers are "really after" (Thoreau again) is intimated through three primary things: PLACE, PEOPLE, and WATER. Consider them with me.

First of all, PLACE of fishing is important. In this book, nearly twenty countries, states, and provinces have been visited. From my life I can identify more than four hundred angled in waters. I have loved these many places and sometimes found myself entranced there.

When I retired from active pastoral ministry a decade ago, I received a plaque that reads,

Life Is Not Measured

By The Number Of

Breaths We Take,

But By The Moments

That Take

Our Breath Away

Some places and conditions provide moments that take us beyond ourselves in a commanding way. Quick to my mind come two such moments touched on in this book.

One is on Mount Misheguk overlooking the Kugururok River in Alaska. The second is standing on basement-of-time metamorphic rocks of the Derwent River in Tasmania. Both were transcendent moments created by place. I've been to some incredible, far-out locales, seen the dawn's early light shimmering over New Zealand's Karamea River, watched the northern lights dance on Keeper Lake in Ontario, been in the shadow of British Columbia's purple mountain majesty, and stared deeply into the iridescent blue-green waters of the Caribbean.

Fishing trips, I do believe, can take folk out of the mundane, put them close to beauty in a special world apart or beyond, however momentarily. Noted author and fly-fisherman Robert Traver says it most impressively: "I fish because I love to. Because I love the environs where trout are found, which are invariably beautiful."

Place, I'm contending, can create *wonder* or *awe*, a great state to be in. It is nonpareil, a true prime suspect as to what we may be after.

Note, though, awe or wonder cannot be coerced. Such happens *to* us, not *by* us. The sense of sublime that I am talking about, comes by grace, usually in an unscripted moment. For instance, I was once on my knees releasing a magnificently colored cutthroat trout, when I heard a honk, looked up, and beheld Canada geese winging through high clouds in tight formation. In that moment I was undone, transported, connected to eternity. It made me want to stay on my knees, as an old hymn puts it, "lost in wonder, love, and praise." What a great way, by grace, to be lost!

Much of soul significance happens in and through special places, even a sense of a *return to one's deepest roots*. My love of lakes and streams in large grasslands and rolling hills may be part of what Harvard scientist E. O. Wilson, in his book *Biophilia*, calls "the savannah gestalt." This is an innate attraction, encoded in our genes, to landscapes resembling the savannahs of Africa, where humanity evolved two million years ago. Vast, open space, like South Park in Colorado, through which a trout stream meanders, may kindle a deep recessed emotional connection to a very ancient past, to primordial roots—which connection we well may be after.

Wow.

"Watery" Savannah-Like Gestalts

Now consider another fruitful category of intimation: PEOPLE.

While the glimmering girl will never be found, she just may exist veiled in those with whom we fish. A person can, of course, fish alone, but most times we do so in company. The stories shared in this book, most certainly, are all bound up with acquaintances, friends, and family. They are the ones who make life interesting, frequently challenging, sometimes ludicrous, but regularly meaningful. Often enough they laugh and cry with us, accepting us "warts and all." They matter. They matter in and of themselves, but especially for the instrumental role they play. They provide *companionship*—even *love*—which now must be high on the "meaning of fishing" suspect list. To be up to your waders with a friend, share a can of sardines, sing too loudly and off-key, and ponder things (politics, religion, or hackle feathers) together is important. The associations make for meaning.

To be deeply connected may be to know *you are not alone in this world*, and that may be to know *you are not alone in the universe*. To believe in your head and trust in your heart that you are connected to the universe is foundational in religious faith. One's in-the-boat companions can intimate the Holy.

The great Jewish philosopher Martin Buber contends that between every I and thou stands a third, that is, God. The folk with whom we break bread, our *com*/with-*pan*/bread-*ions*/friends, make connection to the Third possible.

Between Every I and Thou Is God? . . . or a Woman?

Russian novelist Ivan Turgenev tells a story about a man standing in a crowd listening to a speech. After a while he has this strange feeling that Christ is right behind him. He looks over his shoulder, to conclude, "It was just a man standing there, just an ordinary man with an ordinary face." So he returns to listen to the speaker. Still he feels that Christ is there, right behind him. That is precisely how Christ comes—hidden in the other, yet revealed.

(Christ is for Christians, of course, *the* "Great Mediator"/Intimator. Lest we forget.)

Anthony Surage in *Bringing Back Eden* suggests that "the stranger" whom we meet on the river can be a conduit of grace. If we are but open to that possibility, he says, that stranger can mediate the Holy One.

In my long lifetime I have fished, I know, with over two thousand people. Twelve hundred of them I can still name—see the appendix. In the pages of this book you met Kuster, Hallsten, Spellato, and Onalik in the "Alaska Unplanned" story alone. Colorful characters. For certain, they along with others hold a special place in my heart. They've provided rich meaning. They are fishing's gift, helping me connect better in this world, even to the World Beyond.

Now, let us turn to the third and final mediating category: WATER.

In the closing line of his great novella *A River Runs Through It*, Norman Maclean says, "I am haunted by waters." If "haunted," means "made holy"—and I believe it does—then what Maclean is saying is that water has a special power. There is something about water that draws us to it, holds us fast, and invites us to go deeper.

The pre-Socratic philosopher Thales of Miletus (ca. 624–547 BCE) declared water to be the basis of all things, more so than the other contenders: fire, air, and earth. The world floats like wood on water, Thales held. Certainly 71 percent of the globe's surface is so covered, and beneath the surface of the oceans are vast topography, plant and animal life, and movement. Such things humans are just beginning to appreciate. Maybe we are drawn to water as like to like, the average human body being 60 percent water, our brains 70 percent. All of which is to say that we are of water and are attracted to it in some primal way. We are carried and born in water, often baptized in it. In water we wade, swim, and bathe. By "cool, clear water" thirst is quenched. W. H. Auden observes, "Thousands have lived without love, none without water."

Recently I listened on audiotape to biologist and researcher Wallace Jay Nichols's book *Blue Mind*. The subtitle is *The Surprising Science That Shows How Being Near, In, On, or Under Water Can Make You Happier, Healthier, More Connected, and Better at What You Do*. Nichols contends we are hard-wired to water, drawn to it as by nothing else. We have, he says, a "blue" or water "mind."

(Imagine This Fishing Scene "Blue")

Utilizing the latest research in neuroscience, behavioral psychology, and sociology, he shows how proximity to water reduces stress, fosters well-being, improves creativity, and even increases compassion. If E. O. Wilson in *Biophilia* says savannah-like landscapes take us back two million years to Africa, water somehow touches neurons that recall the beginning of life four billion years ago!

We're talking about what *religio* in the word "religion" means: a "binding back," a return to that from which we came. Though Nichols doesn't say it, it could be God we're talking about. Water intimates the *Creator* and brings us back to humanity's start "in the beginning" (Genesis 1:1).

In 1976 I visited the Whitney Museum of Western Art in Cody, Wyoming. There I was stopped in my museum wandering by a large oil painting called *The Fisherman*. The canvas showed a bare-chested Native American man sitting in the middle of a canoe, his head and body bent forward, looking into the deep. In the fingers of his right hand was a horsehair line going straight down. Where the line broke the surface was an ever-so-slight circle-ripple, the only feel of movement in the painting. There was no hint of breeze on the water nor stir of leaf in the birch trees. The canoe, the man, the sky—everything—was completely calm. Because of that thin cord, however, the viewer still felt there was something moving, something out of sight, beneath the surface, something of great consequence to this fisherman. The fisherman was plumbing the depths.

I was totally mesmerized by the painting, pulled in and pulled down by the horsehair line, taken into What Is Below. Were there music to go with this painting, it could have been Van Morrison's evocative song "The Mystery."

I am contending that the waters we fish can bring us closer to what, in fishing, we really "are after": *Mystery* with a capital M.

At Ring Lake Ranch in Wyoming one summer evening, my clergy colleague Ron Dunn, theologian Brian McLaren, Ring Lake Ranch manager Andy Blackmun, and I had an open conversation about the meaning of fishing. For that occasion, Ron read an original piece called "Just One More Cast." Here is one of its insightful paragraphs:

> *I hold to the premise that there is a connection between my pursuit of fishing and my pursuit of the Holy Mystery of faith. Indeed, it may well be that it is within the element of mystery that this link is forged. For, even as so much of my faith pursuit is enshrouded in mystery, so I have discovered a sense of mystery in the experience of fishing.* '

How well Ron puts this! The preacher in me and the much-traveled, trying-to-be-aware fisherman in me now merge into one. In lieu of an answer to the question, "What's it all about?" or "What is it, Henry David, that we are after?" I tender a one-word response: mystery, deep sustaining Mystery, a.k.a. *God.*

Epilogue

Thank you, my friend, for following this story and these stories.
Vaya con Dios.

Bruce Kuster in Reverie on Dock . . .
Dad and Daughter Going Down the Road

Friends with Whom I Have Fished

A

Tommy Abercrombie

Angie Adams

Melissa White
    Addington

Kyle Addington

Al Almanza

Gary Almeida

Ray Almond

Tim Almond

Bill Anderson

Dave Anderson

Dick Anderson

Doug Anderson

Stuart Andrews

Tim Anglin

Bill Anthony

Bryan Aquillar

Jim Arkebauer

Roger Armstrong

Jim Auman

Austin of Dubois

B

Bob Backus

Jason Baker

Matt Baker

Jocelyn Bakkemo

Rick Baker

Harry Barkdahl

Peg Bartlett

Steve Bassett

Dan Baeti

Bob Ball

Lindy Baer

Terry Belcher

Crosby Bean

Phil Benton

Fawn Bell

Joleen Bell

Rod Bell

Chuck Benson

Carol Bilbrey

Gary Bilbrey

Lou Bintner

Steve Biscontine

Andy Blackmun

Greg Blessing

Bill Boekel

Homer Bollinger

Bali Captain Bogan

Bali Mate Kadet

Richard Bondi

Harry Borowski

Frank Bowman

Dennis Brady

Nancy Brady

Barry Brandt

Mike Brandt

Curt Brekke

Kent Brekke

Kenny Bretag

Travis Brinkhoff

Benjamin Broadbent

Allan Brockway

Ann Brown

Dan Brown

Doug Brown

Steve Brown

Jeff Bullen
Ken Bundy
Karen Burt

Leslie Burton
Joe Butler
Bob Butterly & Son

Otto Butterly
Joan Byers

C

Kelly Cain
Ian Caiozzi
Luke Cammack
Jeff Campagna
JJ Carl
Chris Carlson
Mary Kay Carlson
Dave Carragher
Gary Carbaugh
Rick Carbaugh
Ruth Cacuck
Dave Carragher
Bob Carlton
Jim Carris
Bob Casey

Jane Cauvel
Brian Chan
Ralph Chaney
Miranda Cherry
Matthew Chinchilla
Hal Chorpenning
Sarah Christian
Bob Churchill
Jim Clamp
Tim Clark
Bruce Clatterbaugh
Dick Cleverly
Russ Clewly
Barry Cohen
David Cole

Paul Coleman
Sarah Warren Coleman
Paco & Caspar
  Coleman
Tyan Collins
Jay Colter
Don Cooper
Gavin Cooper
Jim Crimer
Bev Chrisoff
John Chrisoff
Mike Craig
Galen Crowder
Shirley Cruthers

D

Oliver Daley
Steve Dally
Fred Day
Ryan Daniels
Marri Anne Danely
Dick Danninfelser
Steve Davis
Uncle Henry Davis
Russ Davis
Tomas Dawson
Fred Day
Rob DeCosta

Richard Deherrara
Chad DeKaim
Paul DeLaro
Mary Ann Delapp
Jack Dennis
Don Densman
Luis Diaz
Allen Dodge
Mary Dee Dodge
Marianne Donelly
Sara Doud
John Doughty

Paul Dubois
Tracy DuChame
Marsha Duncan
Rich Duncan
Ron Dunn
Jude Duran
Jack Duerson
Dwight of Connecticut
Alex Dyer
Dewey Dyer

E

Jon Eason
Kathryn Eastburn
Don Eberhart
Larry Edwards
Nancy Ekberg
Eydie Elkins
Bob Ellis
Allen Elser

Denise Ellsworth
Mike Emerling
Mike Emerson
Vaughn Emerson
Mel Emeigh
Chuck English
Donn Erickson
Mike Escobar

Jerry Eslinger
Bob Essig
Don Everhart
Benjamin Everett
Nathanial Everett
Ralph Everett

F

Jim Faris
Chuck Fothergiil
Dave Farney
Sherny Farney
John Feek
Steve Ferguson
Michael Feuchter
Annegret H. Feuchter

Marlon Fick
Joe Field
Dennis Fisher
Phil Fiese
Andy Finn
Dennis Fischer
Paul Fitzgerald
Herman Fleishman

Tom Francis
Guy Fredello
Jim French
Nelson Frissell
Sue Frizzell
Dale Fulton
Ben Furimsky

G

Chauncey Gardener!
Abe Gaspar
Georg Gehrung
Tim Geller
Vic Geller
Ed Geuigen
George Gibbins
Clarence Giese
Gilda the Golden!
Bud Gildehaus

Bryan Gillespie
Charles Gillespie
Miriam Glazer
Tricia Gleason
Nora Gledich
John Gordon
Steve Gossage
Ron Granneman
Stan Grater
Mark Gray

Barbara Grinstad
Dick Grinstad
Daphne Greenwood
O'Ray Greybar
Deb Grohs
Everett Groseclose
Charlie Groshans
Jimmy Sue Guggenheim

H

Kea Haas
Peter Hagedorn
Janis Hahn
Matt Halenkamp
Michael Halenkamp
Christine Hall
Roger Hall
John Hallsten
John Hallsten, Jr.
Peter Hallsten
Vic Hallsten
Jennie
   Handt-Henderson
Sally Hill
Dave Harmon
Harmon Family
Lee Harmon
John Harmon
Jet Harper

Ben Hart
Greg Hart
Gary Hart(pence)
Lee Hart(pence)
Gay Hatler
Jack Harvey
Matt Harwood
Stan Harwood
Peggy Harrel
Stuart Haskins
Myron Hayward
Frank Hecert
Steve Hemken
Nathan Henderson
Terry Henderson
Bruce Henry
Dave Herbert
Rich Herzfeldt

Steve Hilbers
Milan Hladik
Del Hokanson
Pete Hokanson
Hannah Hokanson
Kea Hokanson
David Holmgren
Mark Holiday
Cy Holladay
Jim Holladay
Lynn Shelton Holladay
David Holmgren
Gordon Honey
David Hood
Ken Hudson
Sam Hudson
Matt Humphry
Volker Hufsky

I

Italian Guide

J

Jaren Jackson
Tim Jackson
Eric Jacobson
Lisa Jacobson
Ronnie Jacobson
Vic Jacobson
Brent Jakobson
Jeff Jaestrab

George Jamieson
Jamoca Almond Fudge!
Chris Jeffers
Kevin Jeffries
Jim Jepperson
Jerome Jefferson
Darrell Johnson
Dave Johnson

Matt "Bear" Johnson
Jim Johnson
Renner Johnson
Richard Johnson
Shawna Johnson
Judy Jones

K

Don Kast
Brad Kastner
Dave Kastner
Allen Keegan
Jean Keeley
George Kelley
John Kelly
Ryan Kelly
Steve Kern
Carol Keenan
Julie Kiley

Andy Kim
Karel Krivane
Les Kitchen
Charles Kiskiras
Dennis Kleinsasser
Steffan Knapp
George Knox
Jeanie Koeneman
Lynn Koeneman
John Koenig
Frank Koenigsamen

Fred Kolb
Larry Kolz
Burl Kreps
Kathy Kripps
Karel Krivanec
Bob Krumm
John Kurish
Blair Kuster
Bruce Kuster
Gerald Kuster

L

Dave LaFrance
Bruce Lane
Michelle Larkin
Eric Larson
Tom Laswell
Tom Law
Hank Lawshe
Ken "Luby" Lebrand
George LeBus
Marsha Lee
Patty Lee
Dan Leftwich
Becky Leinweber

Dave Leinweber
Lee Lehmkuhl
Neil Lehmkuhl
Don LeTort
Kate Warren Lewis
Mike Lewis
Henry Lewis
Tom Light
Phil Lighty
Bob Limpert
Dan Limpert
Gloria Limpert
Dick Limpert

George Limpert
Robbie Limpert
Robert Limpert
Clete Lipinksi
Dick Littrell
Brad Loper
Cheril White Loper
Ray Lopez
Jim "Stretch" Loughery
Joyce Loughery
Neil Luehring
Al Lutimsky
Audrey Lutimsky

M

Mike of Edinburgh
John Machin
Alyssa Manuliak
Bruce Manuliak
Kim Manuliak

Gabe Magtutu
Mark Mahler
Al Makai
Bob Mapleton
Andrew Markus

Chris Marshall
John Martin
Greg Martin
Paul Martinez
Lisa Mason

Jim Matson
Jim Maurer
Jody McCoy
Luclann McEvoy
Dick McGuire
Brian McLaren
Andreas Meder
Terry Meehan
Gary Mertz
Ayn Miller

Lori Miller
Mark Miller
Tom Minihan
Richie Montelli
Oren Moore
Sandy Moore
Gary Morhess
Dan Moorhusen
James Moorhusen
Jim Moorhusen

Mike Moorhusen
Sunny Moorhusen
Bob Morenski
Mo Morrow
Paul Moraco
Peggy Moraco
Jared Morris
Martin Musil, Jr.

N

Mark Neighbors
Mark Neshit

Terry Nicholson
Dorothy Nye

O

Richard Obey
Donnie Ogden
Glenn Ogden

Ray O'Mara
Victor Onalik
Ian Osborn

Jan Otto

P/Q

Anna Padilla
Dennis Padilla
Josh Painter
Eduardo Pantoja
Anthony Parker
Dave Parker
J. D. Parker
Jiri Pejchar

Jim Perry
John Peters
Bruce Peterson
Connecticut Peterson
Bob Petrik
Marilyn Petrik
John Pierce
Policeman Earl

Joann Porter
Jack Poynter
Ford Price
Willis Price
Sue Prendiger
Richard Pulaski

R

John Rainey
Ruben Rainey
Robert Ramirez

Chris Ramos
Nick Rarick
Bruce Rasmussen

Bob Reese
Carol Reese
Tom Rehling

Dana Resnick

Denny Rickards

Berkeley Rich

Woody Richardson

Gordon Riegel

Lisa Riegel

Carl Roberts

Cale Robinson

Gordy Rockafellow

Nancy Rockafellow

Scott Rockafellow

Sandra Rooney

Murray Ross

Chuck Rudolph

Stuart Rundenell

Buck Rush

Rochelle Ryan

S

Jim Saffer

Victor Saizar

Bob Sales

Bob Salie

Mike Sayler

Kent Saltonstall

Frank Sanborn

Nick Sanborn, Jr.

Nick Sanborn, Sr.

Sherry Sargent

Scott Saunders

Manfred Sauer

Phil Savage

Bill Sayers

Mike Saylers

Diane Schillinger

Rich Schillinger

Bob Schluter

Bill Schleicert

Paul Schwotzer

Bill Scott

David Sears

Harry Sebern

Stan Sedgwick

Alan Severn

Dave Seyfert

Scott Shackelford

Bill Shapell

Benson Shaw

Van Shaw

Sally Sheets

Sandy Shelton

Sid Shelton

Rick Shick

Greg Shoop

Son Shoop

Al Skinner

Bill Smith

Ron Smith

Roy Smith

Erin Sokol

Curtis Songer

Naomi Songer

Mike Spangler

Arnie Sparnins

Mike Spellato

Mike Spillman

Johnny Stafford

Rick Stafford

Rick Steffen

Jackson Straight

Bob Stalcup

André Steenkamp

John Stefonik

Dean Stephenson

John Stoeffels

Mike Sulkesky

Anthony Surage

Chloe Surage

Sophia Surage

Wayan Suwinton

Paul Swanson

T

Jean Tidball

Milt Tiede

John of Tillamook

Tim of L. Powell

Amanda Jean Taylor

Paul Taylor

Peter Terpenning

Rollie Thedford

Tim Their

Christopher Thomas

Jon Tomas

Peter Thomas

Scott Thomas
Sara Thomas
Valerie Thompson
Gervaise "Bill"
    Tompkins

John Toline
Rich Tosches
Cliff Towers
Bob Tucker

Bobbye Tucker
Polly Tucker
Dan Tynan

U

Leonard Urban

V

Jan Vales
Jana Vales
Robert van Ransburg
Carl Vance
Jim Vandermiller

Venezuela *Logona*
    Guides:
Jose, Elias, Alejandro,
    Braulio, Achilles
    Luis
Venezuela *Los Roques*
    Guides:

William, Danny,
    Claudi, Exis,
    Julio, Vladimir
Amanda Verheul
Ben Verheul
Jiri Vlk

W

Doug Wagner
Scott Wagner
Thomas Wagner
Doug Walker
Jim Warn
Bob Warren
Bruce Warren
Jane Warren
Scott Warren
Keith Watson
Craig Waters
David Weddle
Ben "Rusty" Weeks
Bill Weiss
Craig Weisser
Kermit Wells

David Wenzlau
Nancy Wenzlau
Tom Wenzlau
Glenn West
Scott Whitaker
Anita McCullough
    White
Audrey White
Terry White
Becca White
Charlie White
Charley White
Fred White
Jerry White
Jimmie White
Cousin John White

Uncle John White
John Boyd White
Kenneth White
Kenny White
Lolise White
Loree White
Patti White
Pete White
Phyllis White
Sevier White
Yan Jun White
Yangtze White
Charles Wiggins
Joe Willauer
Charlie Williams
Gail Wilson

Ivan Wilson

Jim Wilson

Scott Wilson

Hayley Willson

Lauren Willson

Tom Willson

Brad Winger

Kara Winger

Patty Winter

Russ Winger

Judy Winters

Walt Winters

Joe Wolf

Ken Wolf

Marty Wolfe

Tony Woods

Jack Wooley

Bill Worth

Joe Wulhaur

David Wuthrich

Fred Wuthrich

Paul Wuthrich

XYZ

Joe Yan

Tom Yeakley

Joe York

Roy York

Gary Young

Patrick Young

Robert Younghanz

Brad Yuan

Jürgen Zimmerman

Subject Index

Name Index

Locations and Waters Index

CPSIA information can be obtained
at www.ICGtesting.com
Printed in the USA
FSHW011410060419

9 781532 665486